D0146466

IMAGINING
THEOLOGY

IMAGINING THEOLOGY

Encounters with God
in Scripture, Interpretation,
and Aesthetics

Garrett Green

Baker Academic
a division of Baker Publishing Group
Grand Rapids, Michigan

© 2020 by Garrett Green

Published by Baker Academic
a division of Baker Publishing Group
PO Box 6287, Grand Rapids, MI 49516-6287
www.bakeracademic.com

Printed in the United States of America

Library of Congress Cataloging-in-Publication Data
Names: Green, Garrett, author.
Title: Imagining theology : encounters with God in scripture, interpretation, and aesthetics / Garrett Green.
Description: Grand Rapids, Michigan : Baker Academic, a division of Baker Publishing Group, [2020] | Includes bibliographical references and index.
Identifiers: LCCN 2019031921 | ISBN 9781540961921 (cloth)
Subjects: LCSH: Imagination—Religious aspects—Christianity. | Theology.
Classification: LCC BR115.I6 G745 2020 | DDC 230—dc23
LC record available at https://lccn.loc.gov/2019031921

Figure 1 is based on the figure in J. Jastrow, "The Mind's Eye," *Popular Science Monthly* 54 (1899): 299–312.

20 21 22 23 24 25 26   7 6 5 4 3 2 1

✝

To the inmates of the Church Inside the Walls
at the Radgowski Correctional Institution,
my companions on the Way

Remember those who are in prison,
as though in prison with them.
(Hebrews 13:3)

CONTENTS

ACKNOWLEDGMENTS

How does one acknowledge those who have provided support and inspiration throughout a whole career of teaching and writing theology? I could begin at the beginning with gratitude to my *Doktorvater*, Hans W. Frei, who remained a source of friendship, advice, and encouragement until his death in 1988. His legacy is evident in many places in this book, especially chapter 5. Or I could begin in the present with thanks to my editor at Baker Academic, R. David Nelson, who believed in this project from the outset and helped me mold and focus it into a real book. Without his insightful guidance, it might never have seen the light of day. Our mutual friend Joseph Mangina introduced us and has also supported me personally and academically over many years, through conversations, advice, and his own contributions to Christian theology. Two scholarly societies of which I am a member—the New Haven Theological Discussion Group and the Duodecim Theological Society—have provided me with ongoing opportunities to hear the work in progress of other scholars and on occasion to try out my own ideas before an audience of sympathetic experts.

Equally deserving of acknowledgment are others outside the world of academic theology. They include members of the various churches of which I have been a part, especially Crossroads Presbyterian Church and Bishop Seabury Anglican Church, as well as the incarcerated Christians to whom this book is dedicated. Without being aware of the help they were giving me, these fellow believers have kept my academic work grounded in the corporate worship and fellowship of the body of Christ.

Finally, at the most personal level, I must acknowledge the ongoing love and support of my wife, Priscilla, which has accompanied and undergirded all my work. She has also contributed concretely to this book (and everything else I have written) through her skillful editing of my prose, as only an experienced English teacher could have done, saving me from many a grammatical or stylistic stumble.

1

TOWARD A NORMATIVE
CHRISTIAN IMAGINATION

Theologians have long been occupied with the question of how human beings can know God. Since the European Enlightenment, however, this question has assumed a new and more urgent form. For the Enlightenment inaugurated a radical change of worldview, beginning in seventeenth-century Europe and spreading eventually to the entire world. The factors leading to this change are many and complex,[1] but one of the root causes—the one of greatest importance to Christian theology—was the advent of the "new science," which has evolved into what today we call *modern science*. This new way of thinking about reality had its origin in the revolutionary astronomy of Copernicus (1473–1543), but its powerful impact on modern thinking was first felt as a result of the work of Galileo (1564–1642), who employed the new technology of the telescope to provide empirical proof of the Copernican system. By demonstrating that the mechanics of the heavens (the moons of Jupiter were his prime example) operate according to the same mathematically defined laws governing motion on the earth, he delivered a fatal blow to the Aristotelian-Christian worldview. This way of envisioning the world, as composed of concentric celestial spheres

---

1. For a more extensive overview of the origins of the modern world and its implications for theology, see Garrett Green, "Modernity," in *The Blackwell Companion to Modern Theology*, ed. Gareth Jones (Oxford: Blackwell, 2004), 162–79.

with the earth at its center, had dominated classical and Christian thought for two millennia. It is no accident that the opening battle in the modern war between "science" and "religion" was provoked by Galileo's work. And the controversy has continued to this day: questions about "science and religion" still occasion widespread interest and heated debates among believers, skeptics, and the general public.

The worldview of the new science truly came of age with the epochal achievement of Isaac Newton (1642–1727), whose *Mathematical Principles of Natural Philosophy* appeared in 1687. According to Newton's system, the universe consists of an infinite expanse of space containing material bodies that move in accordance with universal laws that can be described in the language of mathematics, the lingua franca of modern science. This view of the world, unlike the one it replaced, is in principle fully accessible to the natural capabilities of human reason. The theological implication of this new worldview is epitomized in an exchange (perhaps apocryphal) between Napoleon and his former teacher, the mathematician and astronomer Pierre-Simon Laplace. The emperor, having been told that Laplace's book contained no mention of the Creator, asked him, "Where is God in your system of the universe?" Laplace is said to have answered, "Sire, we have no need for that hypothesis." The scientific account, by offering an explanation of the world devoid of theological grounding, thereby called into question not only the authority of the church but the truth of Christianity itself.

The antithesis of "science and religion" runs like a scarlet thread through the history of modern thought from its origins in the new science of seventeenth-century Europe to the global secularism of the twenty-first century. It has captured the imagination of most of the technologically advanced societies of today and seems poised to overwhelm the remaining traditional backwaters that continue to resist its advance. The scare quotes around the two central terms call attention to the way in which our notions of both "science" and "religion," especially in their perceived incompatibility, have been shaped—and distorted—by the very forces that drive the advance of modern culture. If Christian theology is to escape this intellectual and cultural deluge, it will be necessary to deconstruct and demystify the mythical story of how "science" has displaced "religion" as the privileged key to understanding the world today. Only as we are able to see how the advocates of each side have misunderstood both themselves and one another can we regain our cultural bearings and form a truer picture of how modernity has shaped our world. And only then can theology begin to correct the misperceptions of the past and chart a better path forward.

The Metaphysics of Modern Science

Two influential books that appeared late in the nineteenth century epitomize and chronicle the way in which people in the modern West have imagined a struggle between science and religion that has now raged for more than three centuries. John William Draper published his *History of the Conflict between Religion and Science* in 1874, and it was followed two decades later by Andrew Dickson White's massive two-volume *History of the Warfare of Science with Theology in Christendom* (1896). The assumption that such a conflict exists is deeply rooted in the imagination of modernity and is shared both by advocates of "science" and by those who defend "religion." Even those who believe this warfare to be unfounded cannot ignore the battle that continues to rage around them. The issue that should concern us first of all is not who is right, or even whether the whole struggle is futile or unnecessary, but rather how our culture came to view things under this set of images in the first place. E. A. Burtt, author of the monumental study *The Metaphysical Foundations of Modern Physical Science*, maintains that "the ultimate picture which an age forms of the nature of its world . . . is its most fundamental possession." Accordingly, he sets out to discover "the cosmology underlying our mental processes" by exposing the unexamined metaphysical assumptions bequeathed to modernity by the founders of modern science along with their revolutionary new empirical method of understanding the physical world.[2] This new and unacknowledged metaphysics has achieved virtually universal acceptance in the modern world due especially to the authority accorded to Newton for his revolutionary scientific achievements. Modern philosophy, simply taking modern science for granted, has accepted uncritically the metaphysical assumptions of its founders along with their scientific method.[3] Not only philosophers, however, have fallen into this unconscious error but modernity as a whole, including those religious thinkers who have engaged in an ongoing battle with science.

Burtt's detailed demonstration of how these unexamined principles came to be presupposed in the modern world is a major scholarly accomplishment that has not been sufficiently acknowledged and taken into account by other interpreters of modern thought and culture over the past century—most especially by those who wrestle with the problem of "science and religion." Burtt himself was concerned primarily with the way in which these "metaphysical foundations" have affected and distorted modern philosophy. What

2. Edwin Arthur Burtt, *The Metaphysical Foundations of Modern Physical Science*, 2nd ed. rev. (London: Routledge & Kegan Paul, 1932), chap. 1.

3. Burtt, *Metaphysical Foundations*, 17.

disturbs him most of all is the "banishing of man from the great world of nature and his treatment as an effect of what happens in the latter."[4] His complaint: "Man begins to appear for the first time in the history of thought as an irrelevant spectator and insignificant effect of the great mathematical system which is the substance of reality."[5] But this displacement of humanity in the modern era is the consequence of a more fundamental shift in the metaphysics of modernity—namely, the displacement of God. The diction in Laplace's response to Napoleon is a dead giveaway: we modern scientists, he says, have no need for that *hypothesis*. How did the God of the Bible, the God worshiped by Jews and Christians, become the "God-hypothesis"? At least one seventeenth-century European, Blaise Pascal (1623–62), recognized the immense difference between the "God of Abraham, Isaac, and Jacob" and the "God of the philosophers"—by which he surely meant those *modern* philosophers who have adopted the implicit metaphysics of modern science.

The misunderstanding of science by both sides in the "science and religion" debate is rooted in what we might call the *teleological amnesia* of modern science. The revolution in science initiated by Kepler, Galileo, Newton, and their peers is rooted in a methodological innovation first articulated by Francis Bacon in his *Novum Organum Scientiarum* (1620) and taken for granted in all subsequent science. Explicitly departing from Aristotle's fourfold account of causality that had been the standard teaching for centuries, Bacon proposes a new experimental empiricism based entirely on efficient causality. In other words, the modern scientist explains the phenomena of nature inductively by attending to the immediately preceding conditions. Doing science this way, however, means ignoring what Aristotle calls "final causes"—that is, questions of end or ultimate purpose. The modern scientist thus excludes all *teleological* considerations in order to describe how things move and change in the present, how they come about in the light of the preceding conditions. By bracketing consideration of the end or purpose of things (the *why* question), they are able to observe and test the immediate causes of natural phenomena (the *how* question)—and thus to gain greater control over them. The importance of this last point—control—which Bacon emphasizes, can be seen in the stupendous technological advances that have flowed from the findings of modern science. What has happened, however, is that our culture, including many of its influential philosophical and religious leaders, has forgotten that the bracketing of teleology by scientists was a methodological choice, a presupposition of scientific method, not a conclusion induced

4. Burtt, *Metaphysical Foundations*, 78.
5. Burtt, *Metaphysical Foundations*, 80.

from observation of natural phenomena. Having forgotten that questions of purpose and ultimate meaning had been deliberately set aside, people now imagine that science has *discovered* that nature is devoid of purpose. This teleological amnesia has encouraged the widespread modern notion that "science" has proven the beliefs of "religion" to be mistaken or implausible since the natural world is devoid of purpose and is guided by no ultimate end. What has really happened is that a particular scientific method has been mistaken for a metaphysics. The fact that this transformation has mostly occurred unintentionally, even unconsciously, makes it all the more difficult to perceive and to criticize. Through a meticulous examination of the writings of the founders of modern science, Burtt shows how the transformation from method to metaphysics began in the thinking of Galileo, Descartes, and others in the seventeenth century—especially Newton—and came to shape the whole of modern thought and culture.

The "Religious" Misunderstanding of Science

The same misreading of science that seduced philosophers into uncritically adopting the metaphysical assumptions of the architects of early modern science has not been confined to the field of philosophy. Precisely because the underlying sources of confusion were unrecognized even by scientists themselves, the new metaphysics has transformed the thinking of nearly every modern person, including those religious thinkers who set out to defend the Christian faith. The abandonment of teleological explanations in favor of efficient causality in science has encouraged religious apologists to try to defend religion on the same assumption—that is, without recourse to teleological considerations. "With final causality gone," Burtt summarizes, "the only way to keep [God] in the universe was to . . . regard him as the First Efficient Cause," thus leaving behind the understanding of God as Supreme Good.[6] Christian apologists who start down this road today can scarcely avoid arriving at the deism championed by so many of the leading thinkers of the Enlightenment. These well-meaning apologists have unwittingly adopted the metaphysics of modern science without realizing that in doing so they have reduced God to the First Efficient Cause of the world while claiming that they are justifying belief in the Holy One of the Bible. Looking for empirical evidence of God, they fail to see that they are treating God as an explanatory hypothesis, one of the contingent objects of the world (even if called the Supreme Being) that

6. Burtt, *Metaphysical Foundations*, 90.

may or may not exist. If they were to be successful in their arguments, they would find that what they had proved was not God but an idol.

The warfare between science and religion has reached a stalemate because both have been wrongly conceived. A lasting truce will require a demythologizing of both terms. A good place to begin is with a suggestion that Burtt makes about how a scientific method came to be misunderstood as a metaphysical discovery in the first place. He suggests that it resulted from "a misapplication, to the universe at large, of a point of view legitimate enough in a certain field," an error arising from "the unwarranted assumption that because man . . . can know and use portions of his world, some ultimate and permanent difference is thereby made in that world."[7] A proper apologetic strategy for religious believers must begin by acknowledging that empirical science is not equipped to tell us the ultimate nature of reality but is rather a means to better understand the workings of the natural world by bracketing ultimate questions in order to investigate and gain control over its immanent mechanisms. The founders of modern science were surely correct in blaming medieval thinkers for confusing theological principles with empirical accounts of nature. But they and their modern successors have made a similar error by absolutizing their empirical methodology to arrive at conclusions that exceed the legitimate capabilities of science, becoming in effect metaphysical assumptions that carry theological implications. What is needed today is a more modest understanding of the limits of empirical science, together with a better way of distinguishing the realm in which it does its proper work from the realm appropriate to metaphysics and theology.

Imagination in Science and Theology

The most important change in our understanding of science since the founding of modern science occurred in the latter part of the twentieth century. Anyone wishing to think seriously about science today must take into account Thomas Kuhn's *Structure of Scientific Revolutions*.[8] Kuhn proved that

7. Burtt, *Metaphysical Foundations*, 12.

8. Thomas S. Kuhn, *The Structure of Scientific Revolutions*, 2nd ed. (1st ed., 1962; Chicago: University of Chicago Press, 1970). A number of other scholars played important roles in the new understanding of the history and philosophy of science, including Paul Feyerabend, Norwood Russell Hanson, Michael Polanyi, Max Black, Margaret Masterman, and others; but Kuhn's book was primarily responsible for the revolutionary change in the way we think about science. For a more complete account of this movement and its importance for theology, see Garrett Green, *Imagining God: Theology and the Religious Imagination* (Grand Rapids: Eerdmans, 1998).

many of our common assumptions about how science works—notions that have gained virtually universal consensus in the modern era—are mistaken. Through a close examination of the history of science, he shows how actual scientific work proceeds much differently from the common assumption that scientists simply observe nature objectively in order to gather facts that are then verified by experiment and added cumulatively to our store of knowledge about the natural world. His most important contribution is the concept of *paradigm*, which identifies the analogical exemplar of the whole that underlies every particular scientific enterprise. Kuhn draws on the insights of Ludwig Wittgenstein, who used the figure of the "duck-rabbit"[9] to show how the recognition of parts depends on prior apprehension of a whole, the constitutive pattern by which the separate parts can be recognized as such (fig. 1). Wittgenstein's philosophical insight was derived from the work of Gestalt psychologists, who showed why one person viewing an object can see something quite different from another viewer (e.g., one sees a duck where another sees a rabbit). Such examples show how even objective observation is dependent on an implicit grasp of the holistic paradigm that governs what kind of object the observer observes.

Figure 1. The duck-rabbit

Kuhn has brought to light the essential role played by *imagination* in science. The importance of paradigms throughout the history of science demonstrates the necessary contribution of imagination to the ongoing work of science. Most of the time scientific research proceeds without an explicit awareness of the paradigms it presupposes; Kuhn calls this phase "normal science," which consists mainly of "puzzle-solving."[10] Contrary to the commonly held view of science, however, scientists do not simply discard their working hypotheses when experiments fail to verify them. Instead, they continue to pursue their research in spite of experimental anomalies. Eventually, however, the pressure of anomaly—"a phenomenon . . . for which his paradigm had not readied

9. Ludwig Wittgenstein, *Philosophical Investigations*, trans. G. E. M. Anscombe, 2nd ed. (New York: Macmillan, 1958), pt. 2, p. 194.
10. Kuhn, *Structure of Scientific Revolutions*, 35–42.

the investigator"[11]—may lead to a crisis in the normal practice of science, in which the paradigm that has hitherto given shape and direction to scientific research appears to falter. What happens next is unpredictable. Scientists may succeed in overcoming the apparent dilemmas by correcting errors in their previous work or refining existing theories. But it may also happen that some new and unorthodox way of doing science appears on the scene and succeeds in attracting scientists to a new way of thinking on the basis of a quite different paradigm. This event is the "scientific revolution" of Kuhn's title—such as the famous examples of the adoption of Copernican astronomy in the seventeenth century and the transformation from Newtonian to Einsteinian mechanics in the twentieth century. Not all paradigm changes in science are as dramatic as these, but such transformations have occurred and will continue to occur, though often so gradually that the participants may be unaware of them at the time. It is nevertheless the case that all scientific research takes place under the influence of specific paradigms. Following Wittgenstein, Kuhn appeals to the work of Gestalt psychologists, whose experiments have shown "that something like a paradigm is prerequisite to perception itself."[12] In the same way that we remain unaware of our seeing "paradigmatically" until we encounter something akin to the duck-rabbit figure, so scientists may proceed without awareness of the implicit paradigms guiding their research until, say, a series of anomalous experiments calls into question their basic assumptions. Such crises have occurred repeatedly throughout the history of science. Whether in visual perception, scientific work, or religious experience, people remain unaware of the paradigmatic commitments underlying their thinking until some crisis, some breakdown of "normal" experience, gives birth to a new way of seeing.

This dramatic change in our understanding of how science actually works ought to transform the way we view the problem of science and religion. The key element is the recognition of the role played by imagination in both. For the first time since the advent of modern science we catch a glimpse of something *similar* in the work of the natural scientist and the theologian: the essential role of paradigmatic imagination for both enterprises. It is not the case, of course, that this similarity dissolves the real differences between them. On the contrary, recognition of the essential role played by imagination in both scientific and theological thought puts us in a better position to grasp the *real* differences between them, and to see why the long-standing notion of their "warfare" is an illusion produced by an inadequate understanding of both.

11. Kuhn, *Structure of Scientific Revolutions*, 57.
12. Kuhn, *Structure of Scientific Revolutions*, 113.

Let us begin by acknowledging the qualitative difference between knowing the things of this world and knowing those aspects of reality that transcend our cognitive abilities. That such a distinction exists can be illustrated by an everyday analogy. Try to imagine a dog's conception of human beings; let's call it *canine anthropology*.[13] Anyone who has spent time communicating with dogs has learned that they do in fact have knowledge of humans: they can recognize the difference between humans and other animals, and between one human and another; they are able to communicate to us at least some of their needs and desires; we can teach them to obey certain spoken commands— and so on. Yet their canine anthropology does not begin to approach human reality as we know it. And no amount of training or education could ever enable a dog to achieve the kind of knowledge we possess about our own species. Now compare this canine epistemological quandary to the situation of human theology. Our creaturely attempts to know God confront us with a comparable but far greater quandary—not the watered-down, domesticated God of modern deism and religious apologetics, but the biblical God, the Holy One of Israel, the Father of Jesus Christ, the God of the church fathers, of St. Augustine and St. Thomas, Luther and Calvin, and of myriad ordinary believers throughout the ages.

The difference between the two kinds of knowledge sought by theologians and empirical scientists is not simply quantitative but qualitative, for my desire to know God is vastly more complex and problematic than the efforts of my dog (a fellow creature) to know me. There are many ways in which the immeasurable difference between knowing the natural world around us and knowing its Creator, Sustainer, and End has been expressed: the difference between time and eternity, earth and heaven, creature and Creator, imminence and transcendence, contingency and necessity, this world and the world to come. The apostle Paul puts it like this: "For now we see in a mirror dimly, but then face to face. Now I know in part; then I shall know fully, even as I have been fully known" (1 Cor. 13:12). St. Thomas Aquinas distinguishes our knowledge of *being* from our knowledge of *Being-Itself*, who is God. Theologian Katherine Sonderegger, employing another term from scholastic theology, speaks of the divine *aseity*, God's Reality *a se*, in himself and not simply as known from the standpoint of the created world.[14] She puts her finger squarely on the central error of modernist theology, one that has

---

13. It will be helpful in reading the following to have in mind Gary Larson's famous cartoon about human and dog communication (https://terriermandotcom.blogspot.com/2010/07/dogs -are-not-verbal.html).

14. Katherine Sonderegger, *Systematic Theology*, vol. 1, *The Doctrine of God* (Minneapolis: Fortress, 2015), 49–50 and passim.

prevented it from doing justice to the divine aseity: "the importation and concentration of causality into Divine Power," which "forces Divine Will off the stage." In this way God's freedom "has been hopelessly compromised by the notion of Absolute Cause, an efficient Power that can brook no rival." She sees this error epitomized in the theology of Friedrich Schleiermacher, who "has recognized the full collapse and reduction of causality in the modern age into efficient cause, and has embraced it with radical confidence."[15] Here, in the theologian who has had so great an influence on Protestant theology over the past two centuries, we see the consequences of adopting the metaphysical foundations of empirical science into our theology. By trying to conceive God according to the metaphysics of efficient causality, theologians have fundamentally misunderstood the radical difference between the biblical God and the things of this imminent and contingent world. Theology cannot import its metaphysics or its methods from the sciences without distorting its vision of God, the proper object of theology, as its very name implies. The task of the scientist is to imagine the natural world, but the task of imagining God is something altogether different.

There has been, and still is, great resistance on both sides to the claim that imagination is centrally implicated in both natural science and theology. The reason is clear: people commonly assume that what we imagine must be imaginary. This notion, however, is manifestly false. The human imagination serves various purposes that may be distinguished into two broad groups on the basis of its use. On the one hand, imagination can be employed in *fictive* or *fantastic* ways for a variety of purposes, including the literary and aesthetic. But the fictive imagination also has its darker uses, ranging from misrepresentation (whether intentional or unintentional) to deliberate deceit. On the other hand, imagination can be employed *realistically*, in the service of truth. Even at the level of simple visual perception, the realistic imagination works to focus and supplement the data that our eyes take in directly. (I can't see the other side of the cup into which I am pouring my coffee, but I am willing to trust my imagination that it isn't missing or full of holes.) The realistic imagination functions throughout human experience, enabling us to envision the whole of things, to focus our minds to perceive how things are ordered and organized—in other words, it allows us to see what is really there, rather than just a blooming, buzzing confusion. This is the kind of imagination employed by scientists and theologians alike. Of course, the realistic imagination is not infallible and sometimes misleads us. And as already noted, imagination can be deliberately employed to produce unreal, imaginary outcomes, whether

15. Sonderegger, *Systematic Theology*, 1:180–81.

for good or for ill. So it isn't really surprising that many scientists and many religious believers resist the thesis that imagination plays a crucial role in their respective enterprises.

One way to reduce that resistance is to pay close attention to how imagination actually functions realistically in both areas. Philosophers of science have made great strides in the past half century toward that goal in their own field of inquiry. A corresponding account of religious imagination must begin by acknowledging just how different the object of theology is from the objects of empirical science. Accordingly, the theologian and the scientist have very different relationships to their respective objects of study. That difference is concisely expressed in a German term that—regrettably for Anglophones— requires a more complicated explanation in English. We can say, using the German term, that God is *unverfügbar* and that whatever the theologian says about God must therefore take into account God's *Unverfügbarkeit*. The straightforward translation of the verb *verfügen* is "to dispose," implying that *verfügbar* means "disposable." Unfortunately this word has a wide range of meanings in English (are we talking about diapers, perhaps, or beverage containers?), and the theologically significant meaning is rare in current English usage.[16] The definition of the verb *dispose* that comes closest to the German *verfügen* reads as follows: "To make arrangements; to determine or control the course of affairs or events; to ordain, appoint," as in the proverbial expression "Man proposes, but God disposes."[17] The best way to express the meaning of God's *Unverfügbarkeit* in contemporary English is to say that God is *not at our disposal*. Unlike the natural phenomena that the scientist studies (which are *verfügbar*, at our disposal), God cannot be brought under our control, is not subject to our manipulation. We cannot bring God into the laboratory in order to subject him to experimental analysis or search for evidence of his existence in the natural world. Such methods would ignore the sovereign freedom of God, what Sonderegger calls God's aseity, the essential attribute of his nature.[18]

Even though paradigmatic imagination is a necessary component of both empirical science and theology, the vast qualitative differences between their

16. The *Oxford English Dictionary* lists nine definitions of the verb *dispose* (plus numerous subdefinitions), several of them obsolete.

17. A translation of the Latin "*Homo proponit, sed Deus disponit*" (from Thomas à Kempis, *The Imitation of Christ* 1.19). This saying may ultimately derive from the Bible; the closest parallel is Prov. 19:21: "Many are the plans in the mind of a man, but it is the purpose of the Lord that will stand." The Living Bible (TLB) actually translates this verse, "Man proposes, but God disposes."

18. Sonderegger writes that "little else remains in the doctrine of God when His Aseity is lost." *Systematic Theology*, 1:309.

objects of inquiry require them to deploy that imagination very differently. But since both of them understand their use of imagination to be realistic—a means of gaining a better understanding of reality, rather than an exercise in fiction or fantasy—both of them must wrestle with the question of how to govern the use of imagination, how to employ it properly in the service of truth. One reason for the widespread suspicion of imagination, whether in science or religion, is that imagination can be used to serve many different masters, to achieve many different ends. It is, of course, possible to "mis-imagine" reality while seeking to understand it, and some people even appeal to imagination deceitfully, seeking through false analogy or other means to deceive others. What the legitimate seeker after truth needs, therefore, is a way to identify the *normative* use of imagination, some set of rules or guidelines to govern its use and to curb its excesses. The remainder of this chapter will sketch out some of those guidelines for Christian theology.

Normative Imagination in Christian Theology

The first rule for the normative use of theological imagination in Christianity is foundational and underlies all the others:

1. The Bible embodies the concrete paradigm on which all genuine Christian theology is based, enabling the faithful to rightly imagine God.

Christians have affirmed from the earliest times that our knowledge of God is grounded in the Holy Scriptures of the Old and New Testaments. Christian theology is thus a hermeneutical discipline, one that necessarily involves interpretation of a foundational text. But that way of putting things disguises the complexity of the task, for it would be more precise to say that theology requires the interpretation of many *texts*, since the Bible is a collection of sixty-six (or so) writings over many centuries by authors known and unknown, some of which incorporate materials from earlier texts or oral traditions. So before even starting to interpret the Bible, theologians must wrestle with the definition of the biblical canon itself, a task that led to more than three centuries of often contentious debate in the early history of the church and is not a wholly settled matter even today. But the task of defining a canon already *is* interpretation, since it requires us to decide what qualifies a text to be considered canonical.

The principle at stake in this case is the Christian teaching that the Bible is the Word of God, which implies that Christians understand Scripture to be the place where God speaks to us. Everything depends, however, on how we imagine that communication to take place. One popular but wholly in-adequate approach is to claim that Scripture contains the *Words* (plural!) of God—a teaching that would bring Christian reading of the Bible close to the way Islam reads the Qur'an. This doctrine is often called by the misleading term "literalism" but is more accurately labeled the theory of divine *dictation*. It has led to the modern heresy of *creationism*, a particularly contentious the-ory that has shaken the faith of many conscientious but uninformed believers and led critics to accuse the church of being the enemy of science. Sonderegger offers a devastating critique of this popular heresy. "Were Christians to teach a doctrine of inspiration that truly and directly taught divine *dictation*," she writes, "the Divine would be understood to destroy the human through its own manifestation. The human mind would be annihilated, replaced by the Divine Word, a searing and molten Presence that extinguished all creaturely thought and word."[19] Though motivated by the pious intent to affirm the truth of the Bible as the Word of God, this false doctrine is a consequence of the unacknowledged metaphysics of modern science being absorbed into Christian theology. Creationists, confusing scientific language with biblical narrative, claim that the biblical accounts of divine creation contradict the findings of evolutionary science.

The remedy for the hermeneutics of divine dictation begins by recalling that the Bible itself identifies the Word of God not with the words of Scrip-ture but with Jesus Christ (John 1:1–5). He is the Logos, God's own Word, incarnate in the man Jesus of Nazareth. Christians call the Bible the Word of God in a secondary sense, because it contains the witness to Christ the Logos, the testimony of those who "have seen with our eyes" and have "looked upon and have touched with our hands" the living Word of God himself (1 John 1:1). To assert that this testimony contradicts evolutionary science is to make a massive category error, rooted in the unintentional metaphysics of modern science. This error is a major reason for the surviving notion that religion and science are at war. Worse still, creationism encourages readers of the Genesis creation narratives to overlook the real and powerful theological message: that God speaks not simply in the *words* of the Bible but in its embodied language as a whole, including the prescientific thought patterns and images of the ancient Near Eastern priests and prophets who first related these stories. God speaks not by putting words into the mouths of passive ancient authors but by capturing their imagination and enabling them to utter truthfully—using their own culturally specific and time-bound conceptuality—the mysteries of the One Eternal God, Creator of the heavens and the earth.

19. Sonderegger, *Systematic Theology*, 1:142.

One final quibble about creationism: its advocates seem unaware that evolutionary science is not about creation at all. Science does not, and cannot, say anything about the *origin* of the natural world, because that is one issue that cannot possibly be accounted for by appeal to efficient causality. If there is any Christian doctrine that might be affected by evolutionary theory, it is not creation but providence, God's ongoing provision and care for the world he has created. But that is a topic for another day.

One more mistaken hermeneutical theory needs to be headed off if we are to point the way to the normative use of imagination in theology: the view that takes interpretation itself to be the problem. One sometimes hears, especially among conservative Christians, the claim that we ought simply to read the Bible without interpretation. Would that this were possible! Such advice, if followed, would encourage readers of Scripture to ignore their own context as readers, their own assumptions and preconceptions—in a word, their own prejudices. Hans-Georg Gadamer has done us a great favor by showing that *Vorurteile* are not necessarily harmful prejudices but unavoidable and necessary prejudgments that are implicit in all our reading of texts.[20] No appeal to a "literal" reading of the Bible can bypass the need for right interpretation— that is, for a hermeneutic that enables us to find in Scripture a normative way to imagine God. Even the resurrected Jesus turned to interpretation of Scripture in order to open the eyes of the disciples on the road to Emmaus by showing them how the pattern running throughout the entire Scripture is focused on himself (Luke 24:25–27). Calvin gives us a compelling image of how Scripture can be used normatively when he suggests that it functions like spectacles, like a pair of corrective lenses that refocuses our flawed spiritual vision and "clearly shows us the true God."[21] This visual metaphor invites us to use the Bible not simply as something we look *at* but *through* in order to see the world and its relation to God in a new way.

2. Right imagination of God is a movement not only of the head—our mind or intellect—but also of the heart, our feelings and affective responses.

Emphasizing the centrality of imagination in theology can sometimes lead to a serious misunderstanding of Christian experience. The centrality of the visual metaphor (suggested by the word *imagination* itself) can tempt us to overemphasize the rational or intelligible. Scripture, conceived as the spectacles of imagination, may then appear to be primarily a means of *seeing*

20. Hans-Georg Gadamer, *Truth and Method*, 2nd ed. rev. (New York: Crossroad, 1989).
21. John Calvin, *Institutes of the Christian Religion* 1.5.11, trans. Ford Lewis Battles, ed. John T. McNeill (Philadelphia: Westminster, 1960), 63. For a fuller account of Calvin's metaphor and its implications for theology, see Green, *Imagining God*, 106–7.

clearly, which can mislead us into thinking that right imagination is mainly a matter of mind or intellect. But nothing could be further from the truth. Everything depends on the concrete paradigm that is fueling our imagination in a particular case. If, for example, I imagine the world I live in as a battleground in which I am constantly assaulted by forces that threaten to overwhelm me, I will not only *think* in certain ways but also *feel* very differently from my neighbor who imagines herself to be the unique creature of a powerful and loving God who continually watches over her. Imagination is from the outset an integral movement of intellect, will, and affections; there is no need to coordinate or integrate them as though they were separate faculties.

Here is a point at which the empirical scientist and the theologian differ dramatically in their use of the imagination. The responsible scientist must always maintain a *disinterested* stance when conducting research. Any admixture of subjectivity in the outcome, any emotional involvement in the experimental process, can compromise the necessary objectivity of the scientific enterprise. To carry over this scientific virtue into theology, however, leads to confusion and error, as in the attempt by Enlightenment thinkers to construct a religion of reason,[22] purified of all "positivity," of everything "merely" historical or particular in Christianity.[23] Even when trying to understand our fellow human beings, it would be foolish to omit emotional factors. How much more obvious it is that theology, in seeking to know God (a thoroughly personal relationship), must attend to the affective, as well as the intellectual and volitional, dimensions of the relationship.

3. The theological use of imagination must always remain open to the Mystery of God, resisting every temptation to rationalize, demystify, or control the divine.

An even more dramatic difference between the scientific and theological uses of imagination has to do with the question of *mystery*. For the scientist, mystery is something negative, a problem to be solved by further research and experiment. Kuhn describes the essential activity of normal science as puzzle-solving. How different the approach of the theologian, whose object of study is the One Holy God, who in his aseity is not at our disposal, who in his freedom remains ever mysterious, who, we might say, simply *is* Mystery.

---

22. For more about the Enlightenment religion of reason, see James C. Livingston, *Modern Christian Thought*, 2nd ed., vol. 1, *The Enlightenment and the Nineteenth Century* (Minneapolis: Fortress, 2006), chap. 2.

23. For an explanation of the concept of positivity and the distinction between positive and natural religion, see Garrett Green, *Theology, Hermeneutics, and Imagination: The Crisis of Interpretation at the End of Modernity* (Cambridge: Cambridge University Press, 2000), 26–30.

This divine quality is not just a troublesome consequence of our finitude but rather a constitutive attribute of God himself. To say that God is Mystery is not to say (or imply) that God is unknown or unknowable. Divine mystery is not an excuse for agnosticism. Rather, we *know* God precisely *as* Mystery. It is a quality implied by his Eternity. However much "progress" we make in our effort to know God, we will never exhaust the mystery, for he remains the *infinitely* Knowable One.

Such a mystery contains and expresses a truth that is beyond our control. In a culture like ours, in which our collective imagination has been captivated by the marvels of science and its resulting technology, this lack of control appears to be something negative, a limitation to be overcome. From the perspective of the Christian gospel, however, the issue of control looks very different. Theology is a joyful enterprise,[24] for the gracious Lord of Mystery never ceases to extend and enrich our knowledge of himself, which flows forth from its Source in a never-ending outpouring of wisdom and love. For the theologian, a mysterious truth is not a lesser kind of truth: we can affirm it without being able fully to comprehend it. Not only is this kind of knowledge beyond our control, but it cannot be known at all until we abandon the attempt to control it. Theological knowledge is never an achievement but always a gift. We interpret the meaning of the mystery so far as we are able, knowing that we can never exhaust its meaning. The affirmation of mystery by its very nature thus necessitates *humility* on the part of the knower. The wise person is open to the possibility of genuine mystery, which implies that there is more to reality than we are able to comprehend; the foolish person assumes that anything beyond our rational grasp is unreal or untrue.

In theology, unlike science, the mystery surrounding its subject is not a problem but rather a hermeneutical key. God's mystery is an aspect of his *grace*—an expression of his love, not a barrier to be overcome. It is a sign of his infinity: there is always more to be known about God; he is always new without changing or losing his identity. The appropriate theological response to divine mystery, therefore, is not puzzlement but praise.

4. In accordance with its biblical paradigm, theological imagination always remains open to novelty, eschewing every attempt at metanarrative or systematic closure.

The impact of postmodern continental philosophy on academia has encouraged theologians as well as other thinkers to adopt an attitude of "incredulity

---

24. Theology is the truly joyful science, the *fröhliche Wissenschaft*, despite Nietzsche's attempt to claim the title for himself.

towards metanarratives," defined as "totalising stories about history and the goals of the human race that ground and legitimise knowledges and cultural practises."[25] It is important to see why a paradigm (in the sense developed by Kuhn) is not a metanarrative, and why the scriptural canon understood paradigmatically cannot therefore be characterized as a metanarrative.

Expressed in simplest terms, a paradigm tells us what something is *like*. The figure of the duck-rabbit, so revealing to Wittgenstein and his followers, is deliberately constructed so as to balance two visual aspects in order to demonstrate and bring to awareness the "paradigmatic" nature of all our seeing. Viewing the figure according to the duck paradigm causes the viewer to see something wholly different from another viewer who sees it according to the rabbit paradigm—yet both are viewing the same figure. Their experience highlights something true of all seeing, that it depends on a prior but implicit way of organizing the visual data into a meaningful whole. The duck-rabbit is artificially devised to demonstrate this truth and thus has no realistic or moral significance: one way of seeing it is no better or worse than the other. But in real life it can make a huge difference which paradigm is determining our vision. All our seeing, whether we are aware of it or not, is a seeing-as. We may misimagine some aspect of the world, and it might even turn out to be a matter of life or death. *In the twilight the soldier saw the approaching figure as one of his own unit, while his companion saw him as an enemy combatant and ducked for cover just in time.* Christians see the world as the "theater of God's glory" (in Calvin's elegant phrase) while others see it differently—as a living hell, perhaps, or as a place of unlimited opportunity for material gain.

So what does all of this have to do with the Bible? Gestalt experiments have shown that a subject viewing the duck-rabbit for the first time surrounded by images of rabbits is more likely to see it as a rabbit. Christians, immersing themselves in Holy Scripture, find themselves surrounded by a "cloud of witnesses" (Heb. 12:1) all testifying in their various ways to the reality of God and the truth of the gospel of Jesus Christ. But what a diverse and confusing set of testimonies the Bible gives us! We need to think of them not as a series of precise doctrinal instructions (though some of them may be) but as a collection of eyewitnesses, all reporting in their own voices what they have seen and heard, employing their own genres and thought forms. Some readers will hear in this collection only a cacophony of conflicting voices, while others (careless readers though they be) imagine the Bible to be a kind of rule book to be applied randomly and without any attention to context.

25. This summary comes from Ashley Woodward, "Jean-François Lyotard (1924–1998)," *Internet Encyclopedia of Philosophy*, accessed May 17, 2019, http://www.iep.utm.edu/lyotard.

In the natural sciences, as Kuhn has demonstrated, a paradigm retains its usefulness only until the next revolution, when accumulating anomalies open the way for a new and better paradigm to emerge and take its place. Here, too, the theological situation differs because of the character of its object, "the One God's Utter Uniqueness."[26] If a paradigm tells us what an object is *like*, how is a theological paradigm even possible? Where is the theologian to find a likeness to the Utterly Unique? The answer is found in the scriptural witness to Jesus Christ: "He is the image of the invisible God, the firstborn of all creation" (Col. 1:15). Christians affirm that the varied testimonies of the Old and New Testaments are all to be heard in relation to this central focus on Jesus Christ. Viewed in this light, Scripture begins to take on a coherent shape. The apostle Paul expresses it like this: "For God, who said, 'Let light shine out of darkness,' has shone in our hearts to give the light of the knowledge of the glory of God in the face of Jesus Christ" (2 Cor. 4:6). In the sciences, too, a paradigm is open-ended, suggesting new ways in which our knowledge of the natural world might be clarified and extended through further research. A paradigm is not the same as a theory (though it may encourage the development of new theories). No one can say in advance how far and in what ways the paradigm may lead to scientific discovery. In theology the situation is similar, only more so; for the object to be illuminated by the biblical paradigm is itself open-ended, unlimited, and inexhaustible.[27]

Confronted with the task of trying to speak about the One Utterly Unique God, theologians have always acknowledged the necessity of *inspiration*, for it should be obvious that there can be no likeness, and therefore no paradigm, of such a God unless it be revealed by God himself. Thus theologians have followed the Bible in emphasizing the essential role played by the Holy Spirit, the One who inspires the imagination of the witnesses. If the Bible is to be read and interpreted rightly—that is, if theology is to be possible—God's Holy Spirit must not only have inspired the writers of Scripture but must also illumine the minds of its faithful readers. "God alone is a fit witness of himself in his Word," writes Calvin, "so also the Word will not find acceptance in men's hearts before it is sealed by the inward testimony of the Spirit."[28] Such a living and open-ended relationship of the biblical paradigm to its Holy Object and to the believer is unlike a metanarrative or any other kind of premature closure. Any attempt to guarantee its content or to set its

26. Sonderegger, *Systematic Theology*, 1:394.
27. This inexhaustibility finds expression in the final verse of John's Gospel: "Now there are also many other things that Jesus did. Were every one of them to be written, I suppose that the world itself could not contain the books that would be written" (21:25).
28. Calvin, *Institutes of the Christian Religion* 1.7.4 (trans. Battles, 79).

limits systematically—any attempt at closure—would constitute a betrayal of its mission.

5. Because theological imagination is dependent on the Holy Spirit, it is an enterprise of faith, appearing uncertain and circular from a worldly perspective, depending on the certainty of God's revelation for its claim to truth.

When Karl Barth, in his final course of lectures before retirement, set out to describe Christian theology, he noted that it is "not supported by what is usually considered sound evidence" but rather "seems to the onlooker to be situated in mid-air."[29] Barth pictures theology as a series of concentric circles, moving (outer to inner) from the Word, to the Witnesses, to the Community (i.e., the church). At the center, he locates the Spirit, on whom all the others depend. Thus theology can never "seek to secure its operations" but simply does its work without presuppositions, relying wholly on the power of the Holy Spirit.[30]

So central is faith to Christians and to Christian theology that the whole enterprise is known as the Christian *faith* (a better descriptor than the troubled and contested term *religion*).[31] When we speak of faith in the context of modern culture, however, we encounter once again the distorting lens of the metaphysics of modern science. Assuming that all true knowledge is based on efficient causality, people today typically take faith to be just a weaker kind of truth claim, lacking the rigorous evidence found in empirical science. But as we have seen, the spiritual foundation of Christian faith gives rise to a very different kind of truth-seeking and a very different relationship between the knower and the object to be known. Because, unlike the worldly objects studied by natural science, God is Spirit (and therefore free, *unverfügbar*, not at our disposal), the right relationship to him is one of faith—even, we might say, our *epistemological* relationship to him. As such, faith is not a lesser way of knowing God but the right way, the only way.

The way of faith, however, is indirect, for God, unlike the objects of the created world, is invisible, hidden in the world he has made. Sonderegger makes much of this divine attribute, seeing it as exemplifying the *humility* of God. This divine hiddenness results "not from absence but rather from divine presence," she says, claiming furthermore that "this affirmation of

29. Karl Barth, *Evangelical Theology: An Introduction* (New York: Holt, Rinehart and Winston, 1963), 48.
30. Barth, *Evangelical Theology*, 50.
31. For a critical analysis of the modern concept of religion, see chap. 13 below. For a theological critique of religion, see Karl Barth, *On Religion: The Revelation of God as the Sublimation of Religion*, translated and introduced by Garrett Green (London: T&T Clark, 2006).

the One Lord's commanding presence in the midst of His Mystery and Hiddenness is knit into the very structure of biblical revelation."[32] (Notice here how the biblical paradigm informs the imagination of the theologian.) One of the ironies of the modern secular world—the world that has no need of the God-hypothesis—is its unintentional acknowledgment of God's hiddenness. "Modern atheism," Sonderegger writes, "even against its will, glorifies God in this way."[33] Against all modern expectations, the God of the Bible, Holy and Almighty as he is, is no tyrant, no supreme autocrat, compelling his creation to conform to his divine will. On the contrary, Paul writes, "God chose what is foolish in the world to shame the wise; God chose what is weak in the world to shame the strong; God chose what is low and despised in the world, even things that are not, to bring to nothing things that are" (1 Cor. 1:27–28). When *this* God wants to interact with his creation, he arrives on the scene incognito, in the form of a slave (Phil. 2:7), as a newborn child in a stable, as a king who reigns from a cross. What appears to worldly eyes as weakness, however, is in reality the power of Almighty God. "For the foolishness of God," Paul writes, "is wiser than men, and the weakness of God is stronger than men" (1 Cor. 1:25).

The apparent foolishness and weakness of God are also manifested in theology, which, because it is based on faith, appears in this world in the form of uncertainty and circularity. "Naturally," writes Oswald Chambers, "we are inclined to be so mathematical and calculating that we look upon uncertainty as a bad thing. . . . The nature of the spiritual life is that we are certain in our uncertainty, consequently we do not make our nests anywhere. . . . Certainty is the mark of the common-sense life: gracious uncertainty is the mark of the spiritual life."[34] The uncertainty that is endemic to theology reflects the close relationship of faith to hope in the New Testament. As Paul writes to the Christians in Rome, "Now hope that is seen is not hope. For who hopes for what he sees? But if we hope for what we do not see, we wait for it with patience" (Rom. 8:24–25). In empirical science, as in worldly discourse generally, uncertainty is always a negative, an indication that we have not yet attained a full knowledge of whatever it is we are trying to understand. In theology, as in the discourse of faith generally, uncertainty plays a different and positive role, reminding us that certainty about God can never be the product of our own thinking, because all things divine are *unverfügbar*, not subject to our manipulation. Theological certainty is always a gift of *grace*,

32. Sonderegger, *Systematic Theology*, 1:68.
33. Sonderegger, *Systematic Theology*, 1:53.
34. Oswald Chambers, *My Utmost for His Highest*, reading for April 29.

always lying beyond our own devices and desires, not subject to our control—a *gracious* uncertainty.

And yet, as Chambers has expressed it, "we are certain in our uncertainty"— a statement that sounds to modern secular ears like either a patent contradiction or an exercise in circular reasoning. Acknowledging this consternation forthrightly, Barth takes up the challenge. Theology is by formal definition, he states, "the human logic of the divine Logos." It is "science seeking the knowledge of the Word of God spoken in God's work—science learning in the school of Holy Scripture, which witnesses to the Word of God."[35] The word *science* sounds jarring to us in this context, which is testimony to the near-total absorption of the word by the modern, anti-teleological understanding of science.[36] Barth acknowledges the circularity of this theo-logic but argues that not every logical circle is vicious; some are *circuli veritatis*, "circles of truth," or what we might call "virtuous" circles. Theology, he maintains—so long as it remains based on faith—is in fact the *circulus veritatis Dei*.[37]

6. **Theological imagination belongs to the present age, the *regnum gratiae*, the era of our *earthly pilgrimage*, when we "see through a glass, darkly." We will no longer need to imagine God in the world to come, when we shall see him "face to face."**

Theology, as we have seen, because it is based on faith, knows God indirectly, by hearing the testimony of the scriptural witnesses to the Word of God. Imagination, the mode in which we have that indirect knowledge in this world, has no place among the Last Things. Since faith is the "assurance of things hoped for, the conviction of things *not seen*" (Heb. 11:1), we need imagination now because we lack direct vision of the God we worship and seek to know.

The widespread modern suspicion of imagination, rooted in the misleading metaphysics inherited from the founders of modern science, has fostered naïve and distorted understandings of both science and religion. But it has become clear in recent years that both the natural sciences and Christian theology depend on the right use of imagination. That use is governed by paradigms, those concrete likenesses that seed the imagination, opening it to new discoveries by showing us what its object is *like*. The radical differences between these two enterprises indicate *not* that they are competing ways

35. Barth, *Evangelical Theology*, 49.
36. In Barth's native German, *Wissenschaft* has retained more of the older, broader connotations that *science* has all but lost in modern English. In German usage today, all academic disciplines are called *Wissenschaften*.
37. Barth, *Church Dogmatics*, vol. II/1 (Edinburgh: T&T Clark, 1957), 244–47.

of knowing the same reality, but that they both make use of paradigmatic imagination in their separate quests to know very different aspects of reality.

Theologians are (depending on one's point of view) the daring or foolish pilgrims of the Spirit who, leaving behind the comfortable world of familiar ideas and common sense, venture forth, Bibles in hand and heart, in search of the Celestial City that one can approach only by means of a scripturally formed imagination. Like the natural scientist, theologians find orientation and guidance in the paradigms they employ along the way. The sources of their paradigms, the likenesses they discover in the scriptural witness, are open-ended like all paradigms, but never arbitrary. The temptation to indulge their own imaginations and fantasies always lies close at hand and can be restrained only by faithful adherence to the scriptural norm, which has been defined and disciplined by the long tradition of exegesis and articulated in doctrine, which codifies the "grammar" of Scripture. But just as the discipline of grammar does not prevent the poet or philosopher from employing the language in new and creative ways, so the church's doctrine does not confine the theologian to a boring traditionalism but rather provides guideposts and warning signs along the way to new insights into the meaning and application of the biblical witness to real life in the world today.

Theological Explorations in Faithful Imagination

Normative Christian imagination is the employment of the human imagination in ways that remain faithful to the biblical paradigm. The following chapters are offered as examples of how one theologian has tried to carry out that vocation. As such, of course, they represent just a few of the myriad ways in which Christians might interpret their own tradition and the world around them through the eyes of faith. Their arrangement is not sequential or systematic but rather exploratory, seeking to demonstrate though a variety of examples how the theological followers of Jesus might practice their profession today.

PART 1

IMAGINATION AND THEOLOGICAL HERMENEUTICS

2

MYTH, HISTORY, AND IMAGINATION

The Creation Narratives in the Bible and Theology

W hile I was doing graduate studies in theology, Van Harvey's book *The Historian and the Believer* became the focus of a lively debate about what had come to be called the problem of "faith and history." As is so often the case, the subtitle tells us what the book is really about: "the *morality* of historical knowledge and Christian belief."[1] And the book, dedicated to Rudolf Bultmann, is indeed an impassioned moral appeal to the consciences of theologians. "The basic but unspoken issue between the historian and the believer is," in Harvey's words, "a difference concerning intellectual integrity, the morality of knowledge."[2] Especially telling is Harvey's account of the origin of the modern historicist ethic, an insight he attributes to Ernst Troeltsch. Modern historical method, which had created such difficulties for faith, was the outgrowth of a new morality. Paraphrasing Troeltsch, Harvey puts it this way: "A new morality of critical judgment . . . has seized the imagination of the scholar in the Western world and . . . it is this ideal which seems incompatible with the ethic of belief that has dominated

1. Van Austin Harvey, *The Historian and the Believer: The Morality of Historical Knowledge and Christian Belief* (New York: Macmillan, 1966).
2. Harvey, *The Historian and the Believer*, 47.

Christendom for centuries."[3] Harvey's choice of words here—"seized the imagination"—is exactly right, though I doubt he realized its full significance. I'll have more to say about that later on.

"Faith and History" Revisited: The Twilight of Modernity

The Historian and the Believer is a particularly vivid articulation of a typically modern sensibility—one that I believe has been gradually losing its hold on our postmodern imagination. I'm not sure I know what "postmodern" is, but like many others I am drawn to the use of such language by the creeping conviction that (whatever the "post" may herald) we find ourselves living in the twilight of the "modern" world. The metaphor is apt, because the defining image of the moderns has been *light*: they called their movement the Enlightenment and were quick to dub an earlier era the Dark Ages, from which we moderns are now mercifully delivered. Though it is so embedded in our common discourse that we scarcely notice it any longer, the very notion of the modern carries with it a version of Third-Age enthusiasm: the preceding era is conceived as a "middle" age, sandwiched between the ancient and the modern. Did not the original Enlighteners— the *Aufklärer* and *philosophes*—come forward with a passion reminiscent of Joachim of Flora, or even Adolf Hitler, although their Age of the Spirit was to be the Age of *Geist*, their Third Reich the millennium of Reason? "*Sapere aude!* 'Have courage to use your own reason!'—that is the motto of enlightenment."[4]

Before I get carried away by my (or Kant's) rhetoric, let me insert a caveat. I do not want to encourage the popular sport among intellectuals of Enlightenment-bashing. In the first place, it would be masochistic and self-defeating, for the Enlightenment is not just about "them" but "us." Too much has been gained—and precisely by biblical scholars and theologians—in the last three hundred years for us to harbor fantasies of a return to some golden age of naïve faith and cultural unity. If *medieval* is properly not a term of derision, neither should it become one of approbation, something that has happened periodically in the modern age during episodes of Romantic reaction. Paul Ricoeur, whatever one may think of his hermeneutics, has surely given us an apt metaphor to describe what we seek: we who live in the twilight of modernity yearn to discover a "second naïveté," a way of living and thinking

3. Harvey, *The Historian and the Believer*, 38.
4. Immanuel Kant, "What Is Enlightenment?," in *On History*, ed. Lewis White Beck (Indianapolis: Bobbs-Merrill, 1963), 3.

that will allow a new appropriation of our ancient faith without renouncing the critical acumen we have inherited from the Enlightenment.

Myth and History

In an effort to help us think our way forward, out of the dilemmas of the late modern age, we need to reexamine the past in order to better understand how we got into our current predicament. I propose to do so by focusing on a particular locus of Christian doctrine—namely, creation. This topic is both directly pertinent to the issues of faith and history epitomized by Harvey's book and well suited to clarify the relationship between biblical studies and systematic theology. The two flash points in the ongoing modern conflict between the historian and the believer have been the accounts of the creation of the world in the Old Testament and the resurrection of Jesus in the New Testament. Both represent crucial turning points in the biblical narrative that likewise form the basis for central doctrinal affirmations of the Christian faith. Broadly speaking, the nineteenth century seemed fixated on the problem of creation, in which already controversial issues of historical factuality were intensified by revolutions in geology and biology that reached a climax in the debates surrounding Darwin's theory of evolution at the end of the century. Twentieth-century discussion among academic theologians seems more often to have taken the resurrection as the crucial test case for issues of faith and history, leaving the "Genesis and geology" debate to the fundamentalists. *The Historian and the Believer* is a good example of this focus on the resurrection. But I want to return to the less popular example and look again at how problems of faith and history have presented themselves with respect to the doctrine of creation.

The most notorious concept in the long modern struggle to come to terms with the Bible as a historical document is *myth*. Though the word was invented long before the nineteenth century, it took on new life and potency when David Friedrich Strauss redefined it in explicit contrast to *history*, understood in the modern—critical and scientific—sense.[5] In the ongoing attempts at rapprochement between theology and the academic study of religion in our own time, the rubric *myth* stands as a notable exception to the

---

5. David Friedrich Strauss, *The Life of Jesus Critically Examined*, ed. Peter C. Hodgson, trans. George Eliot (Philadelphia: Fortress, 1974). Especially to be recommended are Hodgson's introduction to the Strauss volume and Hans Frei, "David Friedrich Strauss," in *Nineteenth Century Religious Thought in the West*, ed. Ninian Smart et al. (New York: Cambridge University Press, 1985), 1:215–60.

prevailing consensus in matters of methodology and terminology. Textbooks of comparative religion, including ones otherwise free of the old history-of-religions animus against theology, routinely employ *myth* in careless and imprecise ways to cover the sacred narratives of all religious traditions, including (sometimes without any differentiation of internal genres) the Jewish and Christian scriptures.[6] Christian scholars, on the other hand, often continue to speak of the Bible in terms that seem to isolate it from other sacred literature and can appear to outsiders as a form of special pleading, as though "our" sacred writings could not even be studied with the same concepts applied to other traditions.

I want to suggest (reminiscent of Wilfred Cantwell Smith's proposal to retire the word *religion*) that *myth* is too fraught with historical and ideological baggage to be a usable concept in contemporary discussion. Since I doubt that my proposal will be any more successful than Smith's, let me present my argument briefly.

The negative connotations of the term are, rather surprisingly, not a modern innovation. From its origins in ancient Greece, *myth* has been the favored term for untrue religious stories. Only after they lost their power over the religious imagination of the ancient world were the narratives of the Greek and Roman gods called myths. New Testament exhortations to "have nothing to do with irreverent, silly myths" (1 Tim. 4:7; cf. 2 Tim. 4:4; Titus 1:14; 2 Pet. 1:16) are quite consistent with this ancient usage. Scholars and teachers of religion today who—usually under the influence of Eliade—want to use *myth* in a constructive or descriptively neutral sense often rail against the popular definition meaning the opposite of *fact*: "myths of racial superiority" or "ten myths about cancer."[7] But I have heard lecturers make this very point and then go on to violate their own prohibition—for example, by speaking deprecatingly of the "modern myth of inevitable progress." Is it not possible that the powerful resistance among religious believers to describing their scriptures as myth (especially when they

6. One example, noteworthy because it occurs in a textbook that is otherwise a model of conceptual clarity and evenhandedness, is William E. Paden, *Religious Worlds: The Comparative Study of Religion* (Boston: Beacon, 1988). Taking over Mircea Eliade's concept of myth, but without his explicit distinction between biblical and mythic traditions, Paden makes myth a constitutive element of all religions. "In biblical cultures," he writes, "scripture is myth, and *God* is the mythic word par excellence" (73). Though Eliade's conception of myth also raises important critical questions, on this issue he is more careful, contrasting the Western biblical traditions "with the archaic and palaeo-oriental religions, as well as with the mythic-philosophical concepts of the eternal return, as they were elaborated in India and Greece." Eliade, *The Sacred and the Profane: The Nature of Religion* (New York: Harcourt Brace Jovanovich, 1959), 110.

7. These are examples from Paden, *Religious Worlds*, 71.

haven't read Eliade) reflects a greater sensitivity to actual linguistic usage than that displayed by scholars who want to refurbish the concept?

But the real issue is not about diction but rather about a conceptual conundrum surrounding the alleged dichotomy of myth and history. To rationalists of the Enlightenment, the issue was clear-cut and unproblematic: myth could be true insofar as it could be interpreted as allegorical representation of universal truth. Since they generally presupposed that the truth is essentially ahistorical, dispensing with myth (and therefore with historical form) was not a disadvantage but an advantage. Kant's view of myth and history, for example, follows this pattern, remaining basically the same as that of earlier deists like Matthew Tindal. Things got more complicated after Hegel argued that truth is thoroughly historical in a way that does not allow for a neat separation of form and content. And yet in the end he appears to do something very much like that after all, first arguing that religion (in the specific form of Protestant Christianity) is the absolute embodiment of the truth but then suggesting that its form (*Vorstellung*, imaginative representation) remains deficient until it is sublimated (*aufgehoben*) into the pure form of philosophy (*Begriff*, concept).

Not until recently have theologians taken seriously the possibility that Christian truth might depend in some basic and irreducible way on the textual forms or literary genres of the Bible. Hans Frei's *Eclipse of Biblical Narrative* (1974) best exemplifies this theological paradigm shift, and George Lindbeck's arguments in *The Nature of Doctrine* (1984) have provoked discussion of the systematic philosophical and theological issues implicit in Frei's historical work.[8] The challenge of Frei and Lindbeck calls into question not just this or that proposal about myth and history, or biblical form and doctrinal content, but rather the very coherence of a way of thinking that tries to distinguish conceptual content from literary form—certainly in the case of Christian theology and probably in other fields as well. It thereby calls into question assumptions about the relations between language and truth that have been commonplace in religious thought at least since Schleiermacher. The philosophical point is well argued in another significant book, Wayne Proudfoot's *Religious Experience*, even though the author does not share the theological program of Frei and Lindbeck. Proudfoot shows, in my judgment convincingly, the incoherence of taking "experience" to be in any nontrivial sense preconceptual or prelinguistic.[9] Further support comes from the social

8. Hans W. Frei, *The Eclipse of Biblical Narrative: A Study in Eighteenth and Nineteenth Century Hermeneutics* (New Haven: Yale University Press, 1974); George A. Lindbeck, *The Nature of Doctrine: Religion and Theology in a Postliberal Age* (Philadelphia: Westminster, 1984).

9. Wayne Proudfoot, *Religious Experience* (Berkeley: University of California Press, 1985).

sciences, particularly from the work of cultural anthropologists like Clifford Geertz.[10] They show that experience—including religious experience—is a function of culture, especially in its symbol-creating activity. Here, too, the prevailing modern practice of arguing from experience to concepts is reversed. Religion is a system of culturally embedded symbols that give birth to (in Geertz's terms) both the worldview and the ethos—that is, the experience—of the people living in that symbolic world. Understanding such a world thus becomes not a matter of abstracting a "meaning" from the cultural-linguistic nexus of thought and action, but rather a matter of grasping the constitutive patterns that knit that particular social reality into a "world"—a cultural or religious unity. To seek to separate form from content, given this situation, would be an incoherent project. The form *is* the content: that is, the meaning of a religious world is precisely its shape, the concrete web of ideas, social interactions, symbolic forms, and so on, that give it the peculiar qualities that make it what it is and not something else.

From the perspective of contemporary theology, philosophy, and social anthropology, religions are "worlds," ways of living and being, not expressions of prior experience but rather means by which we experience. In that case, there can be no question of distinguishing, for example, the "essence" of Christianity from its "mythic" form. What happens to the problem of "faith and history" in this new intellectual climate (you can call it "postmodern" if you wish)? I'd like to explore that question by turning to the most notorious example of alleged "myth" in the Bible, the accounts of the creation of the world in Genesis. And I want to look in particular at one attempt to make theological sense of it, that undertaken by Karl Barth in his doctrine of creation.

Barth's Theology of Creation

Barth's whole approach to the creation narratives of Genesis appears to be motivated by a determination to avoid two extremes. On the one hand, he is at pains to stress the real historical character of the narratives, insisting that they take place in actual time, that their temporality is no mere form, mythic or otherwise, from which the true content might be extracted by the interpreter. On the other hand, he emphasizes that these narratives cannot be read simply as history in the usual, especially modern, sense of the word. In an effort to avoid the errors of both extremes, he employs the term *saga*

10. See, e.g., Clifford Geertz, "Religion as a Cultural System," in *The Interpretation of Cultures: Selected Essays* (New York: Basic Books, 1973), 87–125.

(German *Sage*), borrowed from Hermann Gunkel and others.[11] Here's how Barth defines it: "an image conceived in visionary-poetic fashion of a concretely unique, spatiotemporally limited, prehistoric temporal reality." Before directly examining this definition of *saga*, it will be fruitful to approach it negatively by noting its opposition to two other terms: *myth* and *history*. I believe that Barth chose the term *Sage* not primarily for its positive meaning but as a relatively neutral placeholder less likely to be misunderstood than other, more familiar terms. He wants to say, first, that the Genesis creation accounts are *not myth* and are *not history*.

The distinction between saga and myth is the more straightforward of the two. Whatever the source of Barth's concept of myth, and however much it may differ from prevailing definitions today, he leaves no doubt about how he understands the term: "The real *object* and *content* of myth," he writes, "are the essential principles of the general realities and relationships of the natural and spiritual cosmos, not bound to particular times and places (in contrast to concrete history)."[12] Although this definition would satisfy few scholars today, it was a position widely held among Barth's contemporaries. It quite accurately describes, for example, Bultmann's view of myth as seen through the lens of existentialist interpretation. Here Barth's point is one that would find widespread support today—namely, that biblical narratives cannot simply be reduced to a nonnarrative meaning, that they cannot be rightly understood as narrative expressions of general cosmic or theological principles. In a time when biblical narrative seems to be emerging from its eclipse, this point should not require an extensive defense.

The more interesting side of Barth's attempt to define the biblical creation accounts as saga emerges from the battle he wages on his other flank: his endeavor to distinguish saga from history. Here Barth's position is more difficult to grasp, a difficulty that becomes a virtual impossibility if one has recourse only to the English translation. The problem is that Barth employs the distinction—so trying to the patience of English speakers—between *Geschichte* and *Historie*. The translators have sometimes erased the distinction entirely by rendering both terms as *history*, and elsewhere have confused the issue by putting "history" in quotation marks for *Historie*, leaving the false

---

11. Karl Barth, *Die Lehre von der Schöpfung*, vol. III/1, of *Die kirchliche Dogmatik* (Zurich: EVZ-Verlag, 1970), 88 (hereafter cited as *KD* III/1). Cf. *The Doctrine of Creation*, trans. J. W. Edwards et al., in *Church Dogmatics*, vol. III/1 (Edinburgh: T&T Clark, 1958), 81 (hereafter cited as *CD* III/1). All translations are mine; for the convenience of the reader I have provided the corresponding reference to the published English translation following each reference to the German original.

12. *KD* III/1, 91 (cf. *CD* III/1, 84) (emphasis original).

impression that *Historie* is not *really* history but only "so-called history." But that is not at all Barth's point. The translators' dilemma stems not from any greater subtlety or profundity in the German but simply from the fact that the various terms have different ranges of meaning in the two languages. The English distinction between *history* and *story* (both corresponding to German *Geschichte*) makes it natural for us to think of *history* as describing real events and *story* as relating fictional, or at least imaginatively rendered, events. The point of introducing the modern word *Historie* was to enable a similar distinction to be made in German. Barth, for example, describes *Historie* as "*Geschichte* that is accessible to the human being because it allows an overview, because he can perceive it and comprehend it."[13] Thus, objectively, *Historie* is "creaturely *Geschichte* in the same context with other creaturely *Geschichte*—an event before which and besides which there are other events that are in principle similar, with which it can be compared and can be incorporated into one image." Subjectively considered, *Historie* is thus "the image of such a creaturely event in its creaturely context." Barth makes the point that this context is precisely what is lacking in the creation narratives. No one could possibly be in a position to relate events that were the origin of all events or to comprehend historically the source of all history. And then comes a statement that is the despair of the translator: "But *Geschichte* that we are incapable of seeing and comprehending is at any rate not *historische Geschichte*."[14] The translators come up with this: "But history which we cannot see and comprehend is not history in the historicist sense"—not bad, but they prove unable to cope with Barth's repeated use of the phrase *unhistorische Geschichte* to describe the Genesis creation accounts, usually settling for "'nonhistorical' history" (with the modifier enclosed in quotation marks). It is no wonder that readers of Barth in English become exasperated by such contradictory language. Surely "nonhistorical history" (with or without quotes) is double-talk that invites the suspicion that the author is trying to have it both ways: modern critical history and naïve ancient storytelling.

I don't have a solution to the translation problem, but I do hope to make Barth's meaning more evident, because I think he offers insight into the issues of faith and history that we late moderns or postmoderns may be in a favorable position to appreciate and develop further. Barth poses the issue of *Historie* and *Geschichte* in the form of a challenge to theologians, one to which I do not think we have so far responded adequately. It is "necessary and required" of us as theologians, he says, to make it clear that "the *Historische* and the

---

13. *KD* III/1, 84 (cf. *CD* III/1, 78).
14. *KD* III/1, 84 (cf. *CD* III/1, 78).

Unhistorische are together and belong together in actual *Geschichte*."[15] He employs two key conjunctions here, *daß* and *wie*: we are obligated both to make clear the fact *that* these two elements are combined in biblical narrative and to explain *how* they belong together.

What kind of distinction is at work here that allows Barth to speak of *historische* and *unhistorische Geschichte*, and to insist that the latter is nevertheless *wirkliche Geschichte*? To begin with the easier part, I think the point of using the neologism *Historie* is clear. It is a technical term for the modern critical discipline of history, designating both the academic practice itself and the object of its research. In other words, it designates *historiography* as distinct from history in a more general sense. Barth is saying in effect that biblical narrative combines historiographic narrative (the kind of history that falls within the competence of the historical scholar) and some other (nonhistoriographic) kind of narrative. And he is asserting that the resulting composite narrative is *true*: it is "real history," *wirkliche Geschichte*. He introduces the term *Sage* precisely in order to designate the nonhistoriographic element in this hybrid narrative.

The fact *that* these two kinds of narrative are combined in the Bible is relatively easy to accept. It is the *how* question that presents us with the greater challenge. I want first to describe Barth's treatment of this issue, and then to offer some suggestions for reconceiving matters in terms of imaginative acts. The outcome, I hope, will be to dissolve the problem of "faith and history," at least in its characteristically modern form exemplified by Harvey's book.

Before it is possible to say how the two elements in the composite biblical narrative go together—what Barth designates as *Sage* and *Historie*—we need to understand what the former, nonhistoriographic category consists in positively. Barth lists two attributes, one of them rather odd: saga, he says, is *divinitorisch* and *dichtend*. He defines *Divination* as "the vision of the historical becoming that precedes historiographic history, a vision that can be surmised from what has come to be, in which historiographic history takes place."[16] Note well: Barth maintains that the authors of the Genesis creation narratives got their material by surmising—literally, by "guessing" ("*sich . . . erraten läßt*")—what must have preceded all knowable history.[17] The biblical authors, Barth is saying, made an inspired guess! And they did so not on the basis of some additional source of information but by interpreting the real world, by extrapolation from the same history that is accessible to the

---

15. *KD* III/1, 88 (cf. *CD* III/1, 81).
16. *KD* III/1, 90 (cf. *CD* III/1, 83).
17. Here the English translators pull no punches: "the vision . . . can be guessed from that which has emerged" (*CD* III/1, 83).

historical scholar. The other attribute of saga, *Dichtung*, is simply "the linguistic shape of this surmising vision"; in other words, it is the literary genre
in which the envisioned narrative is depicted. So the two attributes of saga
are the material and the formal aspects of the same activity, the inspired act
(*Divination*) of apprehending the vision and the creative act (*Dichtung*) by
which that vision takes shape in human language.

Between the polar concepts of myth and history, which had polarized and
paralyzed theology and biblical studies from Strauss to Bultmann, Barth has
inserted the concept of saga. "The biblical creation story is pure saga," he
says in summary, and "as such distinguished from history and likewise from
myth."[18] In driving his point home, however, Barth makes one more important move. He slips in a term that will help us to relate his insights to our
postmodern situation.

One of the best pieces of advice I ever received from my teachers about
reading Karl Barth is never to skip the small print in the *Church Dogmatics*.
Indeed, some of the greatest gems of twentieth-century biblical interpretation, theological analysis, and intellectual history lie buried in those forbid-
ding passages. The term I want to highlight appears first in a brief excursus
at the end of Barth's attempt to delimit biblical saga from historiography. It
occurs in a passage that he cites with evident approval from Adolf Schlatter:

> With all the obscurities of his historical hindsight and his prophetic foresight,
> the biblical narrator is the servant of God, the one who awakens the recollec-
> tion of him and makes known his will. If he doesn't do it as knower, he does
> it as dreamer; if his eye should fail, his imagination [*Phantasie*] steps in and
> fills the gaps as needed. In this way he passes on the divine gift that entered
> into the course of history and makes it fruitful for posterity. The fact that he
> has to serve God not only as knower and thinker but also as poet and dreamer
> is grounded in the fact that he is human and we human beings are unable to
> arrest the transition from thought to poetry.[19]

Later, in his concluding remarks, Barth takes up the term *Phantasie*. Historiography, he insists, is not the only form in which the Bible speaks, because certain
aspects of our creaturely realm are inaccessible to historical investigation. In
an explicitly epistemological passage Barth writes, "The human faculty of
knowledge is not exhausted by the ability to perceive and to comprehend.
To the human faculty of knowledge there also belongs, in its own way just

18. *KD* III/1, 98 (cf. *CD* III/1, 90).
19. Cited in *KD* III/1, 91 (cf. *CD* III/1, 83), from Adolf Schlatter, *Das christliche Dogma*
(1923), 337.

as legitimately, the *imagination*."[20] Emerging into large print at last, Barth concludes his whole subsection on the genre of the biblical creation narratives with an explicit discussion of the role of imagination in Scripture. The ancient Israelite encounter with God that is embodied in these texts, he says, could only have been apprehended and presented by means of the imagination, that is, in the form of vision and poetry—the very terms by which he has defined saga. By "imagining in just this way," he writes, the biblical texts "are inspired, they are the witness of God's self-revelation, they demand faith and can lay claim to faith."[21] Barth goes to great lengths to remove any suspicion that imagination is an inadequate or inferior means as compared with historiography. These narratives are *Holy* Scripture, the "true witnesses to the true God . . . *not in spite of but because* they allow their imagination to govern."[22]

Imagining Creation

What I find most significant, and potentially most useful to theology today, in Barth's treatment of the form of the biblical creation narratives, is the fact that his key category, saga, turns out to be a way of saying that the texts are the product of human imagination. I have no particular attachment to the term *saga* as a genre and will gladly leave that issue to biblical scholars and historians of religion. But the issue of imagination is a theological one, and as such it is independent of the specifically literary, historical, and philological investigation of the texts. What is striking about Barth's doctrine of creation is not that he says the biblical creation narratives are imaginative literature, but that he claims the authority of divine revelation for that literature. The claim is audacious, but its audacity has nothing to do with Harvey's morality of historical knowledge. I want, in conclusion, to show how this difference between the "modern" problem of faith and history and the theological issue of the imagination can help us understand the tasks of biblical and systematic theologians in a postmodern context.

Let me propose a fairly straightforward way to distinguish between the modern and the postmodern—one designed to avoid the pretentiousness that plagues so much talk about postmodernity. The definitive feature of modern thought (i.e., Western thought since the Enlightenment) I take to be the conviction that there is a universal, rational order to the world that is in principle knowable by human beings, however great the practical difficulties

20. *KD* III/1, 99 (cf. *CD* III/1, 91).
21. *KD* III/1, 100 (cf. *CD* III/1, 92).
22. *KD* III/1, 100–101 (cf. *CD* III/1, 92) (emphasis original).

in doing so. A corollary of that thesis, often not explicit but always implicit, is that such knowledge is in principle independent of the act of knowing—once again, in spite of the difficulties involved in making the distinction in actual practice. The model on which this principle is based has been the modern natural sciences, especially as epitomized in the physical sciences after Newton, and later amended to include the life sciences after the acceptance of evolutionary theory by the end of the nineteenth century.

The difference between modern and postmodern assumptions, in this modest use of those terms, can be illustrated by looking at the different reasons various theologians have given for rejecting the category *myth* as descriptive of the biblical message. Earlier rationalists understood myth as a prescientific attempt to explain the world, one that must be rejected now that science has given us the true explanation. The valid religious ideas expressed mythically in the texts must be freed from this inadequate form. Bultmann distanced himself from the rationalist critique, believing that the valid religious content of the Bible consisted not in ideas but in an "existence possibility." But his reason for rejecting mythology remains the same: "modern man" cannot accept a mythological worldview because it involves notions of supernatural causality incompatible with the scientific worldview. Both critiques of myth, those of the older rationalism and of existentialism, rely on the characteristically modern assumption of a universal foundation of life in the world that is knowable (at least in principle) through science. Any set of beliefs incompatible with that epistemological foundation must be rejected. Bultmann makes the typical modernist error of absolutizing the "middle-sized" world of modern science.[23] Barth, too, denies that the biblical texts are myth, but for the very different reason that their narrative form is an essential aspect of their content. This critique not only does not share the modernist criterion, but implicitly denies it by insisting that the biblical writers were able to tell the truth only in a way that cannot be harmonized with modern science.[24] Barth, quite as much as Bultmann, inhabits a world permeated by modern science. But, unlike Bultmann, he does not feel compelled to harmonize the biblical world with scientific assumptions. He—and here he is like most of us postmoderns—simply does not feel the force of Bultmann's insistence that

23. For an elaboration of this modernist error, which I call "mesocosmic parochialism," see Garrett Green, *Imagining God: Theology and the Religious Imagination* (Grand Rapids: Eerdmans, 1998), 74–77.

24. Barth uses strong language indeed in making this point. Engaging in "historical harmonizing" of the Genesis creation stories, he says, amounts to "rape" of the text: "*es könnte nur vergewaltigt werden, wenn es in dieser Absicht gelesen und ausgelegt würde*" (*KD* III/1, 88). The metaphor is sanitized ("do violence to") in the English translation (*CD* III/1, 80).

we choose between the biblical world of myth and our world of electric lights and radios and medical science.[25]

Barth's refusal to choose between the worlds of Bible and science, which produced charges of irrationalism and *sacrificium intellectus* at the time, requires a more careful hearing today. If any intellectual development deserves the designation "postmodern," it is the demise of the conception of science as a unified, value-neutral means of explaining phenomena directly—the very conception that defines the modern. Virtually everyone in the academic world today is willing to acknowledge that "all data are theory-laden," that doing physics and writing history require imagination. Assuming this postmodern turn, I want to show its implications for the problems of "faith and history," with particular reference to the biblical creation accounts.

The polarity of "myth and history," extending from Enlightenment rationalism through Strauss to Bultmann, is a product of the modern sensibility, a variation on the dichotomy between "religion and science" that runs through the thought of the past three hundred years. The problem of "faith and history" is another variation on the same theme, rooted in the unquestioned assumption that scientific rationality, historiography in this case, is the measure and foundation of all knowledge. Harvey's eloquently described "pathos of the modern mind" is just that: a dilemma felt deeply by Christians of the *modern* era who were torn between naïve or uncritical faith and scientific criticism. "From liberal Protestantism to the new hermeneutic," Harvey wrote in 1966, "Protestant theology may be regarded as a series of salvage operations, attempts to show how one can still believe in Jesus Christ and not violate an ideal of intellectual integrity."[26] That ideal now seems to have lost its power.

What makes that modern pathos seem so "pathetic," so melodramatic and yet so naïve, to our postmodern ears today is a radically revised picture of science, one that understands scientific research to be rooted in cultural commitments and social intercourse, dependent on the persuasive power of shared paradigms that give it shape and focus but that cannot themselves be justified by appeal to universal principles. This revisionist account of the history and philosophy of science tends to loosen the grip and blur the edges of the old ("modern") polarities between fact and theory, data and interpretation, *Erklären* and *Verstehen*, science and religion. Stated positively, the thesis is that scientists, like other inquirers after truth, use their imagination

---

25. The reference is to a passage in Bultmann's famous essay, "New Testament and Mythology: The Problem of Demythologizing the New Testament Proclamation," in *New Testament and Mythology and Other Basic Writings*, ed. and trans. Schubert M. Ogden (Philadelphia: Fortress, 1984), 4.

26. Harvey, *The Historian and the Believer*, 103–4.

to discover those paradigms or exemplary patterns that enable them to better understand the world.

In this regard, at least, theologians and biblical scholars are no different. Having overcome what Richard Bernstein calls "the Cartesian Anxiety,"[27] we do not expect (for example) that the paradigm governing our scientific understanding of the origin of species will be the same one governing our theological apprehension of the origin of the world. Relativism no longer threatens to undo our grasp on reality because we no longer imagine that we need universal principles to link all human knowledge systematically or to ground it in incorrigible truth. As Christians we define ourselves by our commitment to Jesus Christ, the paradigm of our knowledge of God, the pattern impressed upon the imaginations of the prophets and apostles and embodied in the canon of the Old and New Testaments, to which we seek to conform our thought and action.

This postmodern orientation requires us to readjust our conception of faith. The decisive issue is not evidence, as it was for the modern world, but rather trust. This insight is not something new; it is the postmodern rediscovery of the premodern doctrine that "the essence of *fides* is *fiducia*," that the assent of faith "is not a theoretical but a practical assent, i.e., an *apprehensio fiducialis*."[28] The "risk of faith," about which our modern theological forebears liked to talk so much, is not a matter of possible historical error (*pace* Harvey) but of choosing the wrong paradigm—of misimagining the world. The audacious claim of Christians is that the biblical writers rightly imagined the world, including its essential relation to God. The proof of that claim, like all paradigmatic claims, is to be found only in its actual use. In the case of a religious paradigm commitment, one involving a claim about the ultimate shape of reality, the only way to prove its truth is to live by it. Christians live out that proof (the only true "proof of the spirit and of power") by faithful imagination—that is, by living in the conviction that the world envisioned in the Bible is the real world. We trust in the faith of the biblical witnesses, which is a way of saying that we trust their imagination.

Imagination, in this comprehensive sense of the term, includes more than Barth's *Phantasie*. He uses the term to designate just one of a number of expressive forms employed by the biblical writers. The Bible speaks imaginatively, he says, but also historically, reflectively, morally, lyrically.[29] But this way of putting

27. Richard J. Bernstein, *Beyond Objectivism and Relativism: Science, Hermeneutics, and Praxis* (Philadelphia: University of Pennsylvania Press, 1985), esp. 16–20.

28. Heinrich Heppe, *Reformed Dogmatics: Set Out and Illustrated from the Sources*, ed. and rev. Ernst Bizer, trans. G. T. Thomson (1950; repr., Grand Rapids: Baker, 1978), 532.

29. *KD* III/1, 102 (cf. *CD* III/1, 93).

things, while rightly emphasizing the literary diversity of Scripture, obscures the sense in which the Bible taken *as a whole* is a work of imagination. Accordingly, Barth's emphasis on the *composite* nature of the creation narratives is misleading insofar as it overlooks their imaginative unity. We see them as a blend of two elements, *Phantasie* and *Historie*, because our imaginations have been trained (as Troeltsch and Harvey recognize) in the modern morality of historical scholarship. Even the modern commonplace of speaking of two accounts of creation, likewise shared by Barth, can lead us to confuse theological with historical-critical interpretation. *Theologically* considered, the opening chapters of Genesis present us with a world, the one world that God created in the beginning. Those whose imaginations are captured by that story respond in faith, which means that they acknowledge the power of that scriptural vision to render truthfully the ultimate shape of reality and thus their own place in it.

Our common Nicene affirmation of belief "in God, the Father almighty, maker of heaven and earth" is one of the ways in which we express that faithful imagination. Equally important, it is also a way of allowing our imaginations to be shaped, to be conformed to the vision we acknowledge. It is no accident that the creed finds its primary application not in doctrine but in liturgy, and that it has always played a prominent role in catechism—that is, in training and nurturing the imagination of each successive generation of believers.

But what does it mean to train the imagination? Here the most useful analogies are found not in the sciences but in the arts. "The art of listening to stories," writes Northrop Frye, "is a basic training for the imagination."[30] This passage is all the more significant because it occurs in a context having nothing to do with religion. Its theological equivalent is the principle that "faith comes from hearing" (Rom. 10:17). Calvin likened Scripture to spectacles, a kind of corrective lens enabling us to see reality without the distortions of sin.[31] But the metaphor of the Bible as lens is overly simple, since it cannot account for our tendency to misread the Bible. Scripture is not the lens itself but rather the vision seen through the lens. It is more like a video taken with a particular lens or filter. The lens is the analog of faith—"the eyes of faith." The danger of taking the Bible itself to be the necessary corrective is that it puts the reader in control. The text becomes *verfügbar*, subject to our disposing—and that is always a misuse of Scripture.[32] Here is precisely

---

30. Northrop Frye, *The Educated Imagination* (Bloomington: Indiana University Press, 1964), 116.

31. Calvin, *Institutes of the Christian Religion* 1.5.11. See chap. 1 above and Green, *Imagining God*, 106–7.

32. For more on *verfügbar* and *unverfügbar*, see chap. 1 above, under "Imagination in Science and Theology."

the point of the old doctrine of the internal illumination of the Holy Spirit. It isn't enough to have the true text unless we also have the proper spectacles with which to read it. Christians are saying something like this about the creation narratives: this is how the prophets and apostles saw the origin of the world with eyes of faith. And since they are our models for faith (we have no more reliable criterion to which we might appeal), we seek to be guided by their example to see our present world through the same eyes. Scripture cannot do that for us, but it can train our imagination to do it. (In this sense medieval theology was right: faith *is* a habit, a skill learned by painstaking trial and error.) Consider an analogy taken from the visual arts: learning to see the world faithfully is like learning to see the world through, say, Van Gogh's eyes. How do you do it? By patient training and practice. You study his paintings and then you look at nature, and if you succeed, you will see nature with "new eyes."

A Practical Postscript

Finally, let me say a few words about the implications of my argument for the relation between the work of biblical scholars and systematic theologians. My thesis has two aspects. First (and most important), *in theory*, our relationship presents no problem at all because our task is the same: to discover how the authors of Scripture imagined God and the world and to interpret their vision so that it might shape the imagination of the Christian community today. Second, *in practice*, our roles are quite different indeed—so different, in fact, that we typically read almost none of the same books or journals, and special consultations need to be devised to get us into conversation. The practical division of labor is unavoidable because of our finitude and the complexity of our world. But it is also dangerous for the obvious reason that we may fail to listen to each other as we go about the different aspects of our common task.

Let me characterize the work of each in a few broad strokes. The biblical scholar specializes in the Bible as concrete text; the systematic theologian in the pattern, the symbolic matrix, which the Bible exemplifies. The biblical scholar studies the Bible as paradigm in the sense of artifact; the systematic theologian studies the biblical paradigm in the sense of normative pattern. Thus they are both studying the same object (the paradigm) but from opposite ends of the image/concept spectrum. Neither can do without the other, for both are really doing the same thing, but each in a one-sided way. The greatest biblical and theological scholars have been the ones who have come closest to grasping this common task in its unity. Perhaps there is a positive lesson to be learned from the disappearance of the "great men" from the faculties of biblical studies and theology. It reminds us that our work is inherently social and communal—a truth that we ought to have learned long ago from our common object of study. For when God, as the story goes, decided to create a world, it turned out that one human creature was not enough. Only when two people, and two different *kinds* of people, populated the earth could the story could go on.

3

WHO'S AFRAID
OF LUDWIG FEUERBACH?

Suspicion and the Religious Imagination

An object first takes on its true intrinsic dignity when the sacred
nimbus is stripped off; for as long as a thing or being is an object
of religious worship, it is clad in borrowed plumes, namely, the
peacock feathers of the human imagination.

—Ludwig Feuerbach, *Lectures on the Essence of Religion*

We . . . need be afraid of no Feuerbach.

—Karl Barth, *Church Dogmatics*

Ludwig Feuerbach appears condemned to play the historical role of
"influence." We read other thinkers of the nineteenth century today—
Hegel, for example, or Kierkegaard, or Marx—for their ideas, for
the insights they continue to bring to contemporary issues. But Feuerbach is
nearly always studied primarily because of the influence he has exercised on
other thinkers—the ones who still attract readers today. James Livingston, for
example, concludes his treatment of Feuerbach in *Modern Christian Thought*
by noting how his "influence on modern thought far exceeds that of thinkers of much greater reputation and popularity." He mentions Feuerbach's
contributions to now familiar themes in existentialism, to the psychological
theories of Sigmund Freud and Erich Fromm, and to the I–Thou philosophy

of Martin Buber, before coming at last to the "most significant of all" the influences: the role that Feuerbach's ideas played in the development of Karl Marx's thought both early and late.[1] Even the critical edition of Feuerbach's works—produced, significantly, in the Berlin of the German Democratic Republic—pays tribute to him primarily as "one of the most outstanding philosophical materialists of the pre-Marxist period . . . and above all as one of the immediate philosophical predecessors of Marx and Engels."[2]

While hardly wishing to deny the importance of such influences, Van Harvey, in *Feuerbach and the Interpretation of Religion*, wants more: convinced that Feuerbach has been the victim of persistent misunderstandings, he wants to rehabilitate him so that his voice can be heard today in the dialog about the meaning of religion. To this end, Harvey proposes to undertake a "rational reconstruction" of Feuerbach's philosophy of religion, not simply a historical account of his thought in the context of his own time and place.[3] Two themes in particular emerge from his attempt to reconstruct Feuerbach's treatment of religion that invite further reflection and response from readers today, not only from those who study religion academically but also from those for whom the interpretation of religion is a matter of *theological* importance. Since I belong to both groups, I propose to take seriously the implications of Feuerbach's theory of religion for both religious studies and historical theology.

The first theme highlighted in Harvey's reading of Feuerbach is *suspicion*. Harvey claims in effect that Feuerbach is the forgotten founder of the hermeneutics of suspicion, and his omission from the canonical list of "masters of suspicion" stems from a failure to understand and appreciate his mature theory of religion. A second theme to emerge from Harvey's retrieval of Feuerbach is the central role of *imagination* in his account of the origin and continuing power of religion in human life and history.

Feuerbach: Neglected Master of Suspicion

One of the more perceptive questions raised by Harvey concerns that now-classic category of Paul Ricoeur, the hermeneutics of suspicion. Why, asks

1. James C. Livingston, *Modern Christian Thought*, 2nd ed., vol. 1, *The Enlightenment and the Nineteenth Century* (Minneapolis: Fortress, 2006), 228–29.

2. Werner Schuffenhauer, preface to *Gesammelte Werke*, by Ludwig Feuerbach (Berlin: Akademie-Verlag, 1981), 1:vii. In the same opening sentence, the editor also pigeonholes Feuerbach as "one of the prominent representatives of classical German *bourgeois* philosophy."

3. Van A. Harvey, *Feuerbach and the Interpretation of Religion* (New York: Cambridge University Press, 1995), 116ff. Subsequent page references to this work are provided parenthetically in the text.

Harvey, is Feuerbach not included along with Marx, Nietzsche, and Freud as one of the "masters of suspicion," those revolutionaries of nineteenth-century thought who changed forever the way we read the authoritative texts of our traditions, especially our religious traditions? He notes that Ricoeur is not alone in denying Feuerbach a place among the suspicious elite and offers some reasons why this should be so. First, Feuerbach's influence on subsequent thinkers has not been as great as that of Marx, Nietzsche, and Freud; and second, his critique "was not part of a larger theoretical framework that was widely appropriated by secular intellectuals and integrated into what we now call the behavioral sciences" (7). More important than either of these factors, however, are a number of widely held misinterpretations of Feuerbach's critique of religion, and it is largely to show that they *are* misinterpretations that Harvey has written his book. He is persuaded that "all of these conventional judgments are partial and misleading truths," and he proposes "to challenge and, if possible, to correct them" (11). Chief among the misreadings of Feuerbach, according to Harvey, is the exclusive identification of his theory of religion with *The Essence of Christianity* (1841), an interpretation that leads either to the neglect of his later works or else to the assumption that those later works merely refine or clarify the theory already articulated in the 1841 book. In fact, according to Harvey's interpretation, in the mature Feuerbach, religion "is no longer explained in terms of self-consciousness alone but in terms of a contingent self confronted with an all-encompassing nature upon which it is absolutely dependent" (162). And Harvey is quite definite in his judgment that the later theory is better (163); it is new and "truly original" (169), he claims, and best of all it breaks finally with the lingering Hegelianism of *The Essence of Christianity*. The later theory "assumes, as the earlier did not, that believers have intellectual grounds, albeit mistaken, for their beliefs" (199). Harvey thinks that Feuerbach makes a useful contribution to the modern academic study of religion because he really "listen[s] to what believers themselves say" (309). (Harvey's hermeneutical charity toward Feuerbach may occasionally over-reach itself; believers might be excused for not appreciating a careful listener who concludes that their hymns, prayers, hopes, and beliefs all amount in the end to no more than "the religious illusion.") Harvey's point is that Feuerbach deserves a hearing for his mature attempt to "let religion itself speak" and then to offer his own interpretation. *Feuerbach and the Interpretation of Religion* is an invitation to do just that, to engage in serious dialog with one of the most important critics of religion in the modern age; and by offering us a fresh and insightful account of Feuerbach's later theory of religion, Harvey's book helps to advance that dialog.

Feuerbach and the Theologians

One of the criteria for rational reconstructions that Harvey borrows from Richard Rorty (whom he credits with originating the distinction between rational and historical reconstructions) is that "they are dominated by questions that have come to prominence in some recent work." Harvey assures us that his reconstruction of Feuerbach's thought springs from just such contemporary concerns; he is also explicit about the fact that in his own case the questions arise "in the field of religious studies in contrast to theology." Despite his own disinterest in theological questions, he nevertheless makes an intriguing observation about Feuerbach's reception by the theologians. "Strangely enough," he remarks, "Feuerbach's work for the most part has been taken seriously only by Marxist philosophers and Protestant theologians and has been virtually neglected by scholars in religious studies" (20). For just this reason he undertakes to explore the implications of Feuerbach's thought for religious studies, by which he evidently means nontheological religious studies. Since I have a rather different take on what properly constitutes the field of religious studies (and how it is related to theology), I want to remove the brackets that Harvey has placed around theological questions. Religious studies is the legitimate domain of all scholars who—out of whatever religious, antireligious, or extrareligious motivations and interests—wish to engage in the serious, public, and academic investigation into the nature, function, and value of religion. For this reason I do not find it strange that theologians (not to mention Marxist philosophers) should be among the first to take Feuerbach's critique of religion seriously. They are, after all, the ones with the biggest stake in the outcome. The attempt to separate the study of religion from theological questions (something, incidentally, that Feuerbach never dreamed of doing) inevitably leads to the neglect of the inescapable question of the *truth* of religious teachings, and hence the integrity of religious believers. Nowhere are these issues more sharply focused than in the themes of suspicion and imagination, especially at their point of convergence. Harvey's rational reconstruction of Feuerbach's interpretation of religion, perhaps in spite of Harvey's own intentions, sheds a revealing light on these issues, including their theological implications.

Harvey's observation about theological interest in Feuerbach requires some qualification as soon as we look more closely at the theological landscape since the nineteenth century. Of the leading twentieth-century theologians, only Karl Barth devoted serious attention to Feuerbach.[4] More remarkable than the

---

4. For bibliographic references to theological responses to Feuerbach in the first half of the twentieth century, see the superb article by John Glasse, "Barth on Feuerbach," *Harvard Theological Review* 57 (1964): 69–96, esp. note 1.

general theological neglect of Feuerbach, however, is the nature of this one exception: Barth's treatment of Feuerbach's theory of religion is overwhelmingly positive. The primary reason for Barth's affirmation of Feuerbach is that he sees him as an ally (though admittedly an unwitting one) in his struggle to free theology from its dangerous infatuation with religion. Barth takes him to be, in the words of John Glasse, "the man whose query does nothing less than locate the Achilles heel of modern theology," a flaw that is most obvious in the case of Schleiermacher but that also afflicts other theologians, including Schleiermacher's critics.[5] Barth mentions specifically G. Menken, J. A. L. Wegscheider, W. L. De Wette, A. Tholuck, and P. Marheineke as other theologians of the day who left themselves open to Feuerbach's reduction of theology to anthropology. He doesn't stop with the generation of Schleiermacher but includes as well later theologians who had the benefit of hearing Feuerbach's critique yet nevertheless persisted in doing theology in a way that perpetuated the "apotheosis of man," thus remaining vulnerable to the Feuerbachian reduction. This history of shame in nineteenth-century theology reaches its culmination in 1900 in the crowning irony of Adolf von Harnack's public lectures on *The Essence of Christianity*, the same title under which Feuerbach had already demonstrated the disastrous consequences of the very path proposed by Harnack.

Barth's endorsement of Feuerbach is decidedly qualified in one respect. While crediting Feuerbach with drawing the inevitable consequence of the theological enterprise of his day, Barth nevertheless refers to it as "Feuerbach's trivial conclusion," wondering how these theologians could have left themselves vulnerable "to that mean insinuation," that "slander."[6] Feuerbach may be right in important respects, says Barth, but his theory of religion remains shallow, "a platitude," "at bottom trite beyond compare."[7] It is surely overstating the case, however, to say, as Harvey does in his introduction, that Barth treats Feuerbach simply "as a *reductio ad absurdum* of liberal theology since Schleiermacher" (20). In the first place, Barth hardly thinks that the identification of religion with human projection is an absurdity, for he endorses this position himself as the negative moment of the dialectic of religion and revelation in his own theory of religion in the

5. Glasse, "Barth on Feuerbach," 72.
6. Karl Barth, "An Introductory Essay," in *The Essence of Christianity*, by Ludwig Feuerbach (New York: Harper, 1957), xx–xxi. This essay, used as an introduction to the English translation of Feuerbach's most famous work, was translated by James Luther Adams from a lecture Barth gave in Münster in 1926, later published as a chapter in *Die Theologie und die Kirche* (Zollikon, Zurich: Evangelischer Verlag, 1928).
7. Barth, "Introductory Essay," xxvii.

Church Dogmatics.[8] Second, Barth by no means restricts his appreciation of Feuerbach to his role in unmasking the error of modern theology.[9] Even his negative comments about Feuerbach appear in the context of a generous appreciation of Feuerbach's intentions. He says, in effect, that if one is going to turn man into God Feuerbach's way of doing it is at least more honest than the theologians' way. Moreover, Feuerbach does greater justice to the concrete reality of human life in the world than do the spiritualizing abstractions of the theologians. He has a "head start over modern theology" because of what Barth calls (negatively) "his resolute antispiritualism" or (positively) "his anthropological realism." Barth calls special attention to the communal nature of Feuerbach's humanism. Perhaps for this reason he treats Feuerbach with greater deference than that other notorious nineteenth-century despiser of Christianity, Friedrich Nietzsche. Whereas Nietzsche represents for Barth the great champion of the isolated individual, of "humanity without the fellow-man,"[10] Feuerbach affirms the unity of human bodily and spiritual reality "in the relation of the I and the Thou." ("It is just because religion is concerned with the assertion of this unity," Barth comments, "that it makes sense and not nonsense" for Feuerbach.)[11] The supreme example of this communal anthropology is surely Feuerbach's interpretation of the Christian doctrine of the Trinity, which Harvey cites. The Trinity, Feuerbach argues,

> is the secret of the *necessity of the "thou" for an "I"*; it is the truth that *no being*—be it man, God, mind or ego—*is for itself alone* a *true, perfect,* and *absolute* being, that *truth* and *perfection* are only the *connection* and *unity* of beings equal in their essence. The highest and last principle of philosophy is, therefore, the *unity of men with men.*[12]

This social understanding of the Trinity shows striking similarities to Barth's own theology, so his admiration is perhaps not surprising. Not only does Feuerbach work "with human honesty and real seriousness"; Barth is willing to say

8. For an account of Barth's theological theory of religion, see Garrett Green, "Introduction: Barth as Theorist of Religion," in *On Religion: The Revelation of God as the Sublimation of Religion,* by Karl Barth (London: T&T Clark, 2006), 1–29.

9. Harvey also errs in assuming that Barth thinks Feuerbach unmasks the secret only of *liberal* theology. Barth makes quite clear that the judgment falls on virtually all theologians, including many of the most conservative of the day.

10. Barth, *Church Dogmatics*, vol. III/2, ed. G. W. Bromiley and T. F. Torrance, trans. Harold Knight et al. (Edinburgh: T&T Clark, 1960), 231–42.

11. Barth, "Introductory Essay," xxiv.

12. Feuerbach, *Principles of the Philosophy of the Future*, trans. Manfred H. Vogel, Library of Liberal Arts (Indianapolis: Bobbs-Merrill, 1966), 72, cited by Harvey, *Feuerbach,* 179.

even that "he works, as it were, with a Christian realism." So "Feuerbach—
however badly he may have done his work—was and is really stronger than
the great majority of modern and most recent theologians."[13] Barth's concern is to pass judgment not on Feuerbach—who, after all, does not claim
to be doing Christian theology—but rather on those thinkers who make
such a claim. "Why has Christian theology," he asks, "not seen these things
earlier and better than Feuerbach, things that it certainly must have seen if it
really knew the Old and New Testament?" Barth is unwilling to join in the
self-serving tut-tutting of the theologians about Feuerbach's atheism until
they have put their own house in order. Barth in effect agrees with Harvey's
judgment that Feuerbach "believed that religion was too important a subject
to leave to the theologians" (6). Barth believes it too—rather, he believes
that *theology* is too important a subject to leave to the theologians, for "the
attitude of the anti-theologian Feuerbach was more theological than that of
many theologians."[14]

Suspicion and Imagination in Feuerbach's Theory of Religion

Feuerbach and the Interpretation of Religion ought, at the very least, to
alter the way scholars henceforth understand the nineteenth-century roots
of religious studies. For Harvey demonstrates convincingly that the hermeneutics of suspicion begins with Feuerbach—and not merely because of his
influence on Marx. Indeed, Feuerbach's ideas on religion lead more directly
to the Freudian than to the Marxian or Nietzschean version of suspicion.[15]
The all-important concept of projection originates with Feuerbach, a debt
acknowledged by Freud, who first turned it into a powerful and influential
(if also problematic and controversial) tool in the interpretation of religion.
(A portion of the credit also belongs to George Eliot, who rendered Feuerbach's cumbersome philosophical term *Vergegenständlichung* in the arresting metaphor of *projection*.)[16] Likewise pointing toward Freud's later theory
is Feuerbach's emphasis on the role of desire in religion, eventuating in the
Glückseligkeitstrieb, a term rife with proleptic Freudian overtones.

13. Barth, "Introductory Essay," xxiv–xxv.
14. Barth, "Introductory Essay," x.
15. Merold Westphal detects three layers in Feuerbach's critique of religion: an explicit
Hegelian one, a proto-Freudian one, and a more obscure Marxian strain, later radicalized by
Marx himself. See Westphal, *Suspicion and Faith: The Religious Uses of Modern Atheism*
(Grand Rapids: Eerdmans, 1993), 123–33, esp. 125.
16. It is ironic testimony to the success of Eliot's translation that her term has found its way
back into current German discourse about religion in the form of *projizieren* and *Projektion*.

More important than these adumbrations of later nineteenth-century theory, however, is Feuerbach's account of the engine of religious projection. By identifying imagination as the "organ of religion," Feuerbach opened a perspective on religion whose significance is only beginning to be grasped today. Had he possessed even an inkling of the possibilities inherent in this thesis—and nothing is more obvious from Harvey's book than that he did not—his treatment of religion might well have taken on a proto-Nietzschean cast. The importance of Feuerbach's thesis that the imagination is the key to understanding how and why human beings are religious lies beyond the horizon of his own narrowly positivist epistemology and stolidly modernist temperament. All one has to do in order to bring out the possibilities of his thesis is to bracket just one unreflected assumption that Feuerbach always takes for granted and (therefore) never attempts to justify: the axiom that *imagination* and *reality* comprise an unproblematic duality, that they are opposed and mutually exclusive terms. In more fashionably contemporary terms, one could call this move a deconstruction of Feuerbach's concept of *Einbildungskraft/Phantasie.*

The crucial connection is the one that links suspicion to imagination. Feuerbach's descriptive thesis is that religion is the product of imagination. But his evaluative thesis is more revealing: *because* religion is produced by the imagination, he claims, we are justified in treating it with suspicion. Why is Feuerbach suspicious of religious ideas and sentiments? Because they are the fruits of imagination and *therefore* cannot be true. Nothing could have been more obvious to Feuerbach; and nothing makes it more obvious to us how much the intellectual world has changed in a century and a half. In reviewing his intellectual development at the start of *Lectures on the Essence of Religion*, Feuerbach contrasts his own position with Hegel's in a way that brings out forcefully the dualism of reason and imagination in his thought. Philosophy, he writes, deals with thought (*Denken*) or reason (*Vernunft*), while religion deals with emotion (*Gemüt*) and imagination (*Phantasie*). Whereas in Hegel religion "merely translate[s] speculative ideas into emotionally charged images," Feuerbach insists on a sharp dichotomy between them. He believes that Hegel missed something important in religion, "an element that is distinct from thought" and that constitutes the "very essence" of religion, which he calls sensuousness (*Sinnlichkeit*).[17] In Hegel, religion

17. Ludwig Feuerbach, *Lectures on the Essence of Religion*, trans. Ralph Manheim (New York: Harper & Row, 1967), 12; *Vorlesungen über das Wesen der Religion: Nebst Zusätzen und Anmerkungen*, ed. Wolfgang Harich, *Gesammelte Werke*, vol. 6 (Berlin: Akademie-Verlag, 1967), 18. In subsequent citations, I have provided shortened titles for references to this work, first to the English translation and then to the German original.

occupies precisely the mediating role between the pure sensuousness of art and the pure conceptuality of philosophy; its defining feature is the ability to mediate between the realms of intellect and sense, a form that he calls *Vorstellung*—traditionally translated "representation" but actually closer to "imagination" in English, as I have argued elsewhere.[18] From the vantage point of the twenty-first century (whether one thinks of post-Kuhnian philosophy of science or of postmodern critiques of the metaphysical tradition), Feuerbach's move hardly seems an advance over Hegel. For although Hegel can be faulted for ultimately subordinating religious *Vorstellung* to the philosophical *Begriff*, thus perpetuating the long-standing Western prejudice for intellect over sense, Feuerbach does it undialectically and from the outset. For him the essence of religion is sensuousness, *not* intellect; and since "emotion and imagination are . . . rooted in sensibility," imagination can yield *only* illusion, leaving the field of truth to pure reason, now stripped of sensuousness—that is, of all relation to the body. So Feuerbach's sensuous anthropology, much praised even by Karl Barth, is not quite what it seems. After wisely noting that *Sinnlichkeit* includes "not only the belly, but the head as well," Feuerbach proceeds to exempt the head from the limitations of *Sinnlichkeit* by presupposing a disembodied faculty of purely intelligible *Denken* and *Vernunft* that evidently gazes directly upon the truth. In the end, for Feuerbach—*Sinnlichkeit* notwithstanding—the head thinks truth, while the belly imagines illusion.

The Beam of Projection and the Grid of Imagination

Harvey titled his book *Feuerbach and the Interpretation of Religion*—rather than, say, *Feuerbach's Interpretation of Religion*—for good reason. His interest is not simply historical, for he thinks that studying Feuerbach not only illumines the origins of religious studies in the nineteenth century but also helps us understand religion today. This constructive and contemporary motivation comes most clearly to the fore in chapter 7, the book's longest, titled "Feuerbach and Contemporary Projection Theories." Here Harvey attempts to cash out the new and improved critique of religion in the later Feuerbach by showing its usefulness for the theory of religious projection, a task he carries out by bringing his "ideal Feuerbach" into "the modern conversation" about the meaning and truth of religion. For reasons that I find puzzling, Harvey has chosen to modernize Feuerbach by focusing on projection—the very concept

18. See Garrett Green, *Imagining God: Theology and the Religious Imagination* (Grand Rapids: Eerdmans, 1998), 14–16.

on which Feuerbach relied so heavily in *The Essence of Christianity* but then abandoned in his later theory (the one Harvey himself finds to be superior). Harvey's strategy leads him to make a problematic distinction between two types of projection, which he dubs the *Beam theory* and the *Grid theory*. The issues become clearer, both in the later Feuerbach and in the contemporary discussion, if we limit the term *projection* to the Beam model and see Grid theory as one way (a rather unclear one, in my judgment) of thematizing the role of imagination in religion. This approach recommends itself because it focuses on a term that was crucial both for Feuerbach (late as well as early) and for religious studies today. The term *imagination* not only more accurately describes religion but also does so in a less tendentious way than the problematic term *projection*.

One of the most useful, and as far as I know original, aspects of Harvey's book is the careful distinction he draws between Feuerbach's early and late critiques of religion.[19] The well-known theory in *The Essence of Christianity*—the version that so impressed the young Karl Marx—was an "inversion of Hegel's philosophy of Spirit" in which religion is "regarded as an involuntary projection inherent in and necessary for complete self-consciousness." In *Essence of Religion* and *Lectures on the Essence of Religion*, Feuerbach (in Harvey's paraphrase) sees religion instead as "an erroneous, belief-like interpretation of the all-encompassing and mysterious nature upon which the self knows itself to be dependent, an interpretation that springs out of the confrontation of the I with the not-I and the desire for recognition by this other" (229). The twofold occurrence of the word *interpretation* is not accidental; rather, it captures the main thrust of the new theory as Harvey presents it. Two other, briefer summary statements make the point even more directly. Whereas in *The Essence of Christianity*, Harvey summarizes, "Feuerbach proposed that religion is a stage in the development of self-consciousness and must, therefore, evolve into philosophy," the later Feuerbach sees religion as "not an involuntary reflex of the self but an interpretation." Even more pithily, Harvey can say that the early theory was "largely a function of . . . the notion of projection," while in the later theory "religion is an interpretative response" to external forces (231). Note that in Harvey's own most careful formulations, "projection" is a feature of the early Feuerbach, while his later theory is described as "interpretation." The contrast, in other words (this time mine, not Harvey's), is between two

---

19. It should be noted, however, that Glasse anticipated Harvey's thesis thirty years earlier: "In the latter work [*Lectures on the Essence of Religion*] Feuerbach viewed God not so much as the essence of man as the essence of Nature." "Barth on Feuerbach," 93n47.

ways of imagining God: in the projected ideal image of the human species, or in the image of a personified nature. Harvey is surely right that these two theories are incompatible with one another, though he is less convincing in his claim that the later one is more persuasive. What remains problematic is Harvey's persistence (unlike Feuerbach) in trying to conceive the issues in terms of projection. In projecting, one begins subjectively and then moves to conceive external reality—precisely the direction of religious "alienation" in the early Feuerbach. What is new about the later theory is the reversal of direction: Feuerbach now sees the religious person as beginning with an experience of the outside world ("nature") and then "processing" or organizing that experience in a particular way. Such a move is rightly called (by Harvey, in discussing Feuerbach) interpretation, not projection. As Harvey says, this kind of religion is an "interpretive response" rather than an "involuntary reflex of the self." Feuerbach's own term *imagination*, despite some serious problems in the assumptions he makes about it, therefore offers a more promising way of talking about religion and its relation to human life and thought.

The Beam model requires little comment, since it encapsulates just what Feuerbach, Freud, and others have long meant by *projection*. Something inward, unconscious, or subjective is displaced as something outward and is taken (i.e., *mis*-taken) by the intending subject to be objective. That, after all, is just what the early Feuerbach said: his word was *vergegenständlichen*, to objectify. The assumption that such a move produces illusion rather than truth appears to be so directly implied by the Beam model itself that attempts to use *projection* to describe religion without at the same time precluding its truth have had a difficult time of it.

More interesting and far more problematic is what Harvey calls the "Grid theory." The problem appears in his very first sentence about it, where he describes this option as "another type of projection theory," an assumption that begs the question at stake. He defines Grid theory accordingly in terms of "the symbolic or conceptual forms that human beings *superimpose* on their experience in order to make it intelligible" (246; emphasis added). Implied by this metaphoric language is the assumption that people first have experience that is *un*formed (outside "symbolic or conceptual forms") and then proceed to "superimpose" forms upon it—forms that are evidently alien to the experience itself—that is, qualitatively other than the "pure" experience prior to the act of imposition. Simply putting the issues this way should make plain why I find Harvey's presentation of Grid theory unsatisfactory. Here is not the place to rehearse the arguments, but such appeals to unformed prelinguistic experience have (for good reason) not had an easy time of it in recent philosophical and social scientific thought.[20] Whether one appeals to Wittgenstein's refutation of private language and demonstration of the *Gestalt*-like holism implicit in our perception and language; or to philosophers of science like Thomas Kuhn, Imre Lakatos, and Paul Feyerabend, who have shown the essential role of models and paradigms in the natural sciences; or to post-Heideggerian philosophers like Hans-Georg Gadamer, Amélie Rorty, and Jacques Derrida, who have exposed the inherent contradictions in appeals to "pure presence" and other claims to have "unformed" access to reality apart from linguistic commitments to already existing traditions and forms of life—whichever of these voices one attends to will make it extremely difficult ever again to think of our relation to the world in terms of merely "subjective" images imposed upon an "objective" reality, however it may be conceived.

Feuerbach's Two Theories of Religious Imagination

One of the most frequent concepts found in Feuerbach's writings, especially in English translation, is *imagination*. When one returns to the primary texts after reading Harvey's book, one is struck by the persistence of the term through all the twists and turns of Feuerbach's developing philosophy of religion. Worthy of particular note is the fact that imagination plays the key role in *both* the early projection theory *and* the late "existential" theory. So pronounced is this consistency in Feuerbach that it ought to relativize our understanding of the change of position highlighted by Harvey. It is no doubt both interesting and important that Feuerbach changed his mind about *how* religious people imagine the world; but even more significant is the fact that Feuerbach never wavered in his conviction that religion is fundamentally imagination—and that for this very reason it is suspect. To see how basic this strain of Feuerbach's thought really is, we need to look at what he says about religion and imagination both in *The Essence of Christianity* and in his later theory, presented most fully in *Lectures on the Essence of Religion*.

20. For an insightful treatment of the relationship between experience and the concepts used to interpret it, see Wayne Proudfoot, *Religious Experience* (Berkeley: University of California Press, 1985). Though Proudfoot, like Harvey, is concerned to expose the errors of "religious apologists," the argument cuts both ways: just as it is illegitimate to appeal to religious experience to justify the concepts that believers use to interpret it, so it is equally untenable to presuppose an essentially nonreligious experience lying behind the language of piety. If "religious beliefs and practices are interpretations of experience, and . . . themselves fit objects of interpretation" (Proudfoot, *Religious Experience*, 41), the same holds for nonreligious or antireligious interpretations of experience, such as those proposed by Feuerbach—and by Harvey himself. *All* data are theory-laden, not just the data cited by religious apologists. See Harvey, *Feuerbach*, 93ff., for his treatment of Proudfoot.

First, a comment on terminology. In discussing German philosophical texts in English, one often faces the difficulty that various German terms—*Einbildungskraft* and *Phantasie* are the most important—correspond to "imagination" in English. In Kant, for example, the technical term for "imagination" is *Einbildungskraft*. In Hegel (and also in the thought of the Young Hegelians, such as David Friedrich Strauss), religious imagination is characterized as *Vorstellung* (in contrast to the conceptual purity of the *Begriff*).[21] Feuerbach employs all of these terms (though *Phantasie* is his favorite), and Eliot has rendered almost all of them "imagination." The question therefore arises whether the translation might be obscuring distinctions made in the original, and whether he might have used the terms differently in his earlier and later writings. Fortunately, Feuerbach himself provides compelling evidence for identifying all of these terms, especially *Einbildungskraft* and *Phantasie*, under the single concept *imagination*. Not only does he alternate in his use of the terms, but more than once he places them in an apposition that clearly shows they are meant as synonyms. This passage from *The Essence of Christianity* is typical: "God exists in heaven, but is for that reason omnipresent; for this heaven is the imagination."[22] In the first two editions, Feuerbach uses *Phantasie*; but in the third and final edition of 1849 he appends the word *Einbildungskraft*, so that heaven is identified as "*die Phantasie, die Einbildungskraft*"—obviously two words for the same thing. One could cite numerous other passages where both terms are employed, but none is plainer than this one. Furthermore, the same usage appears repeatedly in the later Feuerbach. In the twentieth of Feuerbach's *Lectures on the Essence of Religion*, for example, where he is ridiculing the "fetishism" of what he calls "savages [*die Wilden*]," he asks, "what impels men to make gods of snail shells, crab claws, flags, and pennants?" His answer: "Their imagination, whose power is proportional to their ignorance." The one word "imagination" in the translation stands for "*Die Phantasie, die Einbildungskraft*" in the original; and he repeats the appositive when he generalizes the example to all religion: "The theoretical cause or source of religion and of its object, God, is therefore the imagination [*die Phantasie, die Einbildungskraft*]."[23]

21. See Green, *Imagining God*, chap. 1.

22. Feuerbach, *The Essence of Christianity*, trans. George Eliot (New York: Harper, 1957), 202n; *Das Wesen des Christentums*, ed. Werner Schuffenhauer and Wolfgang Harich, *Gesammelte Werke* (Berlin: Akademie-Verlag, 1973), 5:345n. In subsequent citations, I have provided shortened titles for references to this work, first to the English translation and then to the German original.

23. Feuerbach, *Lectures on the Essence of Religion*, 178 (*Vorlesungen über das Wesen der Religion*, 201).

A passage from *The Essence of Christianity* cited by Harvey (42) is characteristic of the younger Feuerbach's theory of religious imagination. After referring to "the impression which the imagination [*Phantasie*] makes upon the feelings [*das Gemüt*]," he specifically declares that the "imagination is the original organ of religion."[24] Feuerbach's actual words are "organ and essence [*Organ und Wesen*] of religion." Eliot's omission from the translation of the key word *Wesen*, the title concept of the book, is a rare but significant lapse, for Feuerbach announces here that the essence of religion—all religion, and not just Christianity—is the imagination. Specifically, he locates religion at the point where the emotions impact the imagination. The job of the imagination is to *represent* the contents of emotion, a task that it carries out by means of images taken from the world of the senses. Another passage, not cited by Harvey, makes clear just how central this imaginative task is to Feuerbach's view of human nature. "Man, as an emotional and sensuous being," he writes, "is governed and made happy only by images, by sensible representations."[25] Feuerbach in fact uses the singular ("image") and emphasizes it: human beings are satisfied, he insists, "only [by] the *image* [*Bild*]." Then follows the definition that Harvey cites: "Mind [*Vernunft*] presenting itself as at once type-creating [*bildlich*], emotional [*gemütlich*], and sensuous [*sinnlich*], is the *imagination*."[26] Here is the hinge where Feuerbach's description of religion turns to suspicion, for this triple characterization of the imagination—*bildlich, gemütlich,* and *sinnlich*—provides three reasons for Feuerbach's prejudice against it. Harvey's language is not too strong: imagination *cheats* reason. Feuerbach, he writes, believes that the "imagination . . . is deceptive in the nature of the case, especially when it becomes allied with feeling and wishing. It can and often does cheat the reason" (43). Even this paraphrase is not strong enough: for Feuerbach, imagination can and *always* does cheat reason. Feuerbach's hermeneutic of suspicion, in other words, is rooted in his prejudice against images, feelings, and—most striking of all in this philosopher of sensuousness—the senses as sources of truth. This prejudice, as we will see, in no way disappears or even weakens in Feuerbach's later theory of religion.

One more feature of the early Feuerbach's interpretation of the religious imagination is worth noting; and this point is one that he will abandon in his later thought. The context for the definition of imagination cited above from *The Essence of Christianity* is christological. It appears as part of Feuerbach's

24. Feuerbach, *Essence of Christianity*, 214 (*Das Wesen des Christentums*, 360).
25. Feuerbach, *Essence of Christianity*, 75 (*Das Wesen des Christentums*, 153).
26. Feuerbach, *Essence of Christianity*, 75, cited by Harvey, *Feuerbach*, 43.

treatment of "The Mystery of the Logos and Divine Image." Immediately following the tripartite definition of imagination, he comments, "The second Person in God, who is in truth the first person in religion, is the nature of the imagination made objective."[27] More literally translated, Feuerbach says that the Second Person of the Christian Trinity "is the *objective essence of the imagination [das gegenständliche Wesen der Phantasie]*" (Feuerbach's emphasis). So Christ is the projection of the human imagination; in Christ the imagination imagines itself as divine. (It is intriguing passages like this one in *The Essence of Christianity* that make me hesitant to agree with Harvey that Feuerbach's later theory is necessarily an improvement.) Here is an interpretation that might indeed provide the basis for a productive dialogue between Feuerbach and Christian theologians today, especially after Feuerbach's overhasty dismissal of the imagination is called into question.

When we turn to the later Feuerbach with the question of imagination in mind, we discover the same basic premise at work. As Harvey notes, "Although the concept of the imagination plays an important role in the *Lectures*, as it did in *Christianity*, it is not treated any more systematically in the latter, unfortunately, than in the former" (181). It is nevertheless quite clear that the theory of religion presented in *Lectures on the Essence of Religion* presupposes the very duality of emotion and thought, imagination and truth, that runs throughout *The Essence of Christianity*. Summarizing his own views in the second lecture, for example, Feuerbach maintains that "the difference between religion and philosophy is ineradicable, for philosophy is a matter of thought, of reason, while religion is a matter of emotion and imagination."[28] Later, in a discussion of animal cults, he argues for his new theory that underlying all religion is "the feeling of dependency," which causes religious believers to propose "a chaos of the most baffling contradictions." "For what reason?" he asks rhetorically. The answer: "Out of superstition." Then follows the familiar dualism: In religion "the alternative between fortune and misfortune, well-being and suffering, sickness and health, life and death depends in *truth* and *reality* [*in Wahrheit und Wirklichkeit*] on certain objects of worship, and on others only in *imagination*, in *faith*, in the *mind* [*in der Einbildung, im Glauben, in der Vorstellung*]."[29] Feuerbach is able to distinguish with such alacrity between superstition (*Aberglaube*) and truth because he presupposes that the former employs imagination (*Einbildung*,

27. Feuerbach, *Essence of Christianity*, 75.
28. Feuerbach, *Lectures on the Essence of Religion*, 12 (*Vorlesungen über das Wesen der Religion*, 19).
29. Feuerbach, *Lectures on the Essence of Religion*, 43–44 (*Vorlesungen über das Wesen der Religion*, 53) (emphasis original).

which he immediately equates with *Glaube* and *Vorstellung*) while the latter conforms to "truth and reality."

Feuerbach Reconstructed: Implications for Religious Studies and Theology

What would it take to make Feuerbach a genuine dialog partner in our own attempts to interpret religion? Harvey has done us a service—including those of us whose interest in religious studies is motivated by a theological passion—by his painstaking efforts to reconstruct Feuerbach's interpretation of religion in terms that make contact with our contemporary questions. In conclusion, I want to suggest some points at which this "ideal Feuerbach" might contribute to our own theorizing as scholars of religion. Like most theorists, his chief virtues are closely linked with his vices; but even the vices of great thinkers can be instructive.

Feuerbach's greatest contribution (his chief "virtue") I take to be his insight into the fundamentally imaginative nature of religious belief and practice. In his passion to reverse the effects of Hegelian spiritualizing, he saw with refreshing clarity the concrete, sensuous substance of religious life—its intrinsic connection to the earth, the body, and the natural world generally. Both secular religion scholars and theologians can surely applaud this emphasis in Feuerbach, for it is a trait as rare in the philosophers of his day as in the theologians. He knew and taught what has taken religious studies another century to discover, that religion is not first of all a matter of ideas and ideals but of images and practices. The corresponding "vice" has already been noted: his unquestioned assumption (so typical of his age in this regard) that such a product of the sensuous imagination could not possibly be the bearer of truth. So the scholar of religion must say to Feuerbach, yes, the imagination is indeed the source of religion, but no, religion is not thereby disqualified from the search for truth. In a time when we have learned that even the physicist, not to mention the anthropologist, must engage the imagination in order to gain rational insight into the world, the scholar of religion today will be more reluctant than Feuerbach to preface "imagination" with "mere." The dialog between Feuerbach and the theologians will be more complex and even more interesting, for he will remind them that religious teachings, whatever their truth value, can never be exempt from critical examination, because they are rooted in imagination and therefore implicated in the complex tangle of human desires and mixed motives. Theologians, in turn, will want to ask Feuerbach how he can be so sure that believers do not imagine the world rightly. Here Barth has shown the way—praising Feuerbach for his "Christian realism" while chastising him for his trivialization of the Christian imagination. But Feuerbach will also be a warning to theologians not to suspend their suspicion too hastily in the endeavor to "retrieve" the religious truths of the past. Along with Marx, Nietzsche, and Freud, Feuerbach offers a salutary reminder to theologians that imagination and desire are inevitably intertwined in a complex web of conflicting motives, not all of which lead to truth. Imagination is surely more than a garb of peacock feathers adorning mundane reality; but the temptation to strut about in borrowed religious finery must always be resisted. The issue that emerges from this dialog, therefore, is the hermeneutics of imagination. If the imagination is not only the source of error, as Feuerbach believed, but can serve the cause of truth as well—indeed, is necessary to our apprehension of truth—how can we tell the difference? Suspicion of imaginative excess is deeply rooted in religious tradition: "The heart is deceitful above all things," says the prophet (Jer. 17:9). Not *whether* to imagine but *how* to imagine rightly is the central theological question to emerge from the conversation with Feuerbach.

Another potential contribution that a reconstructed Feuerbach could make to religious studies and theology involves a less obvious but nevertheless intriguing theme in his writings. Like others before and after him who were influenced by Hegel, Feuerbach understands religion in the framework of a historical process. This theme too reveals both strengths and weaknesses in his interpretation of religion. Potentially useful to scholars of religion is a historical-cultural thesis, evident in a number of passages from both the early and the later Feuerbach, which represents a kind of parallel to Nietzsche's meditations on the death of God. One of the strongest indications that religious objects are unreal, Feuerbach argues, is that each religion demythologizes the gods of earlier ages. "What the present regards as reality [*für Wirklichkeit hält*], the future recognizes to be imagination [*erkennt . . . für Phantasie, für Einbildung*]," he writes in the *Lectures*. "Some day it will be universally recognized that the objects of Christian religion, like the pagan gods, were mere imagination [*nur Einbildung waren*]."[30] Setting aside for a moment the epistemological questions raised by this statement, we can extract a historical thesis that there has been a progressive weakening of the religious imagination over time, something akin to Max Weber's demystification of the world. The thesis that the imaginative force of religion (presumably only in Europe and North America?) has been progressively replaced by rational

---

30. Feuerbach, *Lectures on the Essence of Religion*, 195 (*Vorlesungen über das Wesen der Religion*, 219–20).

explanations could be investigated empirically by scholars of religion without necessarily accepting Feuerbach's deprecation of imagination. Less acceptable today, surely, is the evolutionary scheme and cultural prejudice that form one aspect of Feuerbach's historical thesis. He assumes that "naïve primitive peoples . . . were close to the origin and hence to nature."[31] Such assumptions, of course, were nearly universal among scholars of the nineteenth and early twentieth centuries, including many of those theorists most influential in the development of religious studies as a discipline, and those assumptions can no more be used to discredit his entire theory of religion than theirs.

As in the case of Nietzsche, the implications of Feuerbach's "death-of-God" (or "cooling of religion") theme are especially interesting and potentially fruitful for the dialog with theology. Like Nietzsche, Feuerbach frequently shows more sympathy for orthodox believers than for rationalizing modernist theologians. He compares them as follows:

> The more man is dominated by his imagination, the more sensuous is his god. . . . The difference between the Christian God of the rationalists, of those whose faith is tempered by thought, and the Christian God of the older total believers, is merely that the rationalists' God is more sophisticated, more abstract, and less sensuous than the God of the mystics or orthodox believers, that the rationalists' faculty of abstraction restricts their imagination, whereas the old believer's imagination is stronger than his powers of conceptual thinking. In other words: the rationalists's [sic] faith is determined, or rather limited, by reason . . . whereas the orthodox believer's reason is dominated by his faith.[32]

In *The Essence of Christianity* he even insists that the "Church was perfectly justified in adjudging damnation to heretics and unbelievers." In a wonderfully apt phrase, he accuses "the believing unbelief of modern times" of hiding "behind the Bible" while opposing "the biblical dicta to dogmatic definitions, in order that it may set itself free from the limits of dogma by arbitrary exegesis." In this situation, he notes, "faith has already disappeared, is become indifferent, when the determinate tenets of faith are felt as limitations."[33]

31. Feuerbach, *Lectures on the Essence of Religion*, 89 (*Vorlesungen über das Wesen der Religion*, 102–3). The English translation makes the problem worse: Feuerbach speaks not of "primitive peoples" but of *Naturvölker*; in other passages (see above) he does, however, refer to *die Wilden* and regularly assumes their ignorance.

32. Feuerbach, *Lectures on the Essence of Religion*, 192 (*Vorlesungen über das Wesen der Religion*, 216–17).

33. Feuerbach, *Essence of Christianity*, 251–52 (*Das Wesen des Christentums*, 416–17). Eliot omits one important term from her English translation: Feuerbach speaks of *"die Charakter-losigkeit, der gläubige Unglaube der neuern Zeit,"* thus explicitly identifying the bad faith of theologians as a character flaw.

Here, too, we might ask (with Barth) why the theologians did not discover this truth for themselves, rather than learning it from the mouths of their secular opponents.

More than three decades after his initial engagement in a 1926 lecture with Feuerbach's critique of religion, Karl Barth returned to the topic in volume four of the *Church Dogmatics*.[34] At the culmination of his discussion he remarks (according to the published translation) that we can venture the "good confession of the prophecy of Jesus Christ . . . without embarrassment, and need be afraid of no Feuerbach."[35] In fact, Barth's reference is not to fear but to shame: "*und werden wir uns . . . vor keinem Feuerbach zu schämen haben.*" The brief excursus that follows this remark offers a clue to its meaning, for Barth mentions the so-called ontological argument of Anselm of Canterbury and frankly acknowledges the circularity of theological argument against skeptical critics like Gaunilo and Feuerbach. But this circle, he maintains, is not vicious but virtuous, "a *circulus virtuosus.*" Our reconstruction of Feuerbach's theory of religious imagination, with Harvey's expert help, suggests why the believer can affirm the truth of revelation, without shame or embarrassment, in spite of its imaginative character. Feuerbach saw clearly that imagination was the engine of religion, but he also—like so many others, including theologians of his own time and ours—found the imagination to be a source of embarrassment. It is time to subject this suspicious thesis itself to a dose of suspicion. This "deconstructive" move will make it harder for secular scholars to dismiss theological claims out of hand, just as Harvey's book makes it harder for theologians to dismiss Feuerbach out of hand.

34. For a detailed analysis of the continuities and differences in Barth's early and late treatments of Feuerbach, see Glasse, "Barth on Feuerbach," esp. 82–91. Also to be commended are Glasse's thoughtful concluding remarks (92–96).

35. Barth, *Church Dogmatics*, vol. IV/3, ed. G. W. Bromiley and T. F. Torrance, trans. G. W. Bromiley (Edinburgh: T&T Clark, 1961), 85. For the German original, see *Die kirchliche Dogmatik*, vol. IV/3 (Zurich: Theologische Verlag Zürich, 1959), 94.

4

THE CRISIS
OF MAINLINE CHRISTIANITY
AND THE LIBERAL FAILURE
OF IMAGINATION

Whether you think Christianity is dying or thriving depends mostly on which Christianity you have in mind. A Presbyterian in a Korean megachurch is likely to see things differently from an Anglican in a near-empty country church or an American Catholic whose urban parish has not had a priest for years. Few will deny, however, that the great Protestant denominations that once dominated public and private life in North America, Britain, and northern Europe have fallen on hard times. All of the so-called mainline churches of the United States, Canada, and Europe have been reporting steady declines in membership for several decades now. From the standpoint of theology the situation is particularly sobering, since those same churches have produced most of the leading theologians whose work has long provided the backbone of seminary education. That once-thriving academic tradition continues to produce theology worth listening to, though its voice must now struggle to be heard above the often strident tones of the newer "special interest" theologies-of, each celebrating the unique experience of its particular culture, race, or gender. The dominant strain in the mainline theological tradition has been "liberal," at least in the general sense in which the term is contrasted with "conservative," "evangelical," or

"fundamentalist." I want to take the pulse of the mainline tradition by focusing on one of its more substantial theological projects—one that eschews the
new theological tribalism and speaks forthrightly on behalf of beleaguered
liberal Protestantism in North America today. Douglas John Hall, professor
emeritus at McGill University, has spent his long career articulating, developing, and defending the kind of mainline Protestant theology he learned from
his teachers, including Reinhold Niebuhr and Paul Tillich, who epitomize that
theology at the time of its greatest influence in the church and in the broader
culture. Hall's own theological vision is set forth in the trilogy entitled *Christian Theology in a North American Context* (1991–96). The project described
in that work typifies the theological commitment of the liberal Protestantism
that has defined the once-dominant mainline churches of North America. It
is thus well positioned to illustrate the characteristic convictions of that form
of Christianity and to show both its strengths and weaknesses.

Hall sets himself a prodigious task. Convinced that "we have become very
confused about the core of our belief,"[1] he proposes to write a systematic
theology for "the so-called mainline denominations" (6), or what he calls more
precisely "the churches of once-mainline Protestantism" (8). The key to the
whole project lies in that little word "once," for Hall knows that he speaks to
a tradition in decline, to Christians whose institutions once set the standards
and ideals for the entire culture but who now find themselves a shrinking and
dispirited minority. "I want to speak," he tells us, "to and for the remnants
of 'mainline' Protestantism" (498).

The scope of Hall's project is comprehensive and its genre traditional. The
organization of the central volume follows conventional models, though Hall
covers just three theological loci: the first part develops a doctrine of God,
the second part treats creation (primarily anthropology, or human nature),
and the third presents Hall's Christology. Each of these topics is approached
through a further systematic triad: Hall devotes the three chapters under each
locus to historical, critical, and constructive theology, respectively, though
the lines separating them are often rather blurred. He even allows readers
a systematic choice between the two organizing schemes: they may either
follow Hall's own order by taking up Theology (he uses the capital letter
to distinguish the doctrine of God from the whole field of theology), Creaturely Being, and Jesus Christ in turn; or they may read the three historical
chapters first, before proceeding to the critical and then to the constructive
approaches.

1. Douglas John Hall, *Professing the Faith: Christian Theology in a North American Context*
(Minneapolis: Fortress, 1993), ix. Page references to this volume will be made parenthetically
in the text.

Like the mainline churches themselves, this work of theology retains only the formal outlines of the older tradition while drawing much of its content from contemporary and even secular sources. In this way, it stands within the tradition of modern Protestant liberalism, broadly conceived, despite its sometimes sharp criticisms of liberal theology. In a telling phrase, Hall refers to the mainline churches to which his theology is addressed as "the vaguely liberal denominations" (465–66). His own work could be described as a vaguely liberal theology for the vaguely liberal churches of North America. It is an important work because it is a serious intellectual expression of "once-mainline Protestantism," an attempt to reform and revitalize that flagging tradition out of its own resources. Hall is looking for an alternative that is both true to Christian tradition and credible to the growing number of unchurched people in the United States and Canada. His attempt to provide that alternative shows how intractable the problems are; for in significant ways, Hall's own "vaguely liberal" theology does more to exemplify the inadequacies of modern liberalism than to overcome them.

What ails the mainline churches? Some of Hall's characterizations hit the mark. Deploring the absence of the "biblical sense of the divine remoteness"— what the Oxford Movement called "reserve"—precisely in "the 'liberal' churches of North America," Hall points to "their awesome familiarity, their chatty piousness in the presence of God" (139). He finds this lack of respect for God's hiddenness to be not only a departure from traditional Christian teaching but also a distinct handicap in a modern culture impressed by the absence of God. A recovery of the dialectic of divine presence and absence would thus make the Christian message more credible in our age. He is equally scathing in his attack on the "careless eclecticism" about doctrine that prevails in most Christian churches today, "where the old authority patterns of classical orthodoxy, especially in the once-mainstream Protestant denominations, have given way to a fantastic admixture of thoughts and half-thoughts whose chief virtue is not that they have either depth or consistency but that they lend themselves to quick communication" (223). The sentimental religion of love that predominates in these same denominations, Hall argues, lacks the power to reach modern North Americans, who are confronted daily by reminders of the violence and disorder of the society around them. A primary cause "for the absence from the churches of large numbers of people in our society," he maintains, is "that, given the sophistication of our psychological indoctrination and the hardness of the world we experience daily, Christianity as it is practiced in most once-mainline liberal congregations must seem a terribly naïve, insipid thing" (468). Clearly, Hall shares the scathing judgment of the unchurched outsiders and is seeking ways of revitalizing the theology that guides the mainline churches. Both his insights and his failures are instructive.

Modern liberal Protestant theology originated in the German universities early in the nineteenth century among theologians—Schleiermacher is the most noteworthy—who became convinced that the older orthodoxy had no future. The heritage of the Reformers had led, beginning late in the sixteenth century, to an academic systematizing of Protestant theology, employing many of the concepts and methods of the medieval Scholastic tradition. By the eighteenth century, a rational orthodoxy had emerged that relied, in the words of Hans Frei, "on a philosophical vindication of metaphysical principles, . . . undergirded by the rationalism of [Gottfried] Leibniz and [Christian] Wolff."[2] As a result largely of Kant's critique of metaphysical supernaturalism, the original liberal theologians concluded that rational orthodoxy was dead, since it insisted on an external relationship between God and human beings, a relationship that could not be one of rational cognition according to the Kantian critique of reason. The attempt—actually begun by Kant himself—to translate Christian doctrine out of the conceptuality of metaphysical rationalism into some other, more tenable thought form (Kant called it "practical reason") was the genesis of liberal theology.[3]

Thus from its beginnings, liberalism has been on the defensive against secular modernity. Schleiermacher, often acknowledged as the father of liberal theology, directed his *Speeches on Religion* to his skeptical intellectual colleagues, the "cultured despisers" (in the familiar English translation), or (more accurately) "the educated among its despisers."[4] Hall's project belongs in this liberal tradition, even though (perhaps in keeping with the democratic populism of his North American context) the despisers to whom he speaks are not so cultured, taking their cues less from philosophy than from novels, films, and musicals. Hall's predilection for popular culture leads to some of his more outrageous claims. What are we to make of a theology that prefers the insipid "Christology" of *Jesus Christ Superstar* (534–36) to that of Anselm's *Cur Deus Homo?* (422–28)? Can we trust the judgment (not to mention the taste) of a theologian who cites *Dead Poets Society*, that bathetic romance of the irresponsible teacher, as an example of films "that delve more deeply into

2. Hans W. Frei, "The Academic Tradition in Nineteenth-Century Protestant Theology," in *Faith and Ethics: The Theology of H. Richard Niebuhr*, ed. Paul Ramsey (New York: Harper, 1965), 32.

3. For a fuller exposition and critique of Kant's project, see chap. 9 below.

4. The most widely available edition is still Friedrich Schleiermacher, *On Religion: Speeches to Its Cultured Despisers*, trans. John Oman from the 3rd German ed. (New York: Harper, 1958). Also useful is Richard Crouter's translation of the first edition, published under the same title by Cambridge University Press (1988).

the spirit of contemporary society than almost anything one can hear from the churches" (298)? Hall theologizes in the constant awareness of critical outsiders looking over his shoulder—and into the mainline churches. *His despisers are captivated not by enlightened rationalism but by what he calls the "Sisyphus syndrome"*: these moderns are impressed less by "humanity's exalted self-images than its low self-esteem." According to Hall's cultural diagnosis, "the humanity [with which] Christians are called to engage in this context resembles Sisyphus more than Prometheus" (254–55).

Theological liberalism has always taken its cues from the secular culture, whether it sees that culture epitomized in its cultured despisers or the Sisyphus syndrome. Since it is the cultural "situation"—a technical term used by liberal theologians—that defines the problem, and thus the apologetic challenge for theology, a major part of the theological task is the interpretation and critique of culture. This methodological trait is where the basic liberalism of Hall's theology is most apparent. Like Paul Tillich, one of the theologians he cites most frequently, Hall endeavors to correlate the cultural "situation" with the theological truths to be articulated. The method of correlation leads to a concern for relevance, since the success of the liberal project depends upon a successful correlation between culture and doctrine: if the cultured despisers fail to find the church's message relevant, the theologian has failed. Thus Hall takes as his "mandate for the entire discussion of God . . . to discover whether it is possible to profess belief in a revealing God without suppressing the reality of the divine concealment as it is felt in our present context. To state the question explicitly: Can Christians bear witness to the revealing God in such a way as to sustain a meaningful dialogue with the contemporary experience of God's hiddenness, absence, eclipse, or 'death'?" (47).

The problem with this diagnosis of contemporary experience is its arbitrariness. How is Hall able to make such sweeping generalizations about "the" modern sensibility? No doubt some of it is autobiographical, though he doesn't say; all of us tend to generalize from our own experience. Many of Hall's North American contemporaries will no doubt agree with his characterization of our common experience, but many others—my guess would be many *more*—surely will not. How does one decide? Despite his claim to be speaking about general experience today, Hall's theology of culture bears strong resemblances to the existentialism of Tillich and other theologians from the generation of his teachers. But much has changed in half a century. For one thing, reports of the demise of religious belief, so commonplace then, now appear to have been exaggerated. For millions of our contemporaries, God is experienced not as an absence but as a powerful presence, though seldom within the precincts of "vaguely liberal Protestantism." Both Christianity and Islam are thriving in Africa and other developing countries; and even within Hall's North American context, some Christian groups are growing, while Islam is rapidly supplanting Judaism as the third major *American* faith (behind Protestantism and Catholicism). These considerations should cause us to ponder the meaning of "context" in Hall's argument. Clearly influenced by the popularity of contextual theology, he has sought to delineate the context closest to home, which he designates "North American," a rather cumbersome rubric designed to include his native Canada while excluding the obviously quite different Latin American context. But geography turns out to be a poor indicator of cultural context, for there is little in Hall's theological liberalism that would not be appropriate to the contemporary West European experience, and probably to cultural and academic elites the world over. Indeed, one of the theologians most frequently cited by Hall is Jürgen Moltmann. By contrast, there are few references to North American theologians, and most of these are perfunctory. After an incidental reference to George Lindbeck on the first page of *Professing the Faith*, we find no discussion of his post-liberal theology or his cultural-linguistic theory of religion; nor is attention given to the other narrative and intratextual proposals that have been the focus of much recent American theology. One might at least have expected to hear something about David Tracy, who like Hall has learned much from theological existentialism and has devoted considerable energy to diagnosing the current cultural scene. One could, of course, name many others, but I would especially have liked to hear Hall's response to a theologian like Stanley Hauerwas, who has a quite different—and incompatible—account of what is wrong with Protestant churches in North America today.

The elusiveness of theological "context," however, is only a symptom of a deeper question, one that we must put to the whole tradition of liberal theology. Given that theologians require some sense of the context in which they work, how can they obtain it? What methods may Christians appropriately employ to grasp and interpret the culture in which they live? Cultural linguists like Lindbeck, supported by social scientific theory, have pointed out that context is itself already a function of religious commitment; one cannot *first* establish the cultural context (neutrally, as it were) and only *then* subject it to religious interpretation. A more direct addressing of the methodological question would have clarified Hall's project, but one can nevertheless discern what he might say by examining what he actually says. As a theologian in the Protestant tradition, Hall naturally turns to Scripture. In his criticism of the doctrinal tradition of the church—for instance, in rejecting the God of power that has dominated theology for centuries—he characteristically appeals *both* to its offensiveness to modern sensibilities *and* to its lack of conformity to the

biblical view of God. Repeatedly decrying the "triumphalism" of the dominant tradition, Hall welcomes the recent rediscovery of the suffering God of
the Bible. "At long last," he rejoices, "Christians are being guided by Jesus
(often unawares) back to the God to whom Jesus himself prayed. That God
was set aside by Christendom for centuries . . . and . . . forced into the mold
of triumphant divinity, devoid of pathos" (182–83). Problems arise, however,
at points of tension between modern experience and Scripture. In the case of
divine power and suffering, one wonders to what extent the alleged godless-
ness of modern experience functions as a filter, allowing only one aspect (the
suffering one) of the biblical God to find its way into theology. The suspicion
that the God of the Bible may have been censored so as to better accommodate
contemporary sensibilities appears to be borne out by Hall's unsettling treatment of the resurrection of Jesus. In his conclusion to *Professing the Faith*, he
emphasizes "how difficult—how almost impossible—it is to speak about the
resurrection, especially 'in a North American context'" (549). In a virulent
attack on the church's major feast, he maintains that "in North America it
is Easter that should make Jews and all other minorities nervous; for while
it will seldom[!] incite physical violence, this national feast-day of the New
World contributes much to the atmosphere of untruth that permits America
to overlook and repress the subtle and not-very-subtle violence that it does to
those who are 'other' in its midst" (550). Hall's antipathy to the celebration of
Easter appears to derive from an exaggerated fear of "triumphalism," which
leads him to reject virtually every reference to God's glory. So worried is he
about the excesses of divine power, that he coins the term "resurrectionism"
(96) to identify the error. Though he cites Luther and Bonhoeffer approvingly
on the theology of the cross, his pitting of cross against resurrection upsets
the essential relationship between the two that these theologians sought to
preserve.

The theological use of the Bible, which has long been the Achilles' heel
of Protestant liberalism, is also problematic in Hall's theology. There are
indications that Hall thinks the biblical message must be purged of elements
offensive to modern sensibilities. (How else can the soft-pedaling of Easter
be explained?) Mostly, he simply assumes that the Bible, rightly interpreted,
will speak to the needs of modern North Americans. An implicit hermeneutical principle can be gleaned from certain passages in Hall's theology—a
principle that relies heavily on historical-critical interpretation. For example,
when Hall discovers that the God of the "older Testament," not content to
suffer passively, periodically behaves like a "God of power, a sort of Hebraic
Thor," he concludes that "these depictions cannot be designated normative
for Israel's faith; they represent, rather, *reversions* to earlier or extra-Judaic

material" (152, emphasis added). This historicizing hermeneutic allows him to dissolve the biblical dialectic of divine power and weakness and to assert that "the norm . . . is not the God of battles but the 'still small voice,' the God who waits, the 'defenseless' God" (152). Hall thus corrects the theology of both "older" and "newer" Testaments by filtering out disturbing antiliberal notions of power. How he would respond to criticism of his use of Scripture is also clear from the book: he uses the familiar liberal ploy of implying that the only alternative is "fundamentalism." He is profoundly embarrassed by conservative expressions of Christian faith and even suggests that "a major factor in the decline of Christianity in this context may thus be the association of the Christian religion with its crassest and least sophisticated expressions" (453). But if that is the case, why is it that the vaguely liberal, once-mainline churches languish while the evangelical ones flourish?

Embarrassment at unsophisticated piety is also at the root of another of Hall's revisions of the Bible and tradition, his critique of "otherworldliness" (long a target of liberal polemics). Taking aim at "hundreds of years of Christian spirituality," he inveighs against hymns that draw us "beyond 'the Jordan'" toward "heaven" or "the arms of Jesus." The psychological root of this critique is obvious from the test Hall proposes: "Let anyone who does not think [that these hymns convey such a message] sing such hymns attentively alongside his or her teenage children!" (277). One suspects that sophisticated liberal professors and other cultured despisers may be more important than teenagers as the source of Hall's embarrassment. Apparently forgetting the dangers of otherworldliness some pages later, he calls for a theological response to contemporary secular fatalism about the inevitable doom of the earth: "The power of this public mood demands of Christians of the classical traditions that they break their silence on the question of the destiny of creation" (355). The theological challenge, apparently, is to come up with a sufficiently vague and "sophisticated" version of ultimate destiny so as not to embarrass either the teenagers or the scholars!

Far from being a merely peripheral matter, the phenomenon of liberal embarrassment brings us to the heart of both the failure of mainline Christianity and the inadequacy of liberal attempts to revive it. Hall makes an important—and, I am convinced, quite mistaken—diagnosis of the problem of modern unbelief: "The positivism—or let us say the lack of tentativeness and modesty . . . that informs the traditional Christian profession of God makes it difficult for most of our contemporaries to join the ages of Christendom in declaring, 'Credo in Deum' ('I believe in God')" (91). This is the nub of the issue, for his *tentativeness* is just the problem—in fact, the basic problem of the whole mainline Protestant tradition he seeks to renew. Jesus, Paul, Augustine,

Luther, Calvin, Barth—these great teachers of the gospel were not known for their tentativeness! By subjecting the Bible to norms derived from modern secular sensibility, theologians of the liberal tradition—ironically—rob it of the source of its powerful appeal to people in all ages, including our own: its imaginative integrity, the power of its images, poetry, narratives, myth, metaphor, and hyperbole.[5] Spooked by "sophisticated" secular critiques, liberals have convinced themselves that Christians must scale back their claims and tone down their language, lest they be caught making assertions (especially historical ones) that cannot be proved. In the North American context this liberal worry has its roots in the fundamentalist-modernist controversy of the early twentieth century. Each side maintains its own position by the use of scare tactics: you'd better agree with us modernists (or fundamentalists), or you're liable to fall into fundamentalism (or modernism)! Hall's frequent appeal to the dangers of fundamentalism shows that his thought still moves within the parameters of that old debate. What is striking to the outsider is the implicit agreement of the two sides: both are convinced that the truth of Christian doctrine is to be measured by what can (or cannot) be proved, even though they disagree radically about the evidence. Here the work of another North American theologian, Hans Frei, might have rescued Hall from a devil's choice between fundamentalist literalism and liberal reductionism. Frei shows how biblical narrative became "eclipsed" in the modern era by questions of reference. Both fundamentalists and liberals seek the meaning of the biblical text in some extratextual referent, either in the historical events with which the narratives can be correlated (the conservative option), or else in existential states of consciousness or in moral experience (the liberal option). In both cases what is lost is the biblical story itself.[6] But if the *meaning* of the text *is* the story it tells—its narrative shape—then to lose the story is to lose the meaning, and hence the truth that Scripture conveys. A similar case could be made *mutatis mutandis* for the nonnarrative biblical genres: poetry, prophecy, apocalyptic, and so on. In every case the meaning is to be sought in the intratextual relationships within the biblical canon.

Whatever case might once have been made for liberal theology, its day is now past. While liberals have been revising doctrine to make it sufficiently vague and tentative to suit the tastes of moderns, the central traditions of

5. The extensive philosophical and theological literature on myth, models, metaphors, and paradigms is widely known. For an intriguing insight into the power of biblical and religious hyperbole, see Stephen H. Webb, *Blessed Excess: Religion and the Hyperbolic Imagination* (Albany: State University of New York Press, 1993).

6. Hans W. Frei, *The Eclipse of Biblical Narrative: A Study in Eighteenth and Nineteenth Century Hermeneutics* (New Haven: Yale University Press, 1974).

Enlightenment modernity itself have been undergoing a crisis of confidence. The cultured despisers no longer speak with an air of unquestioned authority (those who still do have become comic figures); some of them are even showing signs of renewed interest in religion. In any event, the old modern certainties are coming unstuck: all the comfortable dualities—objective/subjective, real/fictional, science/religion, fact/value, truth/myth—are under attack and are no longer so easy to distinguish. This postmodern conundrum opens the way for theology once again to participate in serious public dialogue, but it is an opportunity for which the tradition of liberal theology has ill prepared us. The proper response of theologians today is not renewed efforts to correlate the Bible and tradition with the fickle moods of contemporary culture. Rather, we should recognize that context is not something simply given but something created by ourselves and others. Religion, including the gospel of Jesus Christ, is a shaper of human culture, not a passive spectator or victim. Religions are imaginative worlds, and they demand respect for their inherent integrity. Christians have always claimed that the world as imagined in the pluriform integrity of the biblical canon is the *real* world, the world created by divine wisdom and redeemed by divine grace. The church is a school of the imagination, the place where we learn to think, feel, see, and hear as followers of the crucified and risen Messiah of Israel; and her theologians are the grammarians of the Christian imagination, the ones who reflect on the patterns that constitute the world of biblical faith. People's imaginations are not transformed by tentativeness but rather by wholehearted commitment to a vision of the world. Not vagueness but vivid specificity is the key to a healthy theology, for worlds are imagined not in general but only through the concrete particularity of specific images, symbols, metaphors, persons, and stories. Hall is surely right that the "vaguely liberal" churches have become boring, and boredom is a disease of the imagination. It will be cured not by a vague and tentative theology but by one that has the courage of its convictions—a theology with the chutzpah to appeal to the imagination even of its secular despisers, challenging them to enter into the world of the prophets and apostles, of Israel and the church, and to see whether they, too, might discover that it is the real world after all.

5

HANS FREI
AND THE HERMENEUTICS
OF THE SECOND NAÏVETÉ

One brief incident during my graduate studies at Yale stands out in my memory: it must have occurred on December 11, 1968. Three of us grad students, teaching assistants in Mr. Frei's undergraduate course, were walking with him along College Street in New Haven, returning from class to his office in Silliman College. The three of us were laughing and joking about who knows what, when he suddenly stopped in his tracks, turned, and rebuked us for our jollity—something so utterly out of character that I have never forgotten it. "Don't you know," he admonished us, "that yesterday Karl Barth died in Basel?"

We knew, of course, that Barth was the theologian Frei took most seriously. He made frequent reference to him in his teaching and in the few published writings he had produced at that time, and he assigned passages from the *Church Dogmatics* for us to read in his graduate courses. I had come to Yale fresh from a divinity degree at Union Theological Seminary in New York, where I had heard about (but never read) Barth, known there as the leading theologian of neo-orthodoxy, a movement in which many of my teachers at Union had been educated, but which, they believed, was now (thankfully!) fading into obscurity as theology sought to recover its bearings amid the intellectual and cultural turmoil of the 1960s. I recall one prominent theologian at Union telling us that, since the "great parenthesis" of neo-orthodoxy was now safely behind us, theology could get back to the real questions facing modern Christianity.

When I reflect today on the legacy of Hans Frei, what first comes to mind is his teaching rather than his published theology: he was the one who taught us how to read Karl Barth. Frei was the most astute reader of Barth in our time, teaching us as much by example as by anything he said or wrote about Barth's theology. Barth's reception in the English-speaking world was badly distorted from the outset, especially by the misconception that he was a neo-orthodox thinker, one who wanted to repeal modernity in order to reinstate the old orthodoxy. In 1968, and for a long time thereafter, Frei was a voice crying in the wilderness. Almost singlehandedly he reoriented and revivified Barth studies in the United States and Great Britain. And for the most part, he did so unintentionally, not by giving lectures and writing books about Karl Barth but by employing what he had learned from Barth to tackle the theological tasks that he himself found so pressing. Others have excelled as Barth scholars (one thinks of George Hunsinger, Bruce McCormack, and John Webster), but Frei's contribution has been different: less comprehensive but more focused. From the outset, as his doctoral dissertation on Barth's dogmatics shows, he was never an uncritical reader, even of Barth—that is, he was never a Barthian. One might say that he was not so much an interpreter of Barth's theology as one who learned from Barth how to read Scripture and the theological tradition and then spent his career doing it. In this way, he exemplified one of Barth's most cherished virtues: he always kept his sights firmly on *die Sache*, on the real subject matter of theology.

Frei's lectures reflected his way of thinking. He once made a revealing comment to an audience at the beginning of a formal lecture: "No matter how well I prepare," he told them, "I don't like to read from a manuscript; I have to work it out from the notes." Fortunately for us, the lecture was being recorded and is now available to a much wider audience.[1] It turned out to be one of the clearest accounts he ever gave of his theological project, quite likely for the reason that he was speaking freely from notes. As he once admitted in a letter, "I can write decent prose for about three pages, and then complexities inevitably get the better of me."[2] He used the same method when lecturing to classes at Yale. Those of us who served as his teaching assistants can remember arriving at his office just as his undergraduate class was about to begin, only to find him scribbling furiously on a legal-sized yellow pad. This way

---

1. Hans W. Frei, "On Interpreting the Christian Story," in *Reading Faithfully: Writings from the Archives*, 2 vols., ed. Mike Higton and Mark Alan Bowald (Eugene, OR: Cascade Books, 2015), 1:69.
2. Letter to Dennis Nineham, July 1, 1976, in Frei, *Reading Faithfully*, 1:27.

of working may explain why he published so few books and articles but left behind a treasure trove of notes and works in progress; and it testifies to his integrity and humility as a theologian. It also helps to explain why he was such a revered and effective teacher: he continually presented not finished products of his research and scholarship, but rather his active, ongoing struggle to articulate the theological issues that were driving him at the time. By doing so, he modeled the vocation of the theologian.

At the time of his death in 1988, it was easy to think that Frei, having finally published his long-awaited historical work, *The Eclipse of Biblical Narrative*, as well as an original and suggestive theological essay, *The Identity of Jesus Christ*, had been tragically prevented from carrying out the promising task that these works seemed to presage. (I still recall my immediate reaction upon hearing of his death. "But he still had so much more to do!" I blurted out at the time.) Now, however, three decades later, Frei's true accomplishments are coming into focus, thanks in large part to the painstaking work of Mike Higton, who has made available Frei's unpublished lectures and papers, as well as some revealing letters written to friends and colleagues. Higton's report on his archival research in his book *Christ, Providence and History* includes a kind of intellectual biography of Frei, revealing a career spent in pursuit of answers to theological problems that was more focused and sustained than most of us who were his students and friends realized at the time.[3] In what follows I will argue that Hans Frei did more than merely prepare the way for a theological project he did not live to accomplish. On the contrary, he pursued throughout his entire career a most original historical and theological thesis, one that goes a long way toward resolving the greatest dilemma facing Christian theology in the modern era—namely, the problem of faith and history.

Frei worked throughout his career as both a historian and a theologian, but it is clear, especially in retrospect, that the two were complementary. In the Department of Religious Studies at Yale, he oversaw the program in Historical Theology (as distinguished from two other kinds of theology: systematic and philosophical). Frei's work as a historical theologian can be seen as an effort to explicate and defend the orthodox Christian use of the Bible against various voices of modernity that claim to have shown the fallacy or impossibility of such a reading of Scripture. Moreover, Frei endeavored to refute those *Christian theologians* who accepted these flawed critiques and tried to reconstruct Christian teaching in order to accommodate them. He carried out this program not by polemical attacks on the modernizers, but rather by

---

3. Mike Higton, *Christ, Providence and History: Hans W. Frei's Public Theology* (London: T&T Clark International, 2004).

careful, persistent intellectual labor, especially through detailed historical analysis of modern Christian thought since 1700. His stubborn adherence to this task without regard to the prevailing winds of the theological academy is evidence of a kind of faithful Christian integrity that attracted like-minded supporters to his side. To this day those who studied with Mr. Frei (as we always knew him) share a fraternal bond—even when our various theological careers have carried us in quite divergent directions.[4]

Some years ago the philosopher Paul Ricoeur captured the pathos of modern religious thought in an arresting image. He takes note of the impact of modern criticism, which has called into question our inherited faith through the "dissolution of the myth as explanation." While affirming criticism and insisting that "we are in every way children of criticism," Ricoeur nevertheless says that "we seek to go beyond criticism by means of criticism, by a criticism that is no longer reductive but restorative."[5] His solution invokes imagery that has resonated with many of his, and our, contemporaries:

> Does that mean that we could go back to a primitive naïveté? Not at all. In every way, something has been lost, irremediably lost: immediacy of belief. But if we can no longer live the great symbolisms of the sacred in accordance with the original belief in them, we can . . . aim at a second naïveté in and through criticism. In short, it is by *interpreting* that we can *hear* again. Thus it is in hermeneutics that the symbol's gift of meaning and the endeavor to understand by deciphering are knotted together.[6]

If we take with a grain of salt the Hegelian overtones of Ricoeur's triadic schema (virtually inevitable in a modern European thinker), it is hard to deny the appeal of his vision of a "second naïveté": a way to overcome the challenges to traditional Christian belief by various forms of secular critique since the Enlightenment. It epitomizes a goal that so many Christian thinkers over the past three centuries have wanted to achieve.

I want to suggest that we can understand Hans Frei's achievement as a theologian in terms of Ricoeur's vision of a second naïveté. I am speaking metaphorically, for Frei most surely does not seek a second naïveté in the same way that Ricoeur does, by means of a "restorative" philosophical

4. For a fuller account of this sense of familial commonalty among Frei's students, see the lovely description of Frei as teacher in George Hunsinger's brief foreword to the first volume of *Reading Faithfully*. Hunsinger notes how Frei "managed to make each of his doctoral students feel affirmed and encouraged without provoking a sense of rivalry among them" (vii).

5. Paul Ricoeur, *The Symbolism of Evil*, trans. Emerson Buchanan (New York: Harper & Row, 1967), 350.

6. Ricoeur, *Symbolism of Evil*, 351 (emphasis original).

"revivification" of traditional symbols. Frei, in fact, explicitly takes exception to Ricoeur's view, which, he writes, "tends to force realistic description to become metaphor." He calls Ricoeur's philosophical system "dangerous" because it "does not allow realistic narrative a genuinely realistic status."[7] Frei does, however, agree with Ricoeur that the way to a second naïveté involves a *hermeneutical* task. For Frei, the modern critique that presents the greatest challenge to Christian faith is the problem of faith and history, the alleged conflict between the historical claims Christians make about the gospel story of Jesus Christ and the results of modern historical-critical interpretation of the New Testament. Frei's hermeneutical attempt to answer that critique, I am arguing, though different in nearly every way from Ricoeur's own, succeeds in pointing the way to a renewed "naïve" reading of the Gospel accounts of Jesus in spite of the challenges made by historical criticism. One might even describe Frei's approach as "neo-orthodox" in a strictly hermeneutical sense, for his proposal seeks to justify the straightforwardly realistic way that Christians, including premodern Christians, have always read Scripture, modern historical-critical scruples notwithstanding.

The Historical Challenge: Faith and History

Among the many things Frei learned from Karl Barth and then developed in his own work as historical theologian is the importance of David Friedrich Strauss, whose monumental *Life of Jesus* (1835) came to epitomize the problem of faith and history. Though not the first to employ the concept of myth to interpret the New Testament, Strauss was the first to apply it consistently to the Gospel accounts of Jesus's life from beginning to end. In the words of James Livingston, Strauss was the one "who first raised, in such a radical way, the question of the historical accessibility of Jesus. His importance as a theologian is assured if for no other reason than for posing this historical question, for it has remained at the center of theological discussion to the present day."[8] Barth had called Strauss, along with Ludwig Feuerbach, the "bad conscience" of modern theology.[9] Though later scholars have criticized Strauss for overemphasizing the extent of mythology in the Gospel texts, he never intended simply to reduce the story of Jesus to myth. Rather, his method

7. Letter to Gary Comstock, November 5, 1984, in Frei, *Reading Faithfully*, 1:37.
8. James C. Livingston, *Modern Christian Thought*, 2nd ed. (Minneapolis: Fortress, 2006), 1:220.
9. Karl Barth, *Protestant Thought: From Rousseau to Ritschl* (New York: Simon & Schuster, 1959), 389.

was "to test *the historical claims* of the New Testament concerning Jesus" by separating out the historical events from their mythological elaboration.[10] While not denying that there were elements of genuine historical recollection in the narratives, he argued that they were overlaid and supplemented by the mythological imagination that was characteristic of the premodern mind. Strauss believed myth to be "the natural language of religion."[11] Strauss's importance for later theology, however, depends not on the particulars of his methodology or his conclusions but rather on the fact that he questioned the historical reliability of the New Testament writings by introducing a distinction between the scriptural narrative and actual historical events. It would not be long before theologians were wrestling with the relation between the "Jesus of history" and the "Christ of faith."[12]

Barth underscored the importance of Strauss's challenge to later theologians. "One must love the question Strauss raised, in order to understand it"; but most people, he added, "have feared it." Most theologians, Barth claims, instead of facing the issue, have ignored it or tried to find a way around it. And that is why Strauss remains the "bad conscience" of theology. But a final comment in Barth's chapter on Strauss contains an odd twist. "Proper theology," he writes, "begins just at the point where the difficulties disclosed by Strauss and Feuerbach are seen"—and here comes the surprise—"and then laughed at."[13] Frei agrees that proper theology should begin with Strauss's challenge. And there are indications that he also shares Barth's desire, in the end, to laugh at Strauss nevertheless.[14] But how can these two responses coexist?

Many of Barth's critics are convinced that they cannot. Livingston is typical, agreeing with Barth that "too many theologians have avoided and bypassed" Strauss's challenge, and he adds that "chief among these 'avoiders' . . . are Karl Barth himself" and his dialectical followers.[15] There is strong evidence, however, that Hans Frei took both parts of Barth's response to Strauss with equal seriousness. To start with, he followed Barth's suggestion and began his theological endeavors by confronting the problem exposed by Strauss, and then he struggled for many years to find a way that theologians might read the Gospel narrative of Jesus realistically without becoming either skeptics

---

10. Livingston, *Modern Christian Thought*, 1:216 (emphasis original).

11. Livingston, *Modern Christian Thought*, 1:217, paraphrasing Strauss.

12. In a letter to Julian Hartt in 1981, Frei refers to "the seemingly everlasting Jesus of history / Christ of faith juxtaposition." *Reading Faithfully*, 1:33.

13. Barth, *Protestant Thought*, 389.

14. Higton entitles his first chapter on Frei's theology "Laughing at Strauss."

15. Livingston, *Modern Christian Thought*, 1:220.

or fundamentalists. Higton argues that "Frei's work can be seen, without too much distortion, as one long attempt to laugh at Strauss—not because he has found a way of ignoring him, but because he has learnt to defeat Strauss with Strauss's own tools."[16] I am not sure whether Frei used Strauss's own tools, but I do believe that he found a way to overcome the Straussian impasse by developing a hermeneutic of realistic narrative that allowed him to read the Gospel narrative of Jesus Christ and to affirm its truth without ignoring or bypassing the results of historical criticism.

Frei employs a two-pronged strategy—one that, not surprisingly, is both historical and theological. He is best remembered for the historical side. Those of us who studied with him and followed his career before the publication of *The Eclipse of Biblical Narrative* in 1974 had sometimes doubted that the project would ever be completed. When I visited Yale in 1967 as a prospective graduate student, I remember his teaching assistants at the time telling me in hushed tones about the groundbreaking book Frei had long been working on. It was going to electrify the theological world, they said—if only he could ever admit that it was finished and allow it to be published! His perfectionism was legendary. The closer he got to the end, the more he worried that critics would discover some error or omission; and so he continued scribbling on his yellow legal pads. When *The Eclipse of Biblical Narrative* at last appeared in print, it quickly became a major focus of theological discussion. Not least among its attributes was the title, which provided a metaphor to describe how a way of reading the Bible that had long been practiced by Christians up to and including the Protestant Reformers had seemingly vanished in the following two or three centuries—while at the same time hinting that, like the moon, it might eventually reemerge. In an effort to show how the eclipse had come about, Frei included detailed accounts of both hermeneutical theory and literary developments in Europe, primarily in Germany and England. By the time Schleiermacher developed his "hermeneutics of understanding" in the early nineteenth century, Frei concludes, the possibility of reading narrative realistically had been thoroughly eclipsed:

> At that time the search for the subject matter beyond the text had obscured narrative meaning. Now it was the quest for narrative unity or continuity in the consciousness of the author, or in the inner form as represented by the characters' consciousness, which prevented the descriptive or narrative shape from assuming its rightful place.[17]

16. Higton, *Christ, Providence and History*, 35.
17. Frei, *The Eclipse of Biblical Narrative: A Study in Eighteenth and Nineteenth Century Hermeneutics* (New Haven: Yale University Press, 1974), 312–13.

Left hanging in the air at the end of this groundbreaking book is a question that readers were bound to ask: Will the eclipse come to an end at last? Can realistic narrative meaning be rediscovered? And if so, how?

The Theological Response: The Identity and Presence of Jesus

In retrospect we can now see that the historical side of Frei's work was never the main point. He was, after all, a historical *theologian*. And for the remainder of his life it was the theological solution to the problem of faith and history that consumed his energies.

It must have come as a surprise to many of Frei's readers, after the long wait for *Eclipse*, that a second book appeared in print just a year later.[18] *The Identity of Jesus Christ*, it is now clear, represented the other prong of Frei's program, the theological complement to *The Eclipse of Biblical Narrative*. In fact, however, it had been written nearly a decade earlier and published in two parts in an obscure periodical for adult education under the auspices of the Presbyterian Church. For reasons that remain puzzling even today, the second book—despite its importance in Frei's larger project—was not received with the interest one might have expected. It appeared, in the words of one observer, "to a tepid reception, and has been overshadowed since."[19] One reason for its disappointing impact at the time may be the odd process by which it had come into being. Higton, in briefly reviewing its circuitous route to publication as a book in 1975, calls it "this strange project . . . [the] strange accompaniment . . . to the massive and ground-breaking *Eclipse*."[20] Another reason for its failure to capture the imagination of readers could be Frei's own ambivalence. He himself later expressed doubts about the book, and rather than revising his argument and defending its main thesis, he turned to other projects, some of which involved further historical work on nineteenth-century thinkers. Perhaps the success of *Eclipse* and the continuing attention it received diverted his attention from the theological project that was its natural complement. Higton suggests other private and personal issues that consumed his energies,[21] but none of these

18. Frei, *The Identity of Jesus Christ: The Hermeneutical Bases of Dogmatic Theology* (Philadelphia: Fortress, 1975). A new edition, including a foreword by Mike Higton and an introduction by Joshua B. Davis, was published by Cascade Books in 2013. Page numbers are accurate to both editions, unless otherwise indicated.

19. Joshua B. Davis, introduction to Hans W. Frei, *The Identity of Jesus Christ: The Hermeneutical Bases of Dogmatic Theology* (Eugene, OR: Cascade Books, 2013), xxii.

20. Higton, *Christ, Providence and History*, 18–19.

21. Although Frei, by his own account, "felt that he had 'found his voice,'" Higton describes his work in the 1970s as "a strange mixture of confidence and anxiety," including a sense of isolation from his roots in the church. Higton, *Christ, Providence and History*, 19.

speculations (however interesting they may be biographically) contributes to an understanding of Frei's eventual theological accomplishments.

With the help of the considerable evidence now available, but not published during his lifetime, we are now in a position to gain a clearer picture of Frei's *theological* response to the problem of faith and history—the demon with which he had been wrestling since the start of his career. Yet the key to its resolution has all along been hiding in plain sight, we could say, in the concluding chapters of *The Identity of Jesus Christ*. I recall a conversation with him in his office in which he was describing the argument that subsequently appeared in chapter 13 of *Identity*. The heart of the matter is a claim he makes about the relation of Jesus's identity and presence: "To know *who* he is in connection with what took place is to know *that* he is."[22] At the time, I commented to him that it sounded to me like an ontological argument for the presence of Jesus Christ—to which he replied, "Precisely!"[23] This Anselmian insight into the Gospel narrative of Jesus's resurrection, he says in *Identity*, "is the climax of the story and its claim. What the accounts are saying, in effect, is that the being and identity of Jesus in the resurrection are such that his non-resurrection becomes inconceivable."[24] What makes this interpretation of the narrative so intriguing and yet so puzzling is Frei's apparent ambivalence about its fictional or historical status. Recall that much of his attention in *Eclipse* was devoted to developments in fictional writing during the eighteenth and nineteenth centuries. He now brings this same attention to realistic fictional narrative to bear on his reading of the Gospel account of Jesus: "The realistic or history-like quality of the narrative," he writes, "whether historical or not, prevents even the person who regards the account as implausible from regarding it as mere myth. Rather, it is to him a kind of hyperfiction claiming to be self-warranting fact."[25] For a few brief paragraphs, Frei wrestles with this fiction/fact duality. He asks, tantalizingly, "Of what other fact can we say that complete commitment is a way of taking note of it?" And then he adds what I can only describe as the seed of a theological answer to Strauss's challenge:

> But grateful love of God and neighbor is the proper manner of appropriating the presence, based on the resurrection of Jesus, who in perfect obedience to God enacted men's good in their behalf on the cross. That this act is the only manner

22. Frei, *Identity of Jesus Christ*, 145 (emphasis original).
23. The term *ontological* could introduce confusion unless it is made clear (as it was to Frei) that it simply refers to the famous argument of Anselm of Canterbury in his *Proslogion* (ca. 1077), which has been dubbed the "ontological argument" by later interpreters.
24. Frei, *Identity of Jesus Christ*, 145.
25. Frei, *Identity of Jesus Christ*, 143.

of appropriating the resurrection we cannot doubt. In this instance—and in this instance alone—commitment in faith and assent by the mind constrained by the imagination are one and the same.[26]

Then he drops the subject, saying only that "we cannot dwell here on the manner of appropriation." Nevertheless, he does further comment about "the issue of where to make the transition from literary description to factual, historical, and theological judgment."[27] He sees no way to argue from actual historical occurrence to the truth of the biblical narrative, nor any way to argue against it on historical or factual grounds. All we can conclude is that "there is a kind of logic in a Christian's faith that forces him to say that disbelief in the resurrection of Jesus is rationally impossible." Frei's last word is agnostic: we have no way of knowing why some readers of the Gospel narrative believe and others do not. But either way, we can be sure that it is "a matter of faith and not of arguments from possibility or evidence."[28]

For whatever reasons, readers of *The Identity of Jesus Christ* failed to recognize in it Frei's theological response to the historical problem posed in *The Eclipse of Biblical Narrative*. Perhaps they failed to see the importance of the concluding interpretation of Jesus's resurrection because it followed upon a long and rather tedious treatment of the various ways of describing a person's identity. The unclarity may also be due to the fact that *Identity*, though published in book form in 1975, had been composed much earlier, and before completion of *Eclipse*. One can only wonder how differently Frei might have presented his theological response to Strauss had he waited to write it until after working through the historical process by which a realistic narrative reading of the Bible had ceased to be a live alternative. With the aid of archival materials, unpublished at the time of their composition but now available to us, we are able to gain a clearer picture of Frei's proposed resolution of the problem of faith and history.

Two lectures that Frei delivered in the mid-1970s help us to flesh out his theological response to Strauss and his present-day representatives, the historical-critical interpreters of the Bible. Both lectures were delivered from notes, but both were recorded on tape and have now been transcribed and published. The first one, delivered in Toronto in 1974, is not about Frei's own project (at least not directly) but rather about Karl Barth.[29] As Frei describes

26. Frei, *Identity of Jesus Christ*, 146.
27. Frei, *Identity of Jesus Christ*, 150 (2013 ed., 149).
28. Frei, *Identity of Jesus Christ*, 151, 152 (2013 ed., 150).
29. Frei, "Scripture as Realistic Narrative: Karl Barth as Critic of Historical Criticism," in *Reading Faithfully*, 1:49–63.

Barth's hermeneutical convictions and practices, it becomes evident that he sees his own project as an application of Barth's method. Frei has learned from Barth how to read the Bible realistically and put that hermeneutical approach to work in his own interpretation of the passion-resurrection narratives in the New Testament. He begins by recalling Barth's well-known claim in the first edition of his Romans commentary that (in Frei's paraphrase) "he was happy that he did not have to choose between historical criticism and the old doctrine of inspiration, but that if he did he would choose the old doctrine of inspiration."[30] The virtue of the "old doctrine" is its insistence that "the subject matter of the Bible [is] in the text, rather than . . . [in] the peripheries that were behind the text, which was what historical criticism did." Frei further highlights the way Barth uses historical criticism. According to Barth—and Frei clearly agrees—"you look steadily at the text and what the text says, and then you utilize, on an *ad hoc* basis, what the historical scholars offer you" (55). Frei stresses that the use of historical-critical material cannot be systematically described; there can be no general theory of the relationship of theological interpretation and historical criticism. Frei also learned from Barth to see the similarity between fictional writing, such as the modern realistic novel, and the New Testament narrative of Jesus's passion and resurrection. Not that Barth ever spoke explicitly about the Bible and the modern novel, but he "wanted the text always to be literal in that same fashion: it means what it says. It is to be taken literally *whether or not* something happened" (57, emphasis original). It is characteristic of Frei's modesty that he does not claim to be the originator of this insight into the "history-like" quality of biblical narrative but says he learned it by observing how Karl Barth interprets the Bible.

Having clarified and endorsed Barth's way of reading Scripture realistically while making *ad hoc* use of historical criticism, Frei concludes the Toronto lecture by explicitly connecting this insight to the possibility of a second naïveté. And he does so not simply in reference to the passion-resurrection narratives in the New Testament but to the Bible as a whole. Barth's realistic hermeneutic, Frei claims, puts him "in the position to suggest that we must be as naïve as our forebears were before the rise of criticism in the interpretation of the Bible and as naïve as the Bible itself" (57). But this naïveté, just as in Ricoeur's schema, is not precritical—it's not your grandfather's naïveté, we might say today. No, Barth is now in a position "to suggest that

---

30. Frei, *Reading Faithfully*, 1:53. Barth's statement is found in *The Epistle to the Romans*, trans. Edwin C. Hoskyns (New York: Oxford University Press, 1933), 1. Subsequent references to *Reading Faithfully*, vol. 1, will be given parenthetically in the text.

in a certain way we *can be critical*. We are no longer at the same stage as the naïve precritical forebears" (57, emphasis original). The example Frei calls upon is not about Jesus's resurrection but about how we read the creation stories in Genesis. Barth, he says, "did not deny the truth or (in a peculiar, hard-to-get-at sense) the *historicity* of Genesis." He always "insisted that the creation accounts are *Geschichte* but . . . not *historische-Geschichte*."[31] That hard-to-get-at sense is (to use Frei's own terminology) *literary*, like a novel, but is at the same time *true*, and true in a way that cannot be verified or falsified by historical (*historisch*) research. "The Bible," Frei says (without limiting its scope to the Gospel narratives of Jesus's passion and resurrection), "is largely and centrally realistic narrative." Though the question of its narrative realism is a separate issue from its truth, the distinction does not matter for Barth. Frei explains it this way: "Remember that, for Barth, [the Bible] depicts the one real world in which we all live so that to understand the meaning of it is the same as understanding the truth of it. If you understand it rightly you cannot *not* think of it as real." Here Frei once again appeals to his Anselmian argument, but this time in relation not just to the resurrection of Jesus but to the Bible as a whole. "That strange, marvelous little book on Anselm's proof for the existence of God is in a peculiar sense also applicable to Barth as an interpreter of the Bible as realistic narrative." In summary, Barth's ambition—and Frei's—is "to be a *direct* reader of the text, and not of some hypothetical subject matter behind the text." One reads this way "not as an uncritically naïve reader but as a critically naïve reader" (59). Frei concludes his lecture with a reminder that historical-critical exegesis must always be at the service of theological exegesis: "as a handmaid rather than either a mistress or a mother" (60).

The other newly available essay from the 1970s is the tenth annual Greenhoe Lecture that Frei delivered at Louisville Seminary in 1976, entitled "On Interpreting the Christian Story."[32] It contains an especially clear and accessible summary of Frei's overall program in both its historical and theological aspects. But it draws out some surprising theological implications that clarify and extend Frei's thinking in ways that do not appear elsewhere in his published or unpublished writings. These latter reflections are more personal, even autobiographical, than his usual way of expressing himself. More than any of his other writings, this lecture allows us not only to see the overall scope of Frei's thesis but also to learn why he thought it to be so important

---

31. For further discussion on *Geschichte*, see chap. 2 above, under "Barth's Theology of Creation."

32. Frei, "On Interpreting the Christian Story," in *Reading Faithfully*, 1:68–93.

and what difference it ought to make in how contemporary Christians understand their faith and practice.

Frei begins his deliberations as before with Strauss's *Life of Jesus*, but this time he points out that the issue—"the problem of historical revelation and the reliability of the Bible"—had already been raised in the eighteenth century (74). The various attempts to solve it led to "an enormous shift" in how the Bible was interpreted, including loss of the literal sense. When the Reformers talked about the literal sense, they had meant what Frei calls the "*literary-literal*"—that is, the Bible gives us "the right description, not a symbol, not an allegory . . . it meant exactly what it said" (75). This way of reading the Bible included figural interpretation—something that Frei had long emphasized in his teaching and writing. Figuration means that "there are certain things, or certain occurrences, or concepts . . . in the Old Testament (say the law, or Noah's ark) that are what they are; they mean in their own right—and yet . . . they are also figures that will be fulfilled in what they prefigure." Frei stresses that in precritical exegesis "the literal sense actually went hand in hand with the figural sense"; in fact, figural interpretation is more closely allied with the literal sense than with allegory. The text still means what it says even if it sometimes points ahead to other events in the narrative. But when the change came in the eighteenth century, "story began to mean something else," because "the narratives and that which they are about began to separate." As a result, the very meaning of *literal* changed: to this day when people talk about taking the Bible literally they mean that it corresponds to historical events beyond the text. "The literal sense now," Frei writes, "refers us to something 'out there,' which is literally represented by the story." This kind of story can be tested, verified to see if it actually corresponds to external events. One needs to search for evidence in order to confirm its accuracy. "And from this notion," Frei concludes, "historical criticism springs" (76). People tried to bridge the gap between the text and its meaning in various ways (e.g., by naturalist, supernaturalist, or mythical interpretation), but in each case "the representation and that which it represents have a gap between them" (77).

Against this background (which amounts to a concise summary of *Eclipse*), Frei offers an equally concise account of what it means to read the text as realistic narrative. The gap that led to the eclipse of biblical narrative disappears when we read the text realistically. A realistic story, he says, "is like any realistic historical narrative, in that it does not have a subject matter that you can state apart from the narrative itself" (78). In the case of the Gospel story of Jesus, he is precisely the one who is portrayed, through the interaction of character and circumstance, in the story itself. Expressed theologically, "Jesus Christ the person is nothing other than the enactment of his person in his work" (79). If we want to know the facts to which the story refers, we can only respond that they "are facts that we *cannot* have apart from the story." Up to this point the Gospel story is just like a fictional narrative. But what about its *truth*? Frei acknowledges that Christians rightly consider the biblical narrative to be true fact, but "in a way that, although it may bear a family resemblance to the set of empirical facts we call history, is not identical with it." What's more, this fact is "rendered effective to us through the story and we cannot have it without the story in which it is given to us" (79–80). Here Frei makes an unexpected move, one that some might call mystical. Recalling Austin Farrer's characterization of Scripture as "God's self-enacted parable," Frei suggests that a kind of figural reversal occurs when we read the Bible:

> It is as though we, ordinary human beings, were living in a world in which the true reality is one that we only grasp in this life as if it were for us a figure. Yes—but it is *we* who are the figures and it is that reality embodied by the resurrection that is the true reality of which we were only figures. It is as though our sense of reality were to be turned about; it is what is depicted . . . which is real, and it is ordinary world history that is a parable, a figure of that reality. And that is the mystery, it seems to me, of our life into which the story and the facts fit together.[33]

Frei's Solution: On Leaving Things the Way They Are

In the second half of the Greenhoe lecture, Frei's solution to the problem posed by Strauss, the problem of faith and history, comes most clearly into view. Perhaps *solution* is not the right word (*resolution* might be a better choice), because what he finally concludes is that the problem has all along been based on a misunderstanding—a *hermeneutical* misunderstanding. Ever since about 1700, theologians and biblical scholars have been trying to read the Bible the wrong way. They have been trying to take a speck out of believers' eyes without noticing the log in their own. Frei titles this part of his lecture "Interpretation and Devotion: God's Presence for Us in Jesus Christ."[34] But in his very first sentence he suggests an alternative title: "Notes on Leaving Things the Way They Are." It is significant, I believe, that at this point Frei adopts a more personal tone and begins speaking in the first person.

He wants to talk about a problem that affects him not only in his academic studies but also personally. Unlike so many other theologians, he has no wish

---

33. Frei, *Reading Faithfully*, 1:80. I have slightly emended the text and supplied some punctuation in order to make clearer what I believe Frei actually said.
34. Frei, *Reading Faithfully*, 1:80–93.

to make the ancient message of the Bible "meaningful" for our secular world today. By "meaningful," he says, "they usually mean how does one allow it to be a *possibility*" for people today. While admitting some sympathy for that desire, he says that "there always seemed to me something callow and shallow about it that bothered me." As an example, he takes the death-of-God theology of the 1960s. He never took it seriously, he says, though he believed that it "did bespeak a certain problem," most likely the fact that "some ministers, theological students, and theologians found it difficult to pray, and [therefore] . . . said that God was dead." His response contains one of his best one-liners. He said to himself, "Well, all right, if Christianity is going to go out (let us assume for a moment that it depends on what *we* do and not on the grace of God!) it's had a magnificent history and I'd rather see it go out with an orthodox bang than a liberal whimper." For himself, however, "the great problem was always this: How does one express, grasp, and speak— . . . articulate the sense of Christianity? What is its *essence*?" The way he set about solving this problem was to look for "a certain center" of the Bible, in which the gospel message appears most clearly, and then to articulate it as best he could. Acknowledging that others have found that center elsewhere in the Bible, for himself "it is in the Synoptic Gospels" that we find "the identity of the account with what the account is about." Christology is therefore "the center of the New Testament," and it's a high Christology "focused on Jesus Christ as not simply the unique revealer but also the atonement through whose death and resurrection we and the whole world have life." Here "we have in the form of a realistic story the rendering of our salvation." That story obviously claims to be a true story, "but [even] if it is not true *that is still what it means*."[35] On no account is he willing to reopen a gap between the biblical text and its meaning.

He then turns from Christology to the other great issue of modern theology: "*the presence of God in Christ now*." Once again he returns to his "ontological argument," which he describes as follows:

> I put it to myself in a very simple, perhaps rather naïve way, which ultimately derives from the ontological argument of Anselm of Canterbury. I want to tell you how that came about, but let me simply state it: if Jesus is really who the Bible says he is; if that is his identity; then he *cannot not be present*. If he is who the Bible says he is then, having died once, he lives; he is in some manner present, here to us—to be sure in a very unique and unrepeatable manner, and yet he is. (83)

35. All quotations in this paragraph are from Frei, *Reading Faithfully*, 1:80–83 (emphasis original).

Frei has now given us his own interpretation of "the two things that the history of modern theology has been all about" (83). If he is right, he has achieved the goal that Ricoeur taught us to call a "second naïveté." And he has done so in a far more convincing way than Ricoeur ever managed to do. Ricoeur's path to a second naïveté exemplifies the erroneous way of dealing with these twin issues that Frei finds typical of modern theology. That erroneous way "has been to think that human beings are consciousnesses" who can encounter God through limit experiences, and that these experiences are ultimately what the Bible means, though it expresses its message indirectly through symbols, myths, and stories. Frei is characterizing here what his colleague George Lindbeck, writing a few years later, would label "experiential-expressivism."[36] The example Frei uses in the Greenhoe lecture is not Ricoeur but Kierkegaard and Tillich, but he might have picked from any number of others in the past two centuries. He locates the problem at one particular point ("where everything seemed wrong to me"): in order to close the gap between the text and its real meaning, these thinkers must first explain the problem and then its solution by using some kind of technical language. They must supply "a certain technical or theological language" in order to explain what happens in solving this problem (85).

At this point Frei's alternative title comes into play: "Notes on Leaving Things the Way They Are." He takes his cue not from a theologian but a philosopher—one who is not even a Christian. We learn from Ludwig Wittgenstein, Frei tells us, "that language doesn't often work in technical concepts." The mistake that so many modern theologians have made is to think that in order to affirm that Jesus Christ is somehow present to us now they must "*explain* [it] by translating the notion of presence into some explanatory concepts. That is precisely what I think cannot be done, and which I think need not be done. There is, it seems to me, a very ordinary way of talking about the presence of Christ." The job of Christian theology "is simply to talk about the way Christian language is used by Christians, and to ask if it is being used faithfully"—in other words, whether it is faithful to biblical language and the tradition that flows from the Bible. (Though he doesn't point it out, this too is something he learned from Karl Barth.) This task does *not* require us "to *translate* Christian language into a language that will be relevant to our situation." In fact, "the whole metaphor of translation there is misleading." After all, Frei has demonstrated that at its very heart the Bible "*means what it says*—so there is no need to translate it; no need to recon-

---

36. George Lindbeck, *The Nature of Doctrine: Religion and Theology in a Postliberal Age* (Philadelphia: Westminster, 1984), esp. chaps. 2 and 3.

ceptualize it. There may be a need to *redescribe* it, but that's a very different thing."[37]

This realization was a great relief to Frei, as it should be to us, for it liberates Christian theology from so much tedious and misleading conceptualizing and theorizing. Frei puts it this way: "One of the marvelous and—to my mind—startling and liberating little sentences that Ludwig Wittgenstein wrote was when he said, 'Don't ask for meaning, ask for use'" (87). Frei calls it getting rid of a "verbal cramp" (91). One can sense his relief as he approaches the end of his 1976 lecture:

> I am suggesting there is no need for an explanation. I am suggesting there *is* no explanation. I am suggesting that *there is no problem*. I am suggesting that this is precisely the function of Christian language; this is its character, its ordinary use, and, if you will, at the same time its uniqueness: it is both these things. . . . To try to go to a level underneath them, you see, is precisely what I am saying is wrong, and is precisely where the technical theologians have been wrong. And we need to be released from that verbal and conceptual cramp. (92, emphasis original)

Hans Frei has bequeathed to us a theological hermeneutic that does not set us another theoretical or conceptual task but rather sets us free to do the real work of theology.

One more point needs to be made. In Frei's official title for part two of the Greenhoe lecture, he speaks of *devotion*, an uncommon word in his theological vocabulary. After his plea to turn away from technical language to ordinary Christian language, he explains why he has included the term in his title. "I use 'devotion' simply to circumscribe, to have a term for, *Christian language in use*. Christian language in meditation, in public worship, private prayer, in the obedience of the moral life: Christian language in the public and private use of faith" (86, emphasis original). He may have been influenced here too by his reading of Wittgenstein, who reminds us that "to imagine a language means to imagine a form of life"; that "the *speaking* of language is part of an activity, or of a form of life."[38] Once Frei has liberated Christian language from the prison house of theory, we are able to see it (*hear* it!) in its proper context—in the everyday life of Christian men and women in the world. The most important legacy of Hans Frei is his call for an end

37. All quotations in this paragraph are from Frei, *Reading Faithfully*, 1:85–86 (emphasis original).

38. Ludwig Wittgenstein, *Philosophical Investigations*, 2nd ed., trans. G. E. M. Anscombe (New York: Macmillan, 1958), §19 and §23 (emphasis original).

to the academic captivity of Christian theology. At the end of the Greenhoe lecture he provides a one-sentence summary of his thesis that includes a small but significant emendation: "What I am saying is that I don't need to think about *how* he can be present; his identity and his presence are given together in the ordinary usage of Christian practice and Christian language."[39] Here he takes the step that he had hesitated to take in *Identity* when he hinted that the way to "take note" of the story of Jesus's resurrection is by means of a "total commitment."[40] At the crucial Anselmian point in Frei's argument, when it dawns on the reader of the Gospel story that Jesus cannot *not* be present here and now—at just this point, where "commitment in faith and assent by the mind constrained by the imagination are one and the same"— interpretation merges into appropriation so that we can no longer tell them apart. The Christian life is not something we first come to grasp intellectually and then go on to practice; rather, one discovers the truth of the gospel when one hears the call of God and obeys. Knowing Jesus and following Jesus are two sides of one reality.

A Personal Epilogue: Reading the Bible with Prisoners

I no longer live in the academic world. Though I still make occasional forays into its conferences and annual meetings and try to keep up on my theological reading, for the past several years I've spent far more time in prison than in lecture halls. How I ended up as a volunteer prison minister is as much a mystery to me as why I believe the Bible is the Word of God. (Come to think of it, they are probably the same mystery.) For some time now I've felt that the two poles of my present life—working with prisoners and doing academic theology—are about as far from one another as the east is from the west, even though I value them both and don't intend to give up either one. Writing this chapter has taught me that they may be more closely akin than I had thought.

Studying the Bible with Christian inmates has taught me that precritical naïveté is to be found not only in our historical past but also among our fellow believers today. I didn't know that before, because I seldom associated with Christians who didn't have a college degree, if not a doctorate. Now I spend most of my time with men who may have finished high school or may still be working on their GED in prison. In theory, of course, I always knew that a person's standing before the Lord had nothing to do with their formal education; but I still found it hard to believe. Now I know it is true because I

---

39. Frei, *Reading Faithfully*, 1:92 (emphasis added).
40. Frei, *Identity of Jesus Christ*, 146.

see the faith of Christian prisoners every time we read Scripture together, pray together, and worship together. One of the qualities of the second naïveté is that it doesn't need to force criticism upon those who haven't encountered it. Since the Bible "means what it says," we can read Scripture together naïvely and hear the same Word of God. I've become more tolerant of fundamentalists (the real ones, who generally refer to themselves not as fundamentalists but as "fundamental Christians"). I've finally outgrown the fundamentalist-bashing that I learned growing up in mainline churches and heard throughout my career in academia.

One of my biggest surprises in prison has been discovering that theological discussions with inmates are often better—more animated and also more insightful—than class discussions in my college courses. One reason is that many of the inmates know their Bible much better than my college students did (they frequently admonish one another to "stay in the Word"). In fact, some of them know their Bible better than I do. I hear it in conversations with them and also in their prayers, which are often filled with biblical language and allusion. But there's a deeper reason too: prisoners understand that what we are doing when we study the Bible and theology is a matter of life and death. That's why it's easier to teach and preach the Christian gospel in the prison than in the university. I would not have believed it if I did not hear it so often from inmates: "I'm so glad God sent me to prison!" One of the first inmates I worked with (I thought of him as "my Colombian drug dealer" . . . because he was) told us one evening at Bible study that he had just learned from his family that all of his former friends and associates back home were dead. Prison had quite literally saved his life.

The opportunity to ponder the legacy of my old *Doktorvater* has been a blessing—almost like being back in graduate school with Mr. Frei. Best of all, I think I finally understand what he was trying to teach us. Part of the reason is that I've learned more about what he was saying then by reading his newly published *Nachlass*. But the other reason has to do with my change of venue from classroom to prison. As I was working on this chapter, I kept wishing that I could talk things over with Mr. Frei now—now that I'm in a context where I can finally understand what he had been saying all along. I think I know what his response would be. I think he would not be at all surprised at what I've learned in prison. And I'd like to think that he'd be pleased.

PART 2

METAPHOR, AESTHETICS, AND GENDER

6

THE MIRROR, THE LAMP, AND THE LENS

On the Limits of Imagination

Like most important philosophical issues, the question of the limits of imagination appears not only as a topic in philosophical theory but also at the level of daily life. This fact was brought home to me by the film *A Beautiful Mind*, loosely based on the life of mathematician John Forbes Nash Jr. (1928–2015), winner of the 1994 Nobel Prize in economics, who struggled with schizophrenia throughout his adult life. It may be just coincidence that the film is brought to us by Imagine Entertainment, and that its advertising tagline is "He saw the world in a way no one could have imagined." But director Ron Howard's film in fact allows the audience to experience schizophrenia from the inside as a life-and-death struggle over the limits of imagination. Nash's life story is a graphic reminder that imagination is both a powerful force for creativity and an essential ingredient in everyday life—and that without effective limits it can destroy us. Seen through the filmmaker's eyes, schizophrenia emerges as a disease of the imagination—one that attacks precisely the *limits* of imagination, rendering the patient incapable of distinguishing reality from fantasy, "good" imagination from "bad." In the film, schizophrenia accordingly takes on a broader, even universal, significance: not just an affliction of the mentally ill but a metaphor for a central feature of the human condition, for a set of issues that no one, including the philosopher, can evade.

I began my research on the limits of imagination the way students do—with a search on the internet. After entering the keywords *imagination* and *limits*, Google unearthed more than 40 million matching websites in less than a second. Although I did not examine them all in detail, a few of them did turn out to be philosophically suggestive, at least to me as one taught by J. L. Austin and Ludwig Wittgenstein to take seriously the ordinary uses of language. For example, one website development company takes as its motto, "Imagination has no limits"; and this thesis is echoed by the personal website of a young Pakistani man living in Saudi Arabia that boldly proclaims, "Imagination and dreams have no limits." A rather different take on the matter came from a website devoted to "reducing fear and alienation in the workplace," which confidently announces, "The only limits are in the imagination." What this admittedly haphazard exercise in ordinary-language philosophy demonstrates is that people who are not reflecting philosophically are likely to think of imagination sometimes as the source of limits and sometimes as the realm of the limitless. As we shall see, this ambiguity is echoed in the history of philosophical reflection on imagination.

Root Metaphors and the Problem of Limits

In his classic study of Romanticism, *The Mirror and the Lamp*, M. H. Abrams identifies the root metaphors according to which imagination has been conceived—the mirror and lamp of his title—the former essentially mimetic and the latter productive or creative. "If Plato was the main source of the philosophical archetype of the reflector," Abrams writes, "Plotinus was the chief begetter of the archetype of the projector."[1] The shift of emphasis from the former to the latter he takes to be the decisive event in the Romantic theory of knowledge as it emerged around the beginning of the nineteenth century. This intellectual gestalt switch is epitomized in a passage from William Butler Yeats that Abrams places as an epigraph on his title page:

> It must go further still: that soul must become its own betrayer, its own deliverer, the one activity, the mirror turn lamp.

Richard Kearney applies these same two metaphors more broadly to represent the difference between premodern and modern theories of imagination. "The *mimetic* paradigm of imagining is replaced by the *productive* paradigm,"

1. M. H. Abrams, *The Mirror and the Lamp: Romantic Theory and the Critical Tradition* (New York: Oxford University Press, 1953), 59.

he summarizes. "The imagination ceases to function as a mirror reflecting some external reality and becomes a lamp which projects its own internally generated light onto things."[2]

The problem of the limits of imagination varies according to the ways in which the faculty of imagination is conceived. The different root metaphors or paradigms by which the imagination has itself been imagined imply different situations with regard to limits. Each model of imagination entails a different problematic, suggests a different threat. The mimetic paradigm of the mirror, in which representations of the "original" are more or less imperfectly reflected, dominated the most influential accounts of imagination from the time of Plato until the dawn of modernity. In this model the underlying duality of original and copy sets the terms according to which imagination is understood and evaluated. This mimetic or reproductive model of imagination carries with it the threat of *distortion*. How do we know that the reproduction is true to the original? Plato's denigration of the image as a mere copy of a copy epitomizes the problem of limits as it appears in mimetic views of imagination: here the imagination is itself the limiting factor, the source of distortion or deficiency. For Plato the limitation is inherent in imagination's sensuous nature; like the prisoners in Socrates's allegory of the cave, imagination is chained to the bodily senses. Unable to gaze directly on the source of light, it sees only indistinct shadows cast on the wall. The solution implied by this scenario is to break the chains of enslavement to the senses and ascend with the aid of reason to the pure intelligible sunlight of truth. On Plato's view, in Kearney's paraphrase, "reason alone has access to the divine Ideas. And imagination, for its part, is condemned to a pseudo-world of imitations."[3] Rather than inviting or requiring limits, the mimetic imagination itself limits our access to truth. The worry is not that imagination will overreach itself but rather that it may inhibit or interfere with the rational apprehension of truth.

In Kearney's view, as a result of the "onto-theological" alliance of Athens and Jerusalem—the fusion of ancient Greek ontology with the biblical worldview—the fundamental attitude of suspicion toward the imagination continued to characterize the medieval period in Europe.[4] Although the attempt of the iconoclasts to root out all images from Christian life and worship was officially repudiated by the church, the prevailing attitude toward

2. Richard Kearney, *The Wake of Imagination: Toward a Postmodern Culture* (London: Routledge, 1988), 155.

3. Kearney, *Wake of Imagination*, 88.

4. This claim is the main thesis of Kearney's account of the medieval imagination. *Wake of Imagination*, chap. 4.

imagination and the images it produces nevertheless remained, according to Kearney, "essentially one of prudence or distrust."[5] Doctrines governing the veneration of images and proscribing their worship served as necessary theological limits on the imagination.

As with so many issues in modern Western thought, a key turning point in the career of imagination occurred in the philosophy of Immanuel Kant, who is primarily responsible for placing the question of imagination at the center of modern philosophical attention. Kant, who derived his concept of imagination from the psychology of Johannes Nikolaus Tetens (1736–1807), assigns it a crucial role in the *Critique of Pure Reason*, calling it "a blind but indispensable function of the soul, without which we should have no knowledge whatsoever, but of which we are scarcely ever conscious."[6] Because the imagination takes the sensible manifold and synthesizes it into a unified experience, Kant claims that "imagination is a necessary ingredient of perception itself."[7] As a transcendental function, imagination processes what is given to the mind by the senses and makes it available to the understanding: thus it is the link between body and mind. "The two extremes," he writes, "namely sensibility and understanding, must stand in necessary connection with each other through the mediation of this transcendental function of imagination."[8] Kant breaks with the long tradition going back to Plato, according to which the imagination is mimetic, in the unoriginal business of re-presenting something "original." Accordingly, for Kant the imagination takes on an active, as opposed to a merely passive, role; it is no longer simply dependent on a prior original but assumes an "originating" role of its own. Right here is the genesis of the modern problem of limits: if imagination does more than simply reproduce for us what is already there, what are the warrants for its "productions"? How can we trust an admittedly "blind" and largely unconscious faculty that derives its material neither from transcendent reality nor from the senses?

Only when the image of imagination as lamp came to supplant the metaphor of the mirror did the problem of imagination's limits truly come into its own. Kant's discovery of the "productive" imagination can be seen as the watershed. "In so far as imagination is spontaneity," he writes in the second edition of the *Critique of Pure Reason*, "I sometimes also entitle it the *productive* imagination, to distinguish it from the *reproductive* imagination,

5. Kearney, *Wake of Imagination*, 138.
6. Kant, *Immanuel Kant's Critique of Pure Reason*, trans. Norman Kemp Smith (New York: St. Martin's Press, 1968), B103.
7. Kant, *Critique of Pure Reason*, A121n.
8. Kant, *Critique of Pure Reason*, A124.

whose synthesis is entirely subject to empirical laws, the laws, namely, of association, and which therefore contributes nothing to the explanation of the possibility of *a priori* knowledge." The mimetic imagination that had hitherto dominated Western thought is now drummed out of philosophy altogether: "The reproductive synthesis," Kant rules, "falls within the domain, not of transcendental philosophy, but of psychology."[9] The productive imagination, on the other hand, assumes an increasingly central role and lays claim to a greater and greater creativity, not only in Kant's own late writings but even more in the German idealists and the Romantics who succeeded him.

The need for limits is rooted in the suspicion of imagination embedded in both of the principal sources of the concept: the Hebrew Scriptures and the Greek philosophical tradition. Kearney shows how the biblical figure of Adam and the Greek figure of Prometheus both come to represent, each in its own way, the ambiguity of human imagination and therefore reinforce the deep suspicion of imagination that pervades the Western intellectual tradition. "In both instances," Kearney writes, "imagination is characterized by an act of rebellion against the divine order of things."[10] As a mirror, the imagination always runs the risk of producing mere copies, or even distortions, of the original. As a lamp, the creativity of the imagination threatens blasphemy or hubris. The resulting dilemma is how appropriate limits can be set on imagination so as to avoid the excesses of distortion and blasphemy. The challenge, in positive terms, is to find norms by which the imagination might be guided into the pathways of truth. Can there be a normative imagination?

An Alternative Metaphor: Imagination as Lens

According to Kearney's telling of the story of imagination, the answer is negative: there can be no normative imagination—something he sees epitomized in the current plight of the imagination. He proposes a third metaphor as the postmodern successor to both mirror and lamp: the labyrinth of mirrors, in which the imagination produces only endless reproductions, copies of copies of copies where there is no longer any original, a kind of self-deconstruction of imagination that erases the distinction between the imaginary and the real, leading to the collapse of the concept of imagination itself. Kearney's pessimistic conclusion, however, results from his flawed attempt to account for imagination entirely in terms of the metaphors of mirror and lamp. It

9. Kant, *Critique of Pure Reason*, B151–52.
10. Kearney, *Wake of Imagination*, 80.

misses a central feature of imagination, one that has become increasingly evident in the modern period.

Rather than imagining imagination as mirror or as lamp, my proposal is that it be conceived as a focusing *lens*. This image combines features of both the "reproductive" aspect of the mirror (imagination as mimetic) and the "productive" aspect of the lamp (imagination as creative). It also preserves the representational intent of language so that it avoids the postmodern critique of the quest for a nonlinguistic "original" lurking behind our signifiers. Rather, imagination is what allows us to see something as meaningful—that is, filled with meaning, having significance rather than sheer randomness. It turns marks on a page, or sounds in the ear, into meaning-filled language. The imagination allows us to make sense of what we perceive (and this is true from the level of perceptual imagination up to poetic and religious imagination). This function of imagination is encapsulated in the metaphor of the lens, which is something we see *with* rather than something we look *at*. Imagination conceived in this way is the analogical or metaphorical faculty, our ability to see one thing *as* another.

In his more robust account of imagination in the first edition of the *Critique of Pure Reason* (toned down in the second edition), Kant announces that "imagination is a necessary ingredient of perception itself."[11] It is necessary because that sheer sensuous input (what Kant calls the "manifold of intuition") is not yet knowledge because it has no focus, no organization, no shape. It is meaningless, without significance, until the imagination performs its service, which is "to bring the manifold of intuition into the form of an image."[12]

The nub of the issue is what the imagination actually does to accomplish this task. My contention is that Kant never succeeds in bridging the qualitative gap between sensibility and understanding—between matter and mind— and that this failure leads eventually to the postmodern labyrinth of mirrors in which all imagination is imitation because no image is anchored in an "original." Broadly viewed, of course, Kant's problem is the great problem of modern philosophers beginning with Descartes: If "thinking substance" is simply other than "extended substance" (the names for the duality change with the times, but the problem remains), how can they ever be brought into communication, let alone "synthesis" (Kant's preferred term)? The search for the point of synthesis between mind and body is reminiscent of the scientific quest for the atom, the ultimate indivisible unit at the base of physical reality: each time scientists think they have discovered the basic particle, further

11. Kant, *Critique of Pure Reason*, A121n.
12. Kant, *Critique of Pure Reason*, A120.

research uncovers yet more minuscule complexities within it. (The paradox is manifest in the very notion of "splitting the atom," for the word *atom* means—or originally meant—that which cannot be cut or divided.) Kant is engaged in an analogous quest, focusing his transcendental microscope ever more keenly on the point at which sense and understanding touch. His word for this point is "imagination." The specific way in which the imagination brings together sense and understanding is by introducing *schemata*. Kant defines the schema of a concept as the "representation of a universal procedure of imagination in providing an image for a concept."[13] A schema is not an image but rather, in the words of Frederick Copleston, "a rule or procedure for the production of images which schematize or delimit." The image belongs to sensibility, but the schema belongs to the understanding. "The imagination is able to mediate between the concepts of the understanding and the manifold of intuition."[14] Kant appears to be simply multiplying terminology in a futile quest to synthesize what cannot, in the nature of the case, be combined. For the duality reappears at a new, more minuscule level: *how* does the mental "schema" manage to produce the sensible "image"?

Kant is quite explicit that imagination is not passive at this point but active; that is why he calls it the *productive* imagination. But his use of this term introduces a confusion by suggesting that imagination, even in its role in sense perception, *produces* something beyond what it intuits in sense data. If we attend closely to Kant's account of how imagination functions at this critical point, however, it would be more accurate to describe it as a focusing or filtering, rather than a productive, activity. In the case of perception as described by Kant, imagination is not "a lamp which projects its own internally generated light onto things"[15] but rather a lens that focuses the light it receives from the senses, projecting it as a nexus of coherent images. The true lamp-function of imagination, as Abrams rightly emphasizes, is epitomized in Romanticism, where imagination is employed not to *perceive* the actual world but rather to *produce* virtual worlds of its own. It is this creative use of imagination that should rightly be called *productive*. The perceptive and creative uses of imagination constitute different applications of the imaginative lens—applications that run in opposite directions.

Kant's two uses of imagination are related in the same way that Clifford Geertz distinguishes the two functions of cultural models: an "of" sense and a "for" sense. In the first case, a theory or symbol system "models . . .

13. Kant, *Critique of Pure Reason*, B179–80 (A140).
14. Frederick Copleston, *A History of Philosophy* (Garden City, NY: Doubleday, 1964), 6:51.
15. Kearney, *Wake of Imagination*, 138.

relationships in such a way—that is, by expressing their structure in synoptic form—as to render them apprehensible; it is a model *of* 'reality.'" In the second case, the model is employed for "the manipulation of the non-symbolic systems in terms of the relationships expressed in the symbolic. . . . Here, the theory is a model under whose guidance . . . relationships are organized: it is a model *for* 'reality.'"[16] Geertz's example is a dam: a model *of* the dam (e.g., hydraulic theory or a flow chart) enables us to understand its workings; whereas a model *for* the building of a dam, such as a set of blueprints or a scale model, can be used for purposes of design and construction. These opposite (though compatible) uses of models are epitomized in the lens, which I am proposing as the root metaphor for the paradigmatic imagination. One use of a lens (e.g., in prescription eyeglasses) is to focus our visual data in such a way that our eyes perceive it correctly: this use corresponds to Geertz's model-of. A lens may also be used (e.g., in a slide projector) to project an image outwards—the model-for function. In this second case, the projected image, like the blueprint for the dam, can actually be used to construct something (e.g., a painting on a wall) according to the pattern projected from the model. These two activities employ the lens in opposite directions: in the first case, the lens gathers light from the outside, focusing it internally for apprehension; in the second, the lens projects light outwards, replicating it for potential use. This model clarifies a basic confusion about the relationship between the "reproductive" and "productive" imagination in Kant. Expressed in his terminology, the two functions appear to be in conflict, for if the goal is to reproduce the perceived reality correctly, any "productive" activity on the part of the imagination threatens to change or distort what is intuited. But the problem vanishes if we conceive the activity of imagination in terms of filter or focus: the intuited data is not supplemented or mixed with something foreign but rather organized in such a way as to make its structure apparent. Perception, then, employs the imagination in a genuinely reproductive way, allowing the mind access to reality by means of received sense data. On the other hand, the imagination can also be employed creatively, in a truly productive fashion, to conjure images of the unreal—for example, in fantasy, fiction, projections of future possibilities, or for purposes of deception. These two uses of imagination, though complementary, are incompatible: we cannot both apprehend the real world and invent new worlds in the same imaginative act.

In its paradigmatic role, the imagination is like a radio receiver, which "intuits" radio signals and processes them, focusing and organizing them into

16. Clifford Geertz, *The Interpretation of Cultures: Selected Essays* (New York: Basic Books, 1973), 93.

a meaningful pattern. In performing this function it does not add any new content, yet neither is it a merely passive recipient. A lens may actually filter out some data in the process of selecting what has meaning, while discarding mere "noise." This filtering function is essential to the work of imagination; and it is the very opposite of distortion. Electronic audio components, for instance, frequently have the ability to *remove distortion* by filtering out some of the data. The fear that imagination may distort reality assumes that the data come to us "pure" and undistorted, but that is obviously not the case, as these examples make clear. It nevertheless remains a problem that we may not know whether a given "meaningful" product of imagination is "true to reality." But the problem will not be resolved by yielding to the naïve assumption that we can have an unmediated check on the reliability of our experience. The fear that imagination may distort the data must not tempt us into thinking we can short-circuit the imagination, make an end run around it, do without its mediation by some kind of *immediate* access to reality. This temptation is what Derrida calls the quest for a "transcendental signified": it represents a kind of hermeneutical failure of nerve in which we deceive ourselves into thinking that interpretation is optional, that we can just go ahead and examine things directly, without mediation. Critics like Kearney believe that this postmodern polemic against the quest for a transcendental signified leads inevitably to the destruction of imagination itself by erasing the distinction between imaginary and real. "Right across the spectrum of structuralist, post-structuralist and deconstructionist thinking," he writes, "one notes a common concern to dismantle the very notion of imagination."[17] Thus in Kearney's account both the mirror and the lamp give way to the labyrinth of mirrors in which images reflect images ad infinitum with no "original" so that the very notions of illusion and reality lose their meaning.

The lens alternative to Kearney's third metaphor preserves elements of the mimetic and creative models, acknowledging both the reproductive and the productive functions of imagination and showing their interrelationship. This metaphor also acknowledges the "undecidability" of imagination and therefore the inevitability of interpretation, but without the pessimistic consequences of a chartless relativism. Rather than the demise of imagination, this option suggests the ongoing centrality of imagination in all the activities of the human spirit, including the arts, the sciences, and religion. Instead of imagining imagination according to the classical image of the *mirror* or the modern image of the *lamp*, let us think of imagination as a *lens* that gathers up and focuses the data we intuit into coherent patterns. Like the mirror, the

17. Kearney, *Wake of Imagination*, 251.

lens performs a mimetic task, reproducing in an organized gestalt whatever aspect of reality we are apprehending. Like the Romantics' lamp, the lens also performs a creative task, forming the raw material of intuition into meaningful shapes and sounds that we can recognize. The view of imagination that takes the focusing lens as its root metaphor is what I have called the *paradigmatic* imagination, because it names the human ability to apprehend meaningful patterns (Greek *paradigmata*)—indeed, to recognize the constitutive pattern that makes a thing what it is and not something else. Seen in this way, the imagination is paradigmatic also in the sense of being exemplary; it is the ability to see one thing *as* another, to recognize in a familiar or accessible image the heuristic model that illuminates another, more complex or recalcitrant aspect of the world. Thus the paradigmatic imagination is the metaphorical or analogical faculty, the ability to grasp something unfamiliar by recognizing similarity, by seeing that it is *like* something else that we already know.

Paradigms and Limits: The Normative Imagination

As in the cases of the mirror and the lamp, conceiving the imagination under the figure of the focusing lens has implications for the problem of limits. A mimetic view of imagination (as mirror) gives rise to the threat of distortion, so that the problem of limits becomes the problem of accurate imitation or reproduction. When imagination is taken to be creative (as lamp), the need for limits arises because of the threat of excess, the danger that imagination will lose its foothold in reality and take flight in illusion and fantasy. In the former case, the problem concerns the divergence between original and copy; in the latter, it is a matter of distinguishing the imaginary from the real. In a paradigmatic theory of imagination (as lens) the question of limits appears in yet another guise, one which is ambiguous in a way that involves the problems of the other two cases. On the one hand, the question arises, Why this particular lens? How do we know that the paradigm by which we are imagining something is the right one? The worry, as with the mimetic imagination, is distortion. But even if we grant that a particular paradigm is appropriate, how can we know the limits of its application? This worry, as in the case of the creative imagination, involves distinguishing the real from the imaginary, fact from fiction, reality from illusion. Before looking specifically at religious imagination, let us examine cases from the arts and the sciences.

The paradigmatic imagination appears in poetry most characteristically as metaphor. Paul Ricoeur captures what he calls the "enigma of metaphorical discourse" in this pithy summary: "it 'invents' in both senses of the word:

what it creates, it discovers; and what it finds, it invents."[18] It does so in the first place by means of the "eclipse of ordinary reference." One way that a reader recognizes a metaphor is by the impossibility of taking it literally. The metaphor is experienced as a "semantic impertinence" that makes it impossible to read the statement as a case of literal descriptive reference and thereby introduces a second, metaphorical reference by analogy. By means of the metaphor, the poet invites us to see something *as* something else, to view it through a particular metaphorical lens. Ricoeur also stresses the role of "redescription" in metaphorical discourse by means of the "creation of heuristic fiction." Drawing on Max Black's theory of models, he claims that by using metaphor the poet is "describing a less known domain . . . in the light of relationships within a fictitious but better known domain."[19] In this way fiction is drafted into the service of truth-telling, which sounds paradoxical in terms of the ordinary "literal" distinction between fact and fiction. Although in literature it is frequently the case that the "better known domain" is fictitious, this need not be the case, and often is not. What is philosophically interesting here is that metaphorical discourse can tell the truth, whether it employs fiction or nonfiction as the means. (The inverse is also the case: one can lie not only with fiction but also with facts.) The same is true in science, so it is not possible simply to align "fiction" with the arts and "facts" with the sciences. Using Black's theory of models, Ricoeur emphasizes that metaphor (whether employing fact or fiction) allows one to "operate on an object that on the one hand is better known and in this sense more familiar, and on the other hand is full of implications and in this sense rich at the level of hypotheses."[20]

It is significant that in exploring the role of paradigmatic imagination in the arts we find ourselves saying things that are equally true of the natural sciences. For what they have in common is the characteristically imaginative practice of "seeing as." Though one may speak more commonly of metaphor in poetry and of models and paradigms in the sciences, the logic of the two is identical. The philosopher who first brought this aspect of science into prominence was Thomas Kuhn (1922–96), whose work in the history of science provoked him to new insights in the philosophy of science. His description of the ongoing scientific enterprise focuses on the concept of paradigms, and one of their most interesting features has to do with the ambiguity of limits. The typical work of scientists—what Kuhn refers to as "normal or

18. Paul Ricoeur, *The Rule of Metaphor: Multi-disciplinary Studies of the Creation of Meaning in Language*, trans. Robert Czerny (Toronto: University of Toronto Press, 1977), 239.
19. Ricoeur, *Rule of Metaphor*, 244.
20. Ricoeur, *Rule of Metaphor*, 241.

paradigm-based research"—is characterized by "drastically restricted vision." The shared paradigm "forces scientists to investigate some part of nature in a detail and depth that would otherwise be unimaginable." In this sense, it would be correct to say that the role of the scientific imagination is to set limits by focusing attention on "that class of facts that the paradigm has shown to be particularly revealing of the nature of things."[21] Functioning as a model *of* reality, the paradigm enables scientific progress by focusing attention and energy in the direction implied by the likeness embodied in the paradigm. But as scientists follow the course prescribed by the paradigm, they also employ it as a model *for* further research and experimentation; and from this angle it becomes possible to see why the imagination is also rightly called *un*limited. As Ricoeur says of the metaphor, it is "full of implications" and therefore (note the scientific diction) "rich at the level of hypotheses." So rich, in fact, is the successful poetic metaphor or scientific paradigm, that one cannot say—indeed, cannot know in advance—how far, or precisely in what direction, the analogical implications may lead. It is thus quite true to say both that imagination sets limits by its choice of paradigm *and* that imagination knows no limits, because of the open-ended nature of the analogy embodied in the metaphor or model.

Finally, I would like to apply these conclusions about the limits of imagination to the specifically *religious* imagination. Like the arts and the sciences, religions employ imagination in the paradigmatic sense, as a lens through which to view reality. The logic of religious imagination is similar to that of the poetic and scientific imagination; what distinguishes them are the different objects to which each enterprise (art, science, or religion) applies paradigmatic imagination. The task of defining religion is notoriously difficult and contentious, but most scholars of religion are willing to grant the usefulness of multiple definitions for different kinds of analysis. I would like to suggest one such heuristic definition from the perspective of the theory of imagination, convinced that it can illumine certain aspects of religion in order both to distinguish religious from other human activities and to distinguish one religion from others. Stated in simplest terms, my thesis is that a religion offers a way of seeing the world as a whole, which means that it is a way of living in the world, an ultimate frame of reference for grasping the meaning of life and living in accordance with that vision. In John Wisdom's words, religion tells us "what the world is like"[22]—not just in this way or that, not a particular

21. Thomas S. Kuhn, *The Structure of Scientific Revolutions*, 3rd ed. (Chicago: University of Chicago Press, 1996), 24–25.
22. John Wisdom, *Paradox and Discovery* (New York: Philosophical Library, 1965), 54.

aspect or part of the world, but the world *as such*. At the heart of a religious tradition is a paradigm—a complex pattern of interwoven metaphors, models, scenarios, exemplary figures, and so on—employed by the community and its individual members as a template for orientation in human life. The religious paradigm, described in Geertz's terminology, serves as both model-of and model-for, providing the religious community with a *worldview* (a model of reality) and a corresponding *ethos* (what it feels like to live in that world and how one should behave accordingly).[23]

The issue of the limits of imagination also arises within the religious traditions as a *theological* question. I would like to explore briefly how the foregoing analysis of the philosophical issues can be applied to the problem of the limits of imagination in Christian theology. Because of the "positivity" of religious paradigms (their unique particularity and unsubstitutable character), theological discussions are tradition-specific by their very nature. The Christian example to be explored nevertheless has implications, *mutatis mutandis*, for other religious traditions as well.

All three major Western religions have faced the same basic problem: how to imagine the invisible God. Polemics against idolatry and the making of images are deeply rooted in the Hebrew Scriptures, most centrally and succinctly expressed in the Decalogue's prohibition against graven images, and the closely related proscriptions of worshiping other gods and of magical or "vain" invocations of the name of the God of Israel (Exod. 20:2ff.; Deut. 5:6ff.). Similarly, the religion of Islam originated in the Prophet's struggle against the idolatry of the ancient cults on the Arabian peninsula. The issues are more complex in Christian tradition because of the New Testament identification of Jesus as God incarnate, the perfect "image of the invisible God" (Col. 1:15). For Christians (in sharpest contrast with Muslims), the issues of idolatry and images remain distinct, even though related, since iconic representations of Christ (and other figures) can be grounded in biblical revelation; and far from being examples of idolatry, they are among its most effective antidotes.

The first reason for setting theological limits to imagination concerns the invisibility of God. Although the question of divine invisibility has been central throughout the long history of debates about idolatry, iconoclasm, and related topics, it is not the most important question but only a symptom of a more basic theological principle. As the context of the prohibition of images in the Decalogue indicates, the real issue concerns not the metaphysical

---

23. This terminology is taken from Geertz's classic essay "Religion as a Cultural System," in *The Interpretation of Cultures*, 87–125.

question of a divine attribute of invisibility but rather the religious question of accessibility and control over divine power. The God of Israel—as indicated by the very content of his name—is not to be manipulated. Just as the ability to invoke one's deity by name gives the worshiper access to supernatural power, so does the localized physical representation of the deity in wood or stone. One example of this theological question in the history of the church is the Protestant Reformers' rejection of the sacrificial understanding of the mass along with the supporting philosophical theory of the transubstantiation of the Eucharistic elements. The theological nub of the issue is the power that this localization of divine activity puts into the hands of the priestly celebrant (and thereby the institutional church that he serves). While it is accurate to say that the God of the Old Testament is rightly understood to be invisible, it is important to see that invisibility is not a metaphysical quality but is rather an implication of divine freedom.

A second way in which the limits of imagination impinge on Christian theology is christological and pertains to the use of images in Christian worship and doctrine. The general rejection of images in earliest Christianity followed Jewish teaching and practice, and identified the veneration of images with pagan religion.[24] With the increasing need of the common people for tangible models and exemplars, along with the rise of the cult of saints, the church gradually became more hospitable to the use of icons, though opposition continued to be strong. The issue came to a head in the eighth-century Byzantine Empire, when the emperor, under the influence of the powerful iconoclastic party, proscribed the use of images in worship. Although the iconodules (the pro-image party) achieved formal victory at the Second Council of Nicaea (787), strife between the two parties continued into the following century. The theological foundations for what came to be recognized in both the east and the west as the orthodox position on images was laid primarily by John of Damascus (ca. 675–749) and Theodore the Studite (759–826). The iconoclasts argued that a graphic representation of Christ must either depict his divine nature, which is impossible and blasphemous, or his human nature alone, which amounts to the heresy of Nestorianism (separating the person of Christ into "two sons"). John of Damascus countered that the making of images of Christ was legitimated by the incarnation, which transformed material reality and made it suitable for divine purposes, so that the honor given

24. For the following summary see H.-G. Beck, "Bilder III," in *Die Religion in Geschichte und Gegenwart: Handwörterbuch für Theologie und Religionswissenschaft*, 3rd ed., ed. Kurt Galling (Tübingen: Mohr Siebeck, 1957), 1:1273–75; and Symeon Lash, "Icons," in *The Westminster Dictionary of Christian Theology*, ed. Alan Richardson and John Bowden (Philadelphia: Westminster, 1983), 274–75.

to the image is transferred to the original. Indeed, their relationship is not physical but rather a hypostatic union. John lays down the crucial theological distinction governing the limits of imagination: between the *worship* of God and the *veneration* of icons. Idolatry violates this limit by offering to images the worship that belongs to the one God alone. Despite this generally accepted theology of images, the issues have remained alive in Christian tradition and have periodically erupted into controversy—most recently concerning matters raised by feminist theological critique (see chap. 8 below).

The theology of imagination extends the issues raised originally by the use of physical images to other uses of imagination, which are not restricted, of course, to concrete physical objects. The question of limits requires what I call a theology of the normative imagination, which for Christians is governed by the paradigm of Jesus Christ, embodied in the Scriptures of the Old and New Testaments and interpreted in various, often conflicting, ways throughout the history of the church. The theological task is to articulate the grammar of the normative paradigm of the faith, to propose the rules according to which interpretations of the shared paradigm may be evaluated and conflicts among them adjudicated. The complement to this internal theological task is to engage those other (religious and secular) paradigm communities in an ongoing dialogue of mutual interpretation. This task, while surely requiring all the resources of academic endeavor, is not confined to the academy. Like John Forbes Nash in *A Beautiful Mind*, all of us are engaged in an ongoing struggle against those schizophrenic temptations to distort or exceed the imaginative limits within which human life is possible and fruitful.

7

BARTH ON BEAUTY

The Ambivalence of Reformed Aesthetics

M̲y first experience of theological aesthetics took place before I had acquired the technical vocabulary to recognize it for what it was. I spent the year after college studying theology as an exchange student in Germany, where I also began to learn something about the variety of religious sensibilities in the world—even within the limited world of Protestant Christianity. I could see at once that Westphalian Lutherans could never be confused with the suburban Methodists of my hometown in Southern California, and the most striking differences were not doctrinal but aesthetic. After a semester among the churches of Lutheran Germany—where statues, stained glass, and crucifixes abound—I traveled with friends to Switzerland during the winter vacation and was immediately struck by the contrast the first time I entered a Swiss Reformed church (could it have been in Basel?). The soaring emptiness of those Gothic spaces and the brilliant light streaming through their clear windows to illumine a great central pulpit (no altars in *these* churches!) had an impact—an *aesthetic* impact—reminiscent, for all the stylistic differences, of the white clapboard meetinghouses of once-Puritan New England, where I have lived more recently. These two Reformed cousins, of course, share a common Calvinist heritage. And Calvin himself doubted whether "it is expedient to have in Christian churches any images at all," preferring the example of the church's first five centuries ("during which religion was still flourishing, and a purer doctrine thriving"), when "Christian churches were commonly empty of images."[1]

These youthful experiences came to mind as I thought about the aesthetics of the great twentieth-century theologian of the Reformed tradition, Karl Barth. Two influential books on theological aesthetics invoke Barth's name, and both refer specifically to his love of Mozart, a love that leads him to what can only be called a theological appreciation of Mozart's music. Richard Viladesau begins his *Theological Aesthetics* by translating in full Barth's excursus on Mozart's place in theology.[2] A very different book by Frank Burch Brown, *Good Taste, Bad Taste, and Christian Taste*, likewise contains several references to Barth, all but one of which pertain to his Mozart interpretation.[3] Besides its appeal to human interest, Barth's commentary on Mozart, especially the one that occurs in the midst of the doctrine of creation in the *Church Dogmatics*, makes at least one substantive theological point. He attributes to Mozart's music what William Desmond calls an "aesthetic theodicy": "one which affirms the beauty of this world as a concretion of the harmony of the whole."[4] Viladesau translates Barth's summary of Mozart's theodicy in these terms: "He had heard—what we shall only see at the end of time: the total coherence of the divine dispensation."[5]

Though intriguing, this theological fragment sheds little light on Barth's theological aesthetics, and none at all on the crucial issue for Reformed theology, the visual arts. I want to examine his substantive treatment of aesthetic questions in the doctrine of God, especially his theology of beauty as a divine perfection. Though Barth's primary concern is the attribute of divine glory, this consideration leads him to make some fascinating and controversial claims about beauty and the arts.

Barth approaches the idea of God's beauty cautiously and indirectly: beauty as a theological concept is to be treated with a reserve that verges on suspicion—not surprising perhaps in a theologian of Calvin's tradition. His

1. John Calvin, *Institutes of the Christian Religion* 1.11.13, trans. Ford Lewis Battles, Library of Christian Classics 20 (Philadelphia: Westminster, 1960), 112.

2. Richard Viladesau, *Theological Aesthetics: God in Imagination, Beauty, and Art* (New York: Oxford University Press, 1999), 3–5. This prologue is Viladesau's own translation of Karl Barth, *Die kirchliche Dogmatik*, vol. III/3 (Zurich: EVZ-Verlag, 1961), 337–39. For the published translation, see Barth, *Church Dogmatics*, vol. III/3, trans. G. W. Bromiley and R. J. Ehrlich (Edinburgh: T&T Clark, 1961), 297–99.

3. Frank Burch Brown, *Good Taste, Bad Taste, and Christian Taste: Aesthetics in Religious Life* (New York: Oxford University Press, 2000) (see his index for references to Barth).

4. Desmond uses this term to describe Hegel's aesthetics in *Art and the Absolute: A Study of Hegel's Aesthetics* (Albany: State University of New York Press, 1986), 104.

5. Barth, *Kirchliche Dogmatik*, vol. III/3, 338, translated in Viladesau, *Theological Aesthetics*, 3–4.

formal way of making this point is to insist that the beauty of God is not a "main concept" but only a "secondary" or "auxiliary" one.[6] "The concept of the beautiful," he warns, "because of its connection with . . . pleasure, desire, and enjoyment . . . appears to be an especially profane concept, one especially unsuited, even dangerous, for introduction into theological language" (734/651). Despite these hesitations, however, Barth concludes that it would be a far greater error *not* to say that God is beautiful, since to do so would leave a permanent "gap" (*Lücke*) in the theology of the divine perfections. Everything depends on getting the context right.

Barth's doctrine of God begins with a chapter on the knowledge of God, followed by another on the reality of God, within which beauty finds a place. Defining God's being as "the One who loves in freedom," Barth enters upon an extended discussion of the divine perfections. There are twelve in all, arranged in pairs. The first three pairs—identified as "perfections of divine love" (grace and holiness, mercy and righteousness, patience and wisdom)—are complemented by another paired triad of "perfections of divine freedom": unity and omnipresence, constancy and omnipotence, eternity and glory. This final perfection—God's glory—is the immediate context for the doctrine of divine beauty, and he calls it the "quintessence [*Inbegriff*] of all the divine perfections" (725/643). It holds a preeminent position among the divine attributes because only here does God's nature become fully manifest. Barth introduces a significant qualifier (one difficult to render into graceful English): the glory of God is "*der sichtbarwerdende Inbegriff*" of all the perfections— that is, the quintessential point at which all of them finally *become visible*. As we shall see, the fact that the rhetoric of the senses (i.e., aesthetic language) emerges at just this point is highly significant.

So where does beauty come into the picture? To prepare for the answer, Barth first develops the implications of the divine glory, beginning with the assertion that the glory of God is "the fullness of God's divinity," the point at which "the reality of all that God is . . . bursts forth, . . . expresses itself, . . . manifests itself." Glory is therefore "the nature [*Wesen*] of God, for God's essential nature is to make himself known" (725/643). Drawing on seventeenth-century Reformed orthodox theologian Petrus van Mastricht, Barth develops four further implications of the *gloria Dei*:

6. Barth, *Die kirchliche Dogmatik*, vol. II/1 (Zurich: Theologische Verlag Zürich, 1940), 736; cf. Barth, *Church Dogmatics*, vol. II/1, trans. T. H. L. Parker et al. (Edinburgh: T&T Clark, 1957), 652–53. Subsequent references to this volume will be made parenthetically, the page number to the German edition followed by the English edition; though the translations are my own, references to the published English translation are also provided for the convenience of the reader.

1. God's completeness and sufficiency are preeminent, exceeding that of all others; he is differentiated from them as light from darkness.

2. Moreover, as both the source and the radiance of light, God's self-manifestation actually illumines everything else: "As light he penetrates and illumines the darkness, even the outermost darkness, in such a way that nothing is hidden from him but rather that everything is revealed and open."

3. But what reaches us in that self-manifesting radiance is not just something that comes from God but rather "God's *own* presence": God's glory places us before the "face of God."

4. The movement of divine glory reaches its culmination in the fact that God's creatures are taken up into his self-glorification: their existence finds its meaning in their destiny "to respond in the temporal realm, inadequately but truly, to the jubilation with which divinity is filled from eternity to eternity" (728–32/645–49).

What emerges from this four-step elaboration is an economy of divine glory, encompassing the Creator, the creature, and the relationship between them.

The theology of glory, however, is still incomplete. The development up to this point Barth refers to as the *content* of the concept, but the question remains as to its *form*. The "nerve" of the concept of divine glory Barth identifies as God's *Transeuntwerden*, his becoming transeunt[7] or "transitive," rather than remaining immanent. The joy that is immanent in God's being expresses itself outwardly in the creature. The question of form that Barth now asks is "In what way?" (*Inwiefern?*), "By what manner?" (*In welcher Weise?*)—in a word, *How* (*Wie?*) does this transaction occur (732/649)? We ought not to be content with the fact "*that* God is glorious" but must go on to ask "*how*, in what shape [*Gestalt*] and form [*Form*] he is so." But *this* question, "the How of God's glory, his self-glorification," is precisely the question of *beauty*. What makes God's self-disclosure, his radiance, his revelation effective is its beauty; it is "the specifically convincing and persuasive quality of his revelation" (738/654).

At this point it becomes possible to account more precisely for Barth's ambivalence about beauty as a divine attribute. Acknowledging that the idea of God's beauty has roots in pre-Reformation tradition, Barth cites a famous passage from the *Confessions* of St. Augustine:

---

7. The term *transeunt* also appears in English as a variant of *transient*, from the present participle of the Latin verb *transire*, "to go over or across." The relevant sense is listed second by the *Oxford English Dictionary*: "2. Passing out or operating beyond itself; transitive; opposed to *immanent*. (Often spelt *transeunt* for distinction from sense 1.)"

I have learnt to love you late, Beauty at once so ancient and so new! I have learnt
to love you late! You were within me, and I was in the world outside myself. I
searched for you outside myself and, disfigured as I was, I fell upon the lovely
things of your creation. You were with me, but I was not with you. The beautiful
things of this world kept me far from you and yet, if they had not been in you,
they would have had no being at all. You called me; you cried aloud to me; you
broke my barrier of deafness. You shone upon me; your radiance enveloped
me; you put my blindness to flight. You shed your fragrance about me; I drew
breath and now I gasp for your sweet odour. I tasted you, and now I hunger
and thirst for you. You touched me, and I am inflamed with love of your peace.[8]

Barth makes no comment on this passage; but when he goes on to paraphrase
Pseudo-Dionysius's claim that "the Beautiful in its identity with the Good
is the ultimate cause that produces and moves all things," he cannot help
remarking on its "scarcely veiled Platonism." He points out that later tradition, especially in Protestantism, largely ignored the doctrine of God's beauty,
sensing its danger as a theological concept. Before we return to the Augustine
passage, let us first follow Barth's logic to its conclusion. After insisting on the
secondary or auxiliary place of beauty as a theological concept, Barth notes
that in the Bible, and likewise in medieval tradition, God's glory is invariably connected with *joy*. It does not simply awaken awe, reverence, and the
like but also "*happiness, joy, pleasure, desire, and enjoyment*" (737/654). He
concludes that it is not saying too much to affirm that "God radiates such joy
also because he is beautiful," insisting upon the "also" as a reminder "that we
are speaking only of the *form* and *shape* of his glory" (738/654).

But this *also* ("he is also beautiful") and its accompanying *only* ("only
the question of form") threaten to undermine the theology of God's glory
that Barth has so carefully constructed. His grudging endorsement of divine
beauty—he speaks of the "borderline character of this whole discussion"
(741/657)—seems to minimize form in favor of content, to suggest that although God *appears* to be beautiful, the real content of his glory is to be
sought elsewhere (might beauty be only skin deep even for the Almighty?).
We know, of course, that he means to do no such thing, for he rules out such
aesthetic docetism explicitly: "There can be no question of distinguishing between content and form of the divine nature and thus abstractly seeking God's
beauty in the form of his being for us and in himself. . . . He is the perfect
content of the divine nature, which also makes his form perfect" (743/658–59).
Even though Barth makes this assertion, his "also" and "only" speak louder.

8. Augustine, *Confessions* 10.27, trans. R. S. Pine-Coffin (New York: Penguin, 1961), 231–32.
Barth cites the Latin original (734/651).

Worried that the concept of beauty may escape its carefully secondary role, Barth makes one last attempt to keep it in its place. Although we must not neglect "the proposition that God is also beautiful," he warns, it can have no claim to "independent significance." This proposition is "instructive in its place," where it performs its one legitimate role: that of explaining "how God in his glory, in his self-disclosure, makes himself evident [*einleuchtend*]." It does this, he says in conclusion, "*in geziemender Beiläufigkeit*": in a fittingly *incidental* manner, merely in *passing*, in an appropriately *parenthetical* way (751/666).

It is not immediately clear why Barth is so guarded in his affirmation of God's beauty, but there is a hint in the examples he draws from the church's tradition of doctrine and piety. His comment about the "scarcely veiled Platonism" of Pseudo-Dionysius suggests his concern that an abstract concept of (capital *B*) Beauty might displace the self-revealing God of the Bible as the ground of theological truth, in effect making God a function of Beauty rather than the other way around. He comments with evident approval that Dionysius's Platonizing concept of Beauty seems not to have been prevalent elsewhere in the early church, and that the Reformation and Protestant Orthodoxy "completely ignored it." Though medieval and Reformation popular piety sometimes praised God's beauty (he cites "Fairest Lord Jesus" and a hymn by Paul Gerhardt), he maintains that even here such elements were "treated as a foreign body, accepted without an entirely clear conscience and therefore always with a certain suspicion" (734/651). To be sure, Barth never explicitly endorses this suspicion of beauty and in fact concludes that we must nevertheless affirm the proposition "God is beautiful." Even as he makes this point, however, his reluctance is palpable; he does not affirm the proposition directly but couches it as a rhetorical question implying a double negative: Does the biblical witness allow us to affirm God's glory and *not* affirm his beauty (734/651–52)? The implied answer is clearly that it does not—that is, the Bible does *not* permit us *not* to affirm God's glory—but his hesitation is unmistakable, and by implication justified.

I suggest that Barth's ambivalence about the beauty of God springs from a failure to abide by his own theological priorities. Various commentators on Barth's theology have noted the centrality of what he dubbed his "christological concentration." "Christian doctrine," he wrote in the *Christian Century* in 1938, "if it is to merit its name . . . has to be exclusively and conclusively the doctrine of Jesus Christ—of Jesus Christ as the living Word of God spoken to us men."[9] In terms of theological method this principle means that every

9. In Barth, *How I Changed My Mind* (Richmond: John Knox Press, 1966), 43.

doctrine must be thought through in view of its relation to Christology. An example is what he calls "the christological basis of anthropology" in his doctrine of human nature. Thinking about humanity christologically leads him to distinguish between "natural man," the historical and empirical reality we encounter in human life, and "real man," the humanity intended by God and revealed in the human nature of Jesus Christ. "His being as human is . . . that which posits and therefore reveals and explains human nature in all its possibilities."[10] When we apply the corresponding logic to the beauty of God, the ambivalence vanishes, or rather is transformed into something objective and quite different.

To illustrate, let us examine the passage from St. Augustine that stands as Barth's first example of the beauty of God in the tradition. Despite Augustine's well-known admiration for Plato, the passage lacks any trace of the notion of transcendental Beauty such as that found in Pseudo-Dionysius that unsettled Barth. Aside from addressing God directly as *pulchritudo*, Augustine makes no mention of divine beauty in the passage—except by implied comparison with the beauty of creation. "The beautiful things of this world," he writes, "kept me far from you and yet, if they had not been in you, they would have had no being at all."[11] Beauty here functions just as Barth says—as the "persuasive" or "convincing" element—for it lures Augustine along his path. Here, too, there is ambivalence, but it is objective, we could say, not subjective as in Barth's case. Augustine ought to have been lured toward God by the beauty of God, but he allowed himself instead to be seduced by creaturely beauty—even though that beauty, along with the very being of the creatures themselves, owes its existence to God. Notice that Augustine does *not* take the Platonic path by arguing that the reflected beauty of creation drew him upward toward the beautiful divine Original. Far from treating Beauty as a transcendental, he has recognized ("too late," he says) the difference between the beauty of the Creator and created beauty.

In fairness to Barth, he does not neglect Christology in his treatment of the glory of God, and he even relates it explicitly to beauty. The problem is that he fails to see the implications of this Christology for his ambivalence about the concept of beauty. He rounds off his theology of divine glory with a discussion of the incarnation of Jesus Christ. "According to scripture, in

10. Barth, *Die kirchliche Dogmatik*, vol. III/2 (Zurich: Theologische Verlag Zürich, 1948), 69; cf. Barth, *Church Dogmatics*, vol. III/2, trans. Harold Knight et al. (Edinburgh: T&T Clark, 1960), 59.

11. Augustine, *Confessions* 10.27 (trans. Pine-Coffin, 231–32). Though Pine-Coffin's rather free translation verges on paraphrase, his rendering of the passage accords with Augustine's meaning.

Jesus Christ we have to do with *the* revelation of God's glory, with *the* self-declaration of God" (746/661–62); and he cites two examples. The letter to the Hebrews tells us that Jesus Christ "is the radiance of the glory of God and the exact imprint of his nature" (Heb. 1:3), and Paul writes to the Corinthian Christians that God "has shone in our hearts to give the light of the knowledge of the glory of God in the face of Jesus Christ" (2 Cor. 4:6). The content of this glory is the incarnation, which Barth expounds with classically Chalcedonian logic as the condescension of God to sinful humanity by actually *becoming* fully human even while remaining fully divine, and doing so in the unity of Christ's person. It is precisely "the real unity of the divine being [*Wesen*] that has this form—this *beautiful* form, this form that *excites joy*." And "what is mirrored in this definition of the relationship of the divine and the human nature in Jesus Christ is the form, the beautiful form of the divine being." No question remains but that God's beauty is christologically grounded: the trinitarian God "is not only the source of all truth and of all good but also of all beauty. And because we recognize in Jesus Christ that this is so, we have therefore to recognize in Jesus Christ the beauty of God" (748–49/663–64).

Where, then, is the true source of ambivalence about God's beauty? Barth's final point about the Christology of God's glory speaks to this question in his interpretation of the Suffering Servant (750–51/665–66):

> For he grew up before him like a young plant,
> and like a root out of dry ground;
> he had no form or majesty that we should look at him,
> and no beauty that we should desire him.
> He was despised and rejected by men,
> a man of sorrows and acquainted with grief;
> and as one from whom men hide their faces
> he was despised, and we esteemed him not. (Isa. 53:2–3)

Although the beauty of Jesus Christ is "not just any beauty but rather the beauty of *God*," he does not present this aspect to us but rather confronts us with the aspect of the Suffering Servant. The divine beauty of the face of Jesus remains hidden behind the unlovely form of the servant. Here is the true ambivalence of divine beauty, and it is rooted in the relationship of cross and resurrection. When we look upon the face of the Crucified, it is not self-evident that God's glory is revealed there; rather, says Barth, one can have such an insight only if it is given. When one gazes upon the likeness of God in Christ, he asks, "how is one to see that this likeness is beautiful?"

The answer comes in the form of another question: "In this respect too, how is God to be known except by God?" (750/665).

If we apply the "christological basis of divine beauty" to Barth's worry about whether and in what way God can be called beautiful, a clearer picture emerges. The problem is not, as Barth seems at first to suggest, that beauty might be an inappropriate attribute for God; rather, God, who is not only beautiful but the source of all beauty, hides his beauty from us in order to become one with us. Christ Jesus, according to the great kenotic hymn of Philippians 2, "though he was in the *Gestalt* of God . . . emptied himself, by taking the *Gestalt* of a servant, being born in the likeness of men." From this vantage point it becomes clear how misplaced is Barth's emphasis on the "also" and the "only" of divine beauty. Christologically considered, God is not just "also" beautiful but rather beautiful with the whole of his being, by his very nature. God did not "also" become human, and surely not "only" as a matter of form! Aesthetic docetism turns out after all to imply christological docetism. The question is not whether we should call God beautiful but how we are to *perceive* the beauty of the one true God. And this question brings us to that other key concern of aesthetics, the relation of beauty to art.

At the very end of his Christology of divine beauty, Barth drops a bombshell. The iconoclasm implicit in his earlier remarks suddenly erupts in an outburst against the "embarrassing history of the image of Christ" (751/666). Having just concluded that telling "the human suffering of the true God and the divine glory of the true man" is the "function of the face of Jesus Christ alone," he expresses outrage that an artist should try to capture it in paint or clay. The unity of "the suffering God and the triumphant man . . . the beauty of God, which is the beauty of Christ, no human art should try to reproduce." He expresses the "urgent wish . . . to all those ever so well-meaning, gifted, and inspired Christian artists . . . finally to *give up* this unholy undertaking— for the sake of God's beauty." Not only is their ambition presumptuous but quite impossible: "*This* image," he says in a parting shot, "the one genuine image—genuine in its object and genuine in the reproduction of the object— cannot itself be copied again, precisely because, also in its beauty, it speaks for itself!" The Reformed tradition, at least as far as aesthetics is concerned, has apparently not wandered far from Father Calvin.

Yet even Calvin protested, "I am not gripped by the superstition of thinking absolutely no images permissible," even affirming that "sculpture and painting are gifts of God."[12] Karl Barth, too, even apart from his elevation of Mozart to theological status, hints at a more affirmative theological aesthetics, even

---

12. Calvin, *Institutes* 1.11.12 (trans. Battles, 112).

in the case of visual arts. In conclusion I would like to point the way, in four theses, toward a more adequate Reformed aesthetics, partly by interpreting the iconoclastic Barth in the light of the christological Barth, and partly by means of some suggestions of my own.

1. Christian theology may understand art *hermeneutically*: not as idolatry but rather as *interpretation* of the biblical witness. Barth himself offers some models for such an aesthetics. (We can learn about art from Karl Barth more by watching what he does with it than by listening to what he says about it.) When he describes how Christology works in his doctrine of revelation, he uses two paintings from Matthias Grünewald's Isenheim Altar as illustrations, both of which contain images of Christ.[13] Far from decrying the artist's work as an "unholy undertaking," he holds it up as a visual model of good theology, a valid interpretation of the scriptural revelation. Understood hermeneutically, visual art does not invite the viewer to worship God in an aesthetic image but rather points aesthetically toward the God of the Bible.

2. Christian theology may understand art *doxologically*. Artists, along with the rest of creation, are invited by the glory of God "to respond in the temporal realm, inadequately but truly, to the jubilation with which divinity is filled from eternity to eternity." Viewed from this perspective, the work of art is not an *object* of worship but an *act* of worship. The new creature in Christ, writes Barth, "is free for God's glory, not because it could or would become so by itself, but because it has been made free for it by God's glory itself. This creature is thankful" (755/669). Artistic creativity can thus be understood theologically as the exuberant response in the aesthetic mode of the grateful creature to his glorious Creator. In this way, art—even visual art—is taken up into the economy of divine glory.

3. Christian theology may understand art *analogically*. The greatest barrier to a theological affirmation of beauty and the work of art appears to be the irreducibly sensuous nature of the aesthetic experience itself (as even its name testifies). Barth is not alone in identifying beauty with the perception of *Form* and *Gestalt*. Barth's great twentieth-century counterpart in the Roman Catholic tradition, Hans Urs von Balthasar, titles the first volume of his theological aesthetics *Schau der Gestalt*—"Seeing the Form (or Pattern)." Such perception seems incapable of expression in other than sensuous terms. Returning to the passage on the beauty of the Creator and creation in Augustine's *Confessions*, this time examining its rhetoric, it becomes apparent that he employs unabashedly sensual language to describe the supersensible Creator, actually running through each of the five senses in turn. Obviously,

13. Barth, *Kirchliche Dogmatik*, vol. I/2, 137–38; *Church Dogmatics*, vol. I/2, 125.

Augustine is not ascribing sensuous qualities to God but is speaking meta-phorically. Such use of metaphor is not simply ornamental but unavoidable in describing nonphysical beauty. Visual art can thus be understood theologically as visual metaphor. Even so blatant a case as Michelangelo's anthropomorphic Creator in the Sistine Chapel might be acquitted of idolatry by interpreting it as an attempt by the Christian artist to imagine the glory of the Creator in the only way possible for a painter—namely, by showing its *Gestalt*. In other words, might Michelangelo be doing in paint what Augustine does in words: enabling the worshiper to imagine the beauty of God metaphorically?

4. Finally, Christian theology may understand art *eschatologically*. All the senses are not created equal in their theological significance. "Faith comes from hearing," St. Paul tells us (Rom. 10:17), and seeing is reserved for the *visio beatifica*. Perhaps this is why music has found more acceptance in the churches, even by Reformed Christians like Karl Barth, than have the visual arts. And that may offer a clue to the right theological use of the visual arts: might they not serve as the eyes of faith, the media of eschatological vision? If one of the tasks that the gospel enjoins on the church is to enable all peoples to imagine God's future for creation, one way to do that might be to invite us to see through the eyes of artists and envision a world transformed by the grace of God. In the enigmatic mirror of the artist we may from time to time catch a proleptic glimpse of that day when we shall see face to face.

8

THE GENDER OF GOD
AND THE THEOLOGY
OF METAPHOR

The Christian community today finds itself embroiled in controversy about the language it uses to speak of God—in its prayer, its worship, its doctrine, and its theological discourse. Viewed from one angle, the issue of gendered language is only the latest in a long series of challenges that the church has faced since the emergence of an autonomous secular culture in Europe about three centuries ago. Like the challenges raised by Copernican astronomy to the church's official cosmology, by critical philosophy to its metaphysics, by scientific historiography to the authority of its Scriptures, and by liberal and radical political theories to its social ethics—so the challenge raised by feminism today calls into question certain aspects of the church's belief and practice in light of the regnant secular faith in human autonomy. Perhaps the closest analogy in modern history is the theological controversy surrounding the abolition of slavery, in which the centuries-old Christian justification of slavery was for all practical purposes expunged from the tradition.[1] The undeniable fact that the powerful traditions of secular modernity have their roots in European Christianity contributes to the complexity

---

1. Jon D. Levenson discusses the appeals to the Bible by both pro-slavery and abolitionist theologians in nineteenth-century America, especially to the exodus narrative, arguing that "both saw part of the picture—the part that provided biblical support for their own position—but failed to do justice to the remainder." "Liberation Theology and the Exodus," *Reflections*

of these issues, but it does not fundamentally alter the fact that the church throughout the modern period has faced a series of challenges to its doctrine and authority from sources essentially external to its own norms and institutions. Viewing the issue of gender in Christian language—specifically, the masculine gender of God—against this background can help to place it in perspective and may even suggest useful analogies with attempts to resolve similar issues in the past.

There is another sense, however, in which feminist critique of Christian language raises more radical—that is, more deeply rooted—issues of Christian doctrine than other modern controversies. Not since ancient times, when the church first formulated its central dogmas in the face of challenges from the religions and philosophies of Greco-Roman culture, have basic Christian concepts been subjected to such scrutiny. Precisely those ancient teachings— the Nicene doctrine of the Trinity, in particular—now face a challenge unlike any in all the intervening centuries.

Despite the prominence of feminist themes in current theological discussion, the issue of gender-specific language for God has not been accorded the kind of sustained critical attention by theologians that it deserves. Because of the radical nature of the questions involved, failure to address them with theological rigor imperils the integrity of Christian teaching. Some theologians today, in a laudable effort to reverse the long legacy of Christian patriarchalism, are adopting uncritically a view of human language and imagination that is deeply flawed and, if left unchallenged, will do great damage to the coherence of Christian faith and doctrine. Moreover, this view prevents theology from making constructive use of Scripture in the struggle to reform the sexual politics of the Christian community. Increasing numbers of Christians (not all of them theologians) find themselves caught in a dilemma whose nature they only partially understand. On the one hand, they feel uncomfortable—even guilty—using biblical language with its masculine gender for God because so many voices are telling them that such language is oppressive to women, or at the very least that women can't relate to it. On the other hand, they sense the vacuousness of the abstract and impersonal alternatives and the artificiality of proposals to make the language of Christian prayer, liturgy, and Scripture either gender-neutral or gender-balanced. The way out of the dilemma, I propose, is to identify and criticize certain underlying principles—sometimes explicit, more often implicit, but almost never argued—on which proposals to alter the gendered language of Scripture are based. Only then will it become

---

(Yale Divinity School) (Winter–Spring 1991), 5. Levenson's hermeneutical observations on this and other examples of social-political exegesis are instructive.

possible to identify and correct the real errors that have for so many centuries encouraged the subordination of women in the name of Christian doctrine.

In an effort to think through the issue of the masculine gender of God theologically, I want first to make explicit the principles implied by one influential type of feminist theology. My response will take two forms, one critical and one constructive: a critique of proposals to eliminate gendered language for God, followed by an attempt to articulate a sounder theological basis for the reform of Christian teaching and practice in response to the challenge of feminism. I will argue that a Christian theological appropriation of feminist concerns requires not the elimination of the masculine gender of God but its interpretation within the context of biblical narrative. This approach necessitates a rejection of traditional male-centered misreadings, and it articulates how the language of gender actually works in the Bible.

The Double Error of Genderless Theology

The thesis that God is beyond gender enjoys a certain commonsense plausibility that helps to explain why theological resistance to the neutralizing of Christian language about God has been so sporadic and ineffectual. Virtually no one wants to be associated with a position that seems to imply that God is male. The consequent abdication by theological moderates has left the field to the religious right, encouraging the impression that only biblical literalists and social reactionaries have a stake in defending the language of Scripture. This situation leaves a significant segment of the church (I am convinced that it comprises a majority of Christians today) in a dilemma in which they feel forced to choose between the authority of Scripture and the full humanity of women.

I want to propose a way out of the dilemma that requires us to first examine critically certain assumptions and presuppositions lying behind theological proposals to eliminate masculine language for God or to balance it with feminine terminology. For convenience these proposals can be called the theology of the genderless God. Both approaches (eliminating the masculine and balancing the genders) proceed from the same premise: that masculine gender ought not to be predicated of God. Whether one responds by avoiding gendered language altogether or by relativizing it through use of the feminine is a secondary issue that I will not address since I am persuaded that their common premise is wrong.

The theology of the genderless God is doubly flawed. In the first place, it misunderstands the nature of the theological problem raised by feminist critique. At the root of the misunderstanding is an implicit acceptance of a projection theory of religion along with theological implications allegedly following from it. I will outline that theory of religion and its associated theology, and examine its most popular form. This analysis will lead us to the other error of genderless theology: its appeal to a flawed theory of metaphor that compromises the normative function of Scripture for theology.

Role-Model Theology

Projection theories of religion can be traced back to Ludwig Feuerbach, who argues in *The Essence of Christianity* (1841) that "God is the mirror of man."[2] Feuerbach identifies the "mystery of religion" in these terms: "Man . . . projects his being into objectivity, and then again makes himself an object to this projected image of himself thus converted into a subject."[3] Feuerbach's critique of religion was subsequently given a powerful sociopolitical twist by Karl Marx, and still later a psychoanalytic interpretation by Sigmund Freud.[4] Various forms of projection theory are widely held today by sociologists, anthropologists, psychologists, and philosophers of religion. One of the few defensible generalizations that can be made about the contemporary academic field of religious studies is that its practitioners typically assume the validity of some form of projection theory. Whatever the variations in detail (some of them significant), there is widespread consensus that religion is the product of unconscious projection by individuals or societies, that human communities construct their gods as expressions of their personal and social values. All the early proponents of projection theory—Feuerbach, Marx, and Freud—understood it to be a refutation of Christianity in particular and of religion (at least traditional theistic religion) generally. As confidence in the positivist and evolutionary doctrine of science presupposed by these thinkers has declined over the past century, so has the automatic link between projection theory and atheism. Some scholars of religion, such as Peter Berger, have even argued that a "methodological atheism" in the study of religion is compatible with religious belief and theology.[5] More typically, theologians

2. Ludwig Feuerbach, *The Essence of Christianity*, trans. George Eliot (New York: Harper, 1957), 63. For a detailed account of Feuerbach's importance to Christian theology, see chap. 3 above.

3. Feuerbach, *Essence of Christianity*, 29–30. Feminists today might find the translator's rendering of *Mensch* (human being) as "Man" to be ironically appropriate—doubly ironic in view of the fact that the translator was one of the great female writers of the nineteenth century.

4. The classic texts are Marx's "Theses on Feuerbach" and Freud's tract *The Future of an Illusion*.

5. See Peter L. Berger, *The Sacred Canopy: Elements of a Sociological Theory of Religion* (Garden City, NY: Doubleday, 1967). Berger wears his other theological hat in *A Rumor of*

have taken a halfway position (it could be called a methodological agnosticism), maintaining that the socially constructed nature of human religion does not preclude the possibility that it may on occasion achieve a valid apprehension of divine reality. The resulting ambiguity has haunted modern theology since Schleiermacher: if theology describes not the metaphysical realm of the supernatural but human religious consciousness, how can it avoid the anthropological reduction proposed by Feuerbach and his heirs? The theology of the genderless God thus joins a long series of modern liberal theologies that take their departure from human experience and then find it difficult to justify their claim to be talking about God rather than humanity.

The axiom that religion is projection or social construction is not really theological but rather a pre-theological assumption generally taken for granted by the proponents of a genderless God. It is often assumed to entail a theological consequence—a position that I call role-model theology. The gist of the position is captured in Mary Daly's dictum that has become the quasi-official motto of much feminist theology: "If God is male, then the male is God."[6] Here's roughly how the logic of role-model theology goes. Since all religious communities construct their gods as expressions of their social values, a proper theology is one that expresses proper social values. Only such a theology is adequate to a proper religion—namely, one whose god is worthy of emulation by human beings. Since we moderns are committed to the full equality of the sexes, our theology must express that commitment; therefore, we should not speak of God in masculine terms (at least not unless balanced by feminine terms).

Role-model theology can be accommodated in a systematic theology to the extent that it does not conflict with other fundamental convictions. Thus it causes little difficulty for advocates of a liberalism that treats Scripture "more as a resource than as an authority."[7] For Christians who take orthodoxy seriously, however—especially the normative role of Scripture for doctrine—role-model theology leads to a dilemma. If the Bible is the touchstone of right doctrine, then theology must learn its doctrine of God from Scripture, not from the mores of secular culture—not even from egalitarian liberal-democratic culture. Surprisingly, therefore, the most radical feminist theologians escape the dilemma that confronts their more moderate colleagues.

Angels: Modern Society and the Rediscovery of the Supernatural (Garden City, NY: Doubleday, 1969).

6. Mary Daly, *Beyond God the Father: Toward a Philosophy of Women's Liberation* (Boston: Beacon, 1973), 19.

7. Charles M. Wood, "Hermeneutics and the Authority of Scripture," in *Scriptural Authority and Narrative Interpretation*, ed. Garrett Green (Philadelphia: Fortress, 1987), 6.

Theologians like Mary Daly and Carol Christ may be wrong in their claim that the traditions of Christian orthodoxy are sexist to the core, but they cannot be faulted for inconsistency. Believing as they do that Christianity is incompatible with the full humanity of women, they have abandoned it in favor of more promising sources of religious insight. *Christian* feminists are left in a more difficult position, wanting to claim allegiance to biblical traditions while still rejecting the patterns of patriarchy seemingly woven into those traditions at nearly every point. Rosemary Radford Ruether, for example, argues on the one hand that "there are critical elements in Biblical theology that contradict" the sacralization of patriarchy so prominent in other parts of the biblical text.[8] On the other hand, she identifies the "critical principle of feminist theology" as the "promotion of the full humanity of women," without indicating the source or criterion of her anthropological doctrine of "full humanity."[9] The operative norm of her theology turns out to be the "revelatory experience" of women today,[10] before which all other authorities, including the Bible, must be called to account. Implicit throughout her argument is the assumption that the object of worship—what Ruether calls "God/ess"—functions as a role model for human beings.[11]

Blaming the Metaphor

The most sophisticated version of role-model theology generally goes under the name *metaphorical theology*. Like all role-model theology, this position assumes that God must be conceived in a way worthy of emulation by human beings, and it sees the problem as essentially one of language—in particular, the metaphors, models, and images that people use to speak of God. As defined by Sallie McFague, its most influential practitioner, "Metaphorical theology . . . claims that in order to be faithful to the God of its tradition—the God on the side of life and its fulfillment—we must try out new pictures that will bring the reality of God's love into the imaginations of the women and men of today."[12] Traditional ways of speaking about God must be rejected

8. Ruether, *Sexism and God-Talk: Toward a Feminist Theology* (Boston: Beacon, 1983), 61.
9. Ruether, *Sexism and God-Talk*, 18–19.
10. Ruether, *Sexism and God-Talk*, 13.
11. Joseph Epstein, in an amusing but pointed op-ed, questions the theory of role models (which he calls a "psychobabblish term") in human social interaction. "Say No to Role Models," *New York Times*, April 23, 1991. The doubts he raises about human role models apply *a fortiori* to alleged divine ones.
12. Sallie McFague, *Models of God: Theology for an Ecological, Nuclear Age* (Philadelphia: Fortress, 1987), xii.

because they contradict the divine nature, not by anything they assert explicitly but because of the metaphors and images they employ. Though McFague no doubt has quarrels with some of the ideas affirmed by earlier theologians, she directs her attack not against their ideas but their metaphors. She rejects metaphors for God that are "patriarchal," "imperialistic," "triumphalist," and "monarchical," calling such imagery "oppressive" and "opposed to life, its continuation and fulfillment."[13]

This attack on biblical imagery is reminiscent of earlier battles, especially the controversy about demythologization unleashed by Rudolf Bultmann in the mid-twentieth century; but there is an important difference. Earlier critics wanted to replace the images they attacked with more direct ways of expressing the text's meaning, whether with literal language in the case of rationalistic interpreters or with existentialist categories in the case of the Bultmannians. Metaphorical theology, on the other hand, proposes not a demythologizing but rather "a *remythologizing* of the relationship between God and the world."[14] Since theologians are, "as it were, painting a picture," they presumably have the right to choose their own colors. And since "theology is *mostly* fiction," it should be free to change the story as needed to make its point. Accordingly, McFague proposes to replace the offending biblical metaphors with ones better suited to our "ecological, nuclear age": God as mother, lover, and friend. So imagined, God can function as an appropriate role model for Christians committed to the proper social and political goals of feminism, environmentalism, and world peace.

The inherent weakness of role-model theology emerges with special clarity in the theory of metaphor employed by metaphorical theology. The proposal that biblical metaphors for God be replaced or supplemented assumes that one metaphor can substitute for another without loss or change of meaning. McFague, for example, is explicit that her three new divine "models" are intended to replace the trinitarian name of God in which Christians from the earliest times to the present have prayed, worshiped, and baptized.[15] The notion that metaphors are substitutable, however, runs afoul of recent theories of metaphor that stress the unique ability of metaphorical language to say what cannot be said in any other way. Surprisingly, McFague has been an articulate advocate of those theories. In her earlier book *Metaphorical Theology* she presents a compelling argument for the unsubstitutable nature of metaphors. Against

13. McFague, *Models of God*, ix–xi.
14. McFague, *Models of God*, xi (emphasis original).
15. McFague, *Models of God*, 181. Though acknowledging in a note that many theologians, including Karl Barth, Claude Welch, and Robert Jenson, insist that the trinitarian names allow no substitutes, McFague offers no refutation of their arguments (222n1).

the long and influential tradition flowing from Aristotle, she demonstrates the superiority of the modern view—propounded by I. A. Richards, Max Black, and others—that sees metaphor "not as a trope but as the way language and, more basically, thought works."[16] The inconsistency between her own theory of metaphor and her theological proposals seems not to have been noticed either by herself or her critics: after arguing for unsubstitutability in *Metaphorical Theology*, she then argues for substituting metaphors in *Models of God*.

The contradiction originates in a social critique, one with close ties to projection theories of religion. This tendency, much in vogue in recent theory, theological and otherwise, could be called "blaming the metaphor." The thesis is that patriarchal and other abuses are the result of the metaphors by which we think, so that if we change our metaphors, we will change our thought and thus our behavior. For example, Gordon Kaufman credits McFague with showing us "how much our thinking has been unconsciously in the grip of metaphors that (however significant and appropriate they may have been in the historical situations in which they arose and were effective) have now become not only misleading but dangerously destructive."[17] Kaufman does not explain how or why metaphors that were once "effective" came to be so "dangerously destructive"; but his own metaphoric language about metaphors is revealing. They appear as powerful and domineering tyrants, exercising a kind of thought control over us (they have us "in their grip," but we don't know it because they operate "unconsciously"). Such hostility toward the central images of Christian tradition is widespread among theologians, especially those most influenced by feminist critique. The root problem of patriarchalism, according to this account, is the paternal (and, more generally, masculine) metaphors that pervade Christian language. The solution then appears obvious: the offending metaphors must be rooted out, replaced by others more in keeping with our own values and commitments.

But how, one may ask, did theologians come to conclude that *metaphors* are to blame for the social and moral ills of Christianity? The key lies in their prior commitment to role-model theology. If religion functions by constructing divine models to be emulated by humans, a tradition that imagines God as heavenly Father must surely serve to legitimate patriarchy: "If God is male, then the male is God." But at this point a Christian metaphorical theology finds itself caught up in contradiction. If metaphors are uniquely informative—if they enable insights that are unobtainable from any other source—then changing

16. Sallie McFague, *Metaphorical Theology: Models of God in Religious Language* (Philadelphia: Fortress, 1982), 37.
17. Kaufman, review of *Models of God*, by Sallie McFague, *Religion and Intellectual Life* 5 (Spring 1988): 12.

religious metaphors means changing religions. Furthermore, any religion that projects images of God that are as destructive as metaphorical theology contends surely *deserves* to be replaced. Now the only way that the metaphorical theologian can escape the implication that the religion itself—Christianity, in this case—is at fault is to claim that Christians have some other, nonmetaphorical information about God against which to measure the adequacy of the metaphors. But that is just the move precluded by modern metaphor theory, for it returns to a view of metaphor as mere vehicle, a rhetorical ornament, an optional means of expression that may in principle be replaced by another. This is, in fact, the view of metaphor employed by metaphorical theology, whatever lip service it pays to the unsubstitutable character of metaphorical language. At the heart of the theology that calls itself metaphorical is a failure to take metaphor seriously: the metaphorical theologian already *knows* what God is like from other—presumably nonmetaphorical—experience and merely makes use of metaphors as vehicles to express that experience. If one vehicle seems to convey the wrong message, it is exchanged for a more suitable one. This criterion becomes explicit in McFague's assertion that in speaking metaphorically "we are trying to think in an as-if fashion." But that is not the way metaphor works. Christians do not think of God *as if* he were a father; they address him as "Our Father." McFague short-circuits the logic of metaphor by jumping from the valid observation that not all attributes of the metaphoric image are applicable to its meaning to the mistaken conclusion that metaphors are optional, that we can pick and choose our metaphors by asking "which one is better in our time."[18] One of the striking characteristics of living metaphoric speech (whether in poetry, religion, or science) is the accompanying conviction that it is the *only* adequate way to utter the intended meaning. This conviction is more powerful to the extent that a given metaphor is central to the text in which it appears. For the New Testament, and hence for the creeds and doctrines of the church, the metaphoric language of God the Father is very near the center. Thus Christians who confess that "God *is* our heavenly Father" will agree that "we think of God *as* Father" but not that "we think of God *as if* he were a father." The subtle but all-important difference between "as" and "as if" is the difference between truly metaphorical speech and speech that treats its metaphors as mere tropes or ornaments.[19] Theologically, it is the difference between taking Scripture seriously as divine disclosure and treating it as an optional resource for theological construction.

18. McFague, *Models of God*, 70.
19. For an elaboration of the distinction between *as* and *as if*, see Garrett Green, *Imagining God: Theology and the Religious Imagination* (Grand Rapids: Eerdmans, 1998), 137–41.

That some theologians now take for granted a theory of religion originally designed to expose the illusory nature of religious belief and the falsehood of Christian doctrine—that fact alone should be enough to provoke some critical questions about their theologies. Feuerbach, Marx, and Freud did not, after all, expose the dynamics of religious illusion in order to encourage theologians to update their illusions; they sought rather to persuade modern people to give up religious belief altogether. Role-model theology wants to use their antireligious critique (what Paul Ricoeur has dubbed the "hermeneutics of suspicion") to dissolve the images and metaphors of the tradition while exempting its own projections from the same fate. The theology of the genderless God arises from this halfway appropriation of projection theories of religion, one that does not take the critical force of those theories with sufficient seriousness and thus ends by repeating the error that the theories were designed to overcome: the divinizing of human values and institutions—in other words, the very kind of mistake made by patriarchal theology.

As paradoxical as it sounds, traditional patriarchalism and the theology of the genderless God share a common presupposition: that the function of divinity is to provide a model for humanity; that religion is the practice of conforming human behavior to a divine model. These most unlikely of allies, in other words, are both committed to role-model theology. They differ only on the question of what role is to be deified. Religious defenders of male privilege appeal to a masculine God in order to justify the authority of his male representatives on earth. Advocates of a genderless God prefer a divine model of sexual equality, whether in the form of an androgynous deity, a God/dess of ambivalent gender, or an impersonal divine principle beyond masculine or feminine. The usual response of theologians to the feminist critique of religious patriarchalism has been to insist that Christians must choose between these two alternatives: either the male God of patriarchy or the genderless God of feminism. But that is a devil's choice if ever there was one.

Toward a Truly Metaphorical Theology

The original temptation, according to the Genesis narrative, was the human urge to model oneself on God: "You will be like God," said the serpent (Gen. 3:5), who thus became the first role-model theologian. One of the deepest ironies of the creation story is that the human creature who has just been formed in the divine image (Gen. 1:26–27) succumbs to the temptation to become "like God"! Evidently there is more than one way to be like God, and everything hangs on recognizing the difference. The crucial principle is that the logic of the *imago Dei* is not reversible. When God fashions us after his image, it is called creation; when we fashion God after our image, it is called idolatry. It is just this distinction that role-model theology misunderstands—in both its patriarchal and its genderless forms.

Here is the point at which to begin thinking theologically about the critical theories of religion stemming from Feuerbach. The way out of the dilemma posed by genderless theology begins with the recognition that we are being asked to choose between rival idolatries. There is a striking similarity between the kinds of religion described by the critical projection theories and what Scripture and Christian doctrine call idolatry. Both seek to alert us to the alienating effects of humanly constructed models of divinity—the one in the name of human autonomy, the other in the name of divine autonomy. And both are right: idol worship threatens freedom, both human and divine. Christian theologians, however, must part company with the nineteenth-century projection theorists at the point where they absolutize their theories into omnicompetent explanations, and thus dismissals, of all religion. One of the strengths of Latin American liberation theology has been its theological appropriation of Marxist criticism of religion without drawing the orthodox Marxist conclusion that all religion is subject to such criticism. Theologians have employed Marxian insights into the ways in which ruling elites employ religion, including Christian religion, to legitimate their power while insisting that the gospel of Jesus Christ is on the side of liberation.[20] Similarly fruitful results have emerged repeatedly in the twentieth century out of the confrontation of theologians with the religious critiques of Freud and Nietzsche—both of whom were as uncompromisingly hostile to Christian teaching as was Karl Marx. No more thoroughgoing rejection of "religion" is to be found, for example, than in the dogmatic theology of Karl Barth.[21]

A truly Christian theology, as Luther reminded the church of his day, must always be a theology of the cross. Theologians need that reminder again today as they think through the theological implications of the feminist challenge. The wrong kind of theology—Luther called it the theology of glory—wants to know God apart from the crucified Jesus. If role-model theology is

---

20. One can appreciate this theoretical contribution while nevertheless wishing that those same theologians were equally critical of the legitimizing theories of the left. There is also a widespread tendency among liberation theologians to adopt the assumptions of role-model theology.

21. The classic discussion is in §17 of the *Church Dogmatics*, but Barth's rejection of "religion" was a consistent theme from his earliest writings to the end of his career. See my translation of Barth's theology of religion and critical introduction to it, entitled *On Religion: The Revelation of God as the Sublimation of Religion* (London: T&T Clark, 2006).

subjected to this test, its root error becomes clear: by attempting to model human behavior after the image of God without regard to the image of God on the cross, this kind of theology wants to directly imitate the God of glory. Patriarchal theologians model themselves after God the Father as though he could be abstracted from the crucified Son of God. The devotees of this theology want the privileges of divine fatherhood without its sacrifices; they want to share God's power but not his powerlessness.

Projectionist theories of religion can serve a useful *negative* function in Christian theology by exposing the dynamics of the universal human religious tendency toward idolatry. To take these theories as *positive* indicators of the content of Christian doctrine, however, would be to deny the fundamental affirmation of Christians throughout the ages that the gospel is God's own communication of himself to those who have ears to hear. Because God has chosen to reveal himself in the flesh as a fully human reality, we come to know him in the same way that we know other human agents: through his self-identification in the interaction of character and circumstance—in a word, narratively—as he is depicted in the words and images of faithful witnesses.[22] Such a story can, of course, be told only in a culturally embodied manner, and that means that it will reflect the customs and social patterns of the concrete human community in which it unfolds. The error of role-model theology is to confuse form with content: to assume that the cultural language of the story, rather than the narrative depiction of the protagonist, is the theologically normative content. I do not wish to minimize the difficulties of making the distinction; the attempt to do so, however, is as unavoidable as it is controversial. Interpretation—the name for this process—is therefore the very lifeblood of theology, and a task which the Christian community cannot shirk or minimize without endangering the gospel it seeks to proclaim. Because the texts of Scripture are metaphorical, the theologian must assume an analogy between its story and ours—between what the text meant and what it means. But since the cross is the root metaphor of Christian interpretation, that analogy is never a direct one between human perfections and divine qualities. Robert Jenson relates this hermeneutical principle to the issues of gender and religious projection:

> The assumption that it is a deprivation not to address God in one's very own gender is a case of humankind's general religious assumption of direct analogy from human perfections to divine qualities. In the faith of the Bible, this direct line is, for our salvation, broken. Indeed, Christianity's entire soteriological

22. See Hans W. Frei, *The Identity of Jesus Christ: The Hermeneutical Bases of Dogmatic Theology* (Philadelphia: Fortress, 1975), esp. chaps. 4 and 9.

message can be put so: God's self-identification with the Crucified One frees us from having to find God by projection of our own perfections.[23]

The chief usefulness of the hermeneutics of suspicion is precisely to expose such direct analogy to critique. The actual analogies of the Bible—shocking to the sensibilities of role-model theology—can employ as metaphors for divine activity the most trivial, base, or terrible features of earthly reality: a thief (1 Thess. 5:2), vomiting (Jonah 2:10), a corrupt judge (Luke 18:2–8), a poisonous snake (Amos 9:3). Jenson points out that "the gospel is free to take its analogies sometimes from human perfections and sometimes from human imperfections, depending on theological need. Sometimes it takes them from death and sin, by no means thereby ranking these above life and virtue." And he suggests that we view the metaphor of fatherhood against this ambiguous background.[24]

A theology that aims at being both consistently metaphorical and authentically scriptural must reject both role-model theology and the substitution theory of metaphor. It may employ the variations of projection theory, like other critical theories, as aids in Christian self-criticism and the Christian critique of culture, as long as the theories remain subject to properly theological criteria. Its negative task will be the critique of all idolatry—that is, of every attempt to construct models of God out of human religious, moral, or cultural experience. But it will undertake this critical task in the service of the far more important constructive task of exploring and elaborating the biblical paradigm so that its meaning and implications can be heard in the present. Metaphors in theology, as in the natural sciences, are neither ornamental nor optional. A defensible metaphorical theology must therefore begin by acknowledging the normative status of the biblical paradigm and its constituent metaphors and images for Christian thought, teaching, and practice. Christians acknowledge and seek to live by the vision of reality embodied paradigmatically in the canon of the Old and New Testaments. Faith, understood as the human response to the self-revelation of God in the imagination of the prophets and apostles, has no other access to God by which it might judge the adequacy of biblical metaphors. It understands its task accordingly to be not the construction of a new paradigm that better expresses our contemporary sensibilities (that would be idolatry) but rather the interpretation of the metaphorical matrix of Scripture in order to bring it more clearly into relation with life in the world today.

23. Jenson, *The Triune Identity* (Philadelphia: Fortress, 1982), 16.
24. Jenson, *Triune Identity*, 16.

The Kenotic Masculinity of God

Christian theologians since the advent of modernity have had to wrestle repeatedly with the "scandal of particularity," the seemingly indissoluble link between Christian truth claims and certain concrete specifics of history, culture, and person. Modern thinkers have been scandalized by Christian particularity because of its apparent arbitrariness and resistance to universalizing generalities. From the deists of the seventeenth and eighteenth centuries to proponents of interreligious dialogue today, the calls have not ceased for Christians to give up their stubborn allegiance to historically and culturally specific particulars in the name of religious harmony and universal truth. But the Christian community has been right to resist pressures to interpret its confession as one symbolic expression of a more abstract and general religious truth. The odd presence of Pontius Pilate in the creed (the only mortal so included other than the Virgin Mary and the incarnate Christ) is a constant reminder that Christian faith has to do centrally not with religious and moral generalities but with decisive historical particulars.

Theologians today who would never dream, for example, of revising liturgies to play down the Jewishness of the central symbols of Christian faith are nevertheless eager to disguise the masculinity of the same symbolism, even in the case of the incarnate Christ. Why is it that those who do not balk at a New Testament that accepts slavery as part of the social order and employs it metaphorically are embarrassed to pray "Our Father"? The reasons, of course, have to do with topics of currently pressing social and political concern. Yet the same offensive particularity clings to Scripture and doctrine whether one focuses on class, gender, or ethnicity. And in all such cases, the temptation to abandon the awkward particularity of the Bible in favor of an abstract conception of deity must be resisted. Christian faith means having one's imagination grasped by the story of God and the world as told by the prophets and apostles and proclaimed by the Christian community throughout the ages. Why that story rather than another is a question for which the theologian has no answer—except the one implicit in the narrative itself: that *this* story is not just another figment of the imagination but God's own story; in short, that this story is *true*. The challenge of feminist critique is one more reminder that Christians know God only in this stubbornly particular way, by imagining him as the One whose identity is depicted in the narrative of Israel and the church. Since that depiction is thoroughly metaphorical, God's identity is mediated to us in these specific images—which, like all true metaphors, convey a meaning that is inseparable from their particularity and cannot therefore be replaced either by literal paraphrase or by different metaphors.

Theology, as the intellectual response to the God of this particular narrative, is not properly in the business of rewriting the story or designing divine models with an eye to their suitability to contemporary sensibilities. Rather, the job of the theologian is to interpret the story, to say what it means in terms that can be understood by people of the theologian's own generation.

How, then, is the church to respond to the pressing demands of feminist critique for a theological hearing? What does the predominantly masculine grammar of the biblical God mean to us who live, not in a traditional patriarchal society, but in one increasingly committed to the equality of the sexes on all levels and to a much greater flexibility of gender roles than ever known in the past? The most valuable contribution of feminist theology has been to cast a new and critical light on traditional ways in which the metaphor of divine fatherhood has been misused to legitimate patriarchal institutions and practices. The appropriate response to this critique is not to reject the metaphor, as proposed by role-model theology, but rather to correct the distortions of male-centered misreadings. This critical contribution of feminism opens the way for us to reread the biblical texts with new eyes in order to discover how patriarchal metaphors actually function in their scriptural context.

One of the failings of metaphorical theology has been its tendency to treat metaphors atomistically, as though they were independent units of thought, each containing an intrinsic meaning. The irony of this approach is that it misses the metaphoric nature of the metaphor; it makes the mistake of literalism by focusing attention on the image itself (the "vehicle" in I. A. Richards's terminology) rather than the subject matter that the metaphor wants to illumine (the "tenor"). An interpreter, for example, may be so taken by the masculinity of the metaphor "Father" as to miss its point, which may depart from, or even invert, the common meaning of the word as used nonmetaphorically. When Christians call God "Father," it is always a shorthand for "the Father of Our Lord Jesus Christ." In other words, Christians are not referring generally to God as *a* father but rather are addressing him in solidarity with Jesus as "*Our* Father." The meaning of the metaphor is accordingly to be sought in the story of the one whom Jesus calls Father.

If we attend to that story, we discover a protagonist very different from the authoritarian patriarch exalted by androcentric tradition and vilified by feminist critique. *This* God does not jealously hoard his power. As husband he does not beat his unfaithful wife but cries out with the pain of a jilted lover and redoubles his efforts to win her back (Hosea 2).[25] As Father he "did not

25. Brian Wren picks precisely this imagery from Hosea as "an example of a God-metaphor ripe for change." *What Language Shall I Borrow? God-Talk in Worship: A Male Response to*

spare his own Son but gave him up for us all" (Rom. 8:32). As Son he did not claim the prerogatives of power and lord it over his subjects but "emptied himself, by taking the form of a servant. . . . He humbled himself by becoming obedient to the point of death, even death on a cross" (Phil. 2:7–8). As Spirit he incorporates us into the mystical body of Christ, in whom "there is neither slave nor free, there is no male and female" (Gal. 3:28). As king he does not isolate himself in heavenly splendor but wills to dwell with his people, to "wipe away every tear from their eyes" and to deliver them from all that oppresses them, even from death itself (Rev. 21:4).

Anyone who claims that masculine metaphors such as these are "oppressive to women" is interpreting them out of context, treating them as isolated units of meaning rather than integral elements of a living narrative. The theological cure for such abstract thinking is reimmersion in the concrete text of Scripture, in all its bewildering and liberating particularity. In its concentration on isolated metaphors, contemporary feminist hermeneutics (together with much of liberation theology generally) has often overlooked the dramatic dialectics of power and weakness in the biblical narrative. To say without qualification or irony that God favors the weak and poor is to invite a fundamental misreading of the dynamics of the story.[26] God's choosing of the scattered tribes of Israel to be his people presupposes that he is Creator of all nature and Lord of all history; without the latter assertion, the theological point of the former is lost. The one who forgives sin is the same one who establishes the law and rules with justice; that is precisely what gives his forgiveness its poignancy and its meaning. The God who goes into exile with

---

Feminist Theology (New York: Crossroad, 1990), 109. Because social and cultural mores change, Wren reasons, metaphors must change to keep up with the times. "When I realize that I live in a society in which men subordinate women and that God does not intend this or wish it to continue," he comments, "Hosea's imagery presents problems." The patriarchal assumptions of the text "give a distorted model for relationships between women and men." But Wren's problem is the reflection of his application of role-model theology to the text. The scriptural point of the text is not to provide us with a model of sexual relationships, distorted or otherwise. Rather, the prophet is talking about *God*. That he does so in the language of his own culture goes without saying (what other language might we expect him to use?). Understood in the prophet's context (and that's what it means to understand a text), his metaphor proclaims the love of God. Wren is correct that this metaphorical language will be misunderstood if taken naïvely—that is, without regard to its historical context. That is why Christian faith, based as it is on a historical revelation, must continually *interpret* the proclamation of Scripture: that is the job of theologians and preachers. To suggest as Wren does that we abandon the text because its cultural assumptions are foreign to us would lead, if applied consistently, to the abandonment of the Bible itself. The properly theological response to Hosea's text is not to *blame* the metaphor but to *interpret* it.

26. Levenson demonstrates how such distortion has taken place in the use of the exodus story by liberation theologians. "Liberation Theology and the Exodus," esp. 7–9.

his people is the same God who uses his people's enemies as instruments for their chastisement. The Crucified Man is himself the Messiah who comes to deliver Israel. Jesus's obedience unto death is the act of the very one who is Lord of life. The self-emptying of God presupposes his fullness; his weakness presupposes his strength; his "femininity" presupposes his "masculinity."

To tinker with the pronouns or alter the metaphors of such a narrative is to risk losing or seriously distorting its meaning.[27] One of the lessons of the modern theory of metaphor, ignored by metaphorical theology, is that true metaphors are open-ended, constantly yielding up new meaning to those who live by them faithfully and attend to their nuances in changing situations. Any theology that thinks it knows in advance what biblical metaphors will mean has not paid attention either to modern theories of metaphor or to the history of interpretation. To treat the Bible as Holy Scripture, as the place where one expects ever again to hear the living voice of God, is the characteristic stance of the Christian community and the special responsibility of its theologians. Part of that responsibility is refusing to foreclose on the meaning of the text in advance, wrestling with it as with a divine messenger until it blesses us at last. If it sometimes seems more like our enemy than our deliverer, we are at least in the company of Job, of Jeremiah, and of Jesus, all of whom we know through that very text.

Too many theologians and church leaders, misled by the popularity of role-model theology and the stridency of political pressure groups inside and outside the churches, have jumped to premature and simplistic conclusions about the meaning of the metaphorical language of Scripture, liturgy, and doctrine. A more nuanced reading of the sources reveals a subtler and more complex picture than the prevailing ideology would lead us to believe. It is noteworthy that in a Bible whose cultural setting is so thoroughly patriarchal one never encounters an explicit appeal to the masculinity of God for any purpose whatever. Even in the history of doctrine one is hard-pressed to find such appeals. On the contrary, all major Christians bodies have long held (in the words of the Anglican Thirty-Nine Articles) that "there is but one living and true God, everlasting, *without body*, *parts*, *or passions*." That misogynists and powerful males in church and society have taken scriptural authorization of their views for granted is obvious; that their assumptions are justifiable on the basis of the texts is doubtful. Once again, the precedent

27. It is a fact worth pondering that the politically correct revisers of Scripture, liturgy, and hymns do not ordinarily propose similar improvements (for example) to Shakespeare. Why is it that the literary classics of culture are treated with greater respect for their integrity than the Bible? Aesthetic considerations are surely not definitive for theological hermeneutics, but any interpretation that ignores them should be treated with suspicion.

of slavery is instructive. The fact that Christian slaveholders for centuries appealed to Scripture for support did not prevent Christians in the modern period from concluding that they had been wrong—nor did it lead them to reject the powerful metaphorical language of master and slave in the Bible.

But the more important reason for retaining the masculine grammar of God is positive and constructive. In view of the ironic dialectics of power in the Bible, a change in gender would obscure precisely that aspect of the biblical message most needed in an age sensitized by feminist and liberationist critiques: the ironic reversal of power—including masculine power. Susanne Heine points out that gender is crucial to the meaning of Jesus's vicarious representation. "A woman," she writes, "could not represent the humiliated because she herself is already where these people are. [Vicarious] representation involves the voluntary renunciation of power and privileges."[28] An image of a suffering female would not challenge the powers of this world because she would merely be one more victim. The point is nevertheless uttered by a female voice in Mary's triumphant response to the announcement of her Son's advent: "He has brought down the mighty from their thrones and exalted those of humble estate" (Luke 1:52). To the extent that the problem is "masculine," one might argue, the solution must be expressed in masculine terms. God himself—the Mighty One of Israel, the Heavenly King, the God of the Fathers—sends his Son and heir to be the scapegoat, the Victim. Far from justifying male dominance, this symbolism calls it under judgment. In the words of Paul, "God chose what is low and despised in the world, even things that are not, to bring to nothing things that are, so that no human being might boast in the presence of God" (1 Cor. 1:28–29). But such language is not an undialectical celebration of weakness, for Paul also insists that "the weakness of God is stronger than men" (v. 25).

Feminist theologians seem generally to have missed the irony of biblical patriarchy. But it is even more obvious that it has been missed by patriarchs through the ages, who have humorlessly and unimaginatively adopted the patriarchy of Scripture as a "model." Instead of repeating their error by inventing new models, theologians today would do better to borrow a page from black slave religion by rediscovering the liberating power of the Bible against its misuse by its self-appointed spokesmen.[29] Just as words have defi-

28. Susanne Heine, *Matriarchs, Goddesses, and Images of God: A Critique of a Feminist Theology*, trans. John Bowden (Minneapolis: Augsburg Fortress, 1989), 138. I have emended the translation to bring out the fact that Heine's term *Stellvertretung* refers explicitly to *vicarious* representation.

29. See Albert J. Raboteau, *Slave Religion: The "Invisible Institution" in the Antebellum South* (New York: Oxford University Press, 1978), esp. chap. 6.

nitions but no meaning until they are used by people speaking in sentences, so the specifics of culture—the Jewish man Jesus, or the Roman practice of capital punishment by crucifixion—have no meaning apart from the narrative of which they are constituents. More specifically: they have no *theological* meaning apart from their scriptural context. But they do have other kinds of meaning—historical and sociological, for example—which means we can discover from biblical texts that first-century Judea was a patriarchal society (a cultural-historical fact); but this fact has no theological meaning in itself. That meaning emerges from *how* the cultural particular is *used* in the biblical narrative. The metaphor of language is not arbitrary, nor does it originate with contemporary philosophical predilections, for Christians have called Jesus the *Word* of God from the start: "In these last days he has spoken to us by his Son" (Heb. 1:2). In order to rightly understand the message of any text we must rid ourselves of inappropriate connotations associated with the vocabulary employed and attend to the text itself. This is all the more necessary in the case of the Bible, which when read as *Scripture*, sets the context for our understanding of God, the world, and ourselves.

In the face of the feminist challenge, Christian theologians need to insist on a subtle but important distinction: God is not male; yet the appropriate language in which to describe, address, and worship him is nevertheless masculine.[30] Such masculinity is one grammatical aspect of the paradigmatic biblical narrative through which he has disclosed himself to Israel and the church. Read in context, however, this masculinity turns out to be "kenotic," an aspect of the divine self-emptying[31] by which God divests himself of all majesty, dominion, and power in order to overcome the powers (masculine and otherwise) of this world. Those whose imaginations are captured by this story will continue to receive it, in all its scandalous particularity, as the gift of God. For it enables them to do what would otherwise be impossible: to know, to love, and to praise the one true God, Father, Son, and Holy Spirit, in human—and that can only mean in culturally particular—language.

---

30. Anthropologists distinguish between *sex*, a biological characteristic, and *gender*, its cultural elaboration. An instructive example of how the distinction can be used to shed light on the universal social subordination of women to men is the influential article by Sherry B. Ortner, "Is Female to Male as Nature Is to Culture?," in *Woman, Culture, and Society*, ed. Michelle Zimbalist Rosaldo and Louise Lamphere (Stanford, CA: Stanford University Press, 1974), 67–87. I am using the qualifier *male* as a sexual (natural) term and *masculine* as the corresponding gender (cultural) term. The difference is too often ignored in contemporary theological writing.

31. The New Testament term is *kenosis*; cf. Phil. 2:7.

PART 3

MODERNITY AND ESCHATOLOGY IN CHRISTIAN IMAGINATION

9

THE ADULTHOOD
OF THE MODERN AGE

Hamann's Critique of Kantian Enlightenment

When Immanuel Kant announced his famous definition of enlightenment in 1784, he enshrined a metaphor that had long been a favorite self-definition of European modernity and was destined—in large part as a result of Kant's essay—to become the quasi-official criterion of what it means to be modern. Kant defines *Aufklärung*, as virtually every textbook tells us, as "man's emergence from his self-incurred immaturity," and he explains immaturity as "the inability to use one's own understanding without the guidance of another."[1] At the heart of Kant's definition is a metaphor—or, as we shall see, a combination of two interrelated metaphors. Enlightenment, Kant is saying, is analogous to the passage from the status of minor child to the status of adult. Enlightened modernity is the adulthood of the human race.

When Johann Georg Hamann, in the same month that Kant's essay on enlightenment appeared, wrote a thank-you note to a friend for sending the essay to him, he raised profound questions about the assumptions of the

---

1. Immanuel Kant, "An Answer to the Question: 'What Is Enlightenment?,'" original German in *Kant's Gesammelte Schriften, Akademieausgabe*, vol. I/8 (Berlin, 1912), 35 (hereafter cited as *AA*); English translation in *Kant's Political Writings*, ed. Hans Reiss (New York: Cambridge University Press, 1970), 54 (hereafter cited as Reiss).

Aufklärer, and he did so precisely in terms of Kant's central metaphor of the passage from childhood to adulthood. Hamann's remarkable letter[2] exemplifies what has often been said about him: that he anticipated, in uncanny ways, criticisms of the Enlightenment that were not generally recognized until long after his lifetime.[3] Indeed, as I hope to demonstrate, Hamann's letter in December 1784 adumbrates several themes that have been elaborated by contemporary commentators on enlightenment. Without the benefit of historical hindsight, Hamann recognized the limitations and dangers lurking in Kant's optimistic endorsement of enlightenment, especially as embodied in his focal metaphor. Hamann's own term for that image—*Gleichnis*, a word that entered the German language as the translation of Latin *parabola* and has never lost its biblical associations—already sets him apart from Kant, who surely did not understand himself to be speaking in parables but rather in clear philosophical concepts. Acknowledging his willingness to be guided by Kant in matters of the understanding (though, significantly, "with a grain of salt"), Hamann identifies the metaphor as the focus of his disagreement with Kant. He can "tolerate gladly," Hamann writes, "seeing enlightenment, if not explained, at least elucidated and expanded more aesthetically than dialectically, through the analogy [*Gleichnis*] of immaturity and guardianship." Before examining Hamann's own "aesthetic" reading of the analogy, we need to attend to the imagery it employs.

Readers of Kant in English translation are likely to misconstrue the controversial metaphor, or even to overlook it entirely. The crucial concept, *Unmündigkeit*, is generally rendered in English as "immaturity." The trouble with that translation is that it subtly shifts the underlying analogy from a legal[4] to a psychological context. Likewise unavailable to the English reader is the common image linking the correlative terms *Vormund* ("guardian" or "tutor" in most English translations) and *Unmündige* ("immature ones"). Their common root—*Mund* ("mouth")—indicates that the underlying meaning of *unmündig* is being unable to *speak* on one's own behalf. For that purpose one has need

2. All quotations from this letter that appear in this chapter come from my annotated translation of Hamann's "Letter to Christian Jacob Kraus," in *What Is Enlightenment? Eighteenth-Century Answers and Twentieth-Century Questions*, ed. James Schmidt (Berkeley: University of California Press, 1996), 145–53.

3. Frederick Beiser's comment is representative: "Judged by twentieth-century standards, Hamann's thought is often striking for its modernity, its foreshadowing of contemporary themes." *The Fate of Reason: German Philosophy from Kant to Fichte* (Cambridge, MA: Harvard University Press, 1987), 17.

4. Elfriede Büchsel notes that "*Mündigkeit* and *Unmündigkeit* are primarily concepts from the legal world." "Aufklärung und christliche Freiheit: J. G. Hamann contra I. Kant," *Neue Zeitschrift für systematische Theologie* 4 (1962): 141.

of a *Vor-mund*, a legally sanctioned "mouthpiece" to stand *in front of (vor)* him as official spokesman. The closest equivalent in English is the status of being a *minor*, a term with the appropriate legal connotations and for which *guardian* is indeed the correlative term. Not only minor children, however, are *unmündig*. A senile old person might also be assigned a legal guardian. Even more important, *Unmündigkeit* (unlike minority) is tied not only to age but also to gender. As both Kant and Hamann make explicit in their comments on the "fair sex," women were considered *unmündig* and therefore (in Kant's view) prime candidates for enlightenment. Hamann's intriguing (if cryptic) comments about Kant, women, and his own daughters suggest that one of the later theoretical perspectives he anticipates is feminism.

A major drawback of translating *Unmündigkeit* as "immaturity" is its pejorative implication of childish demeanor. It may be the case that persons deprived of the legal right to speak for themselves suffer the psychological consequence of immature behavior, but the German term emphasizes the legal rather than the psychological or behavioral nuances of *immaturity*. The absence of adequate English equivalents also obscures the persistence of the metaphor in modern thought and culture. Few English speakers, for example, would suspect a connection between Kant's definition of enlightenment and Dietrich Bonhoeffer's reflections from a Nazi prison about the "world come of age." Yet Bonhoeffer's language is the same as Kant's: he speaks of *die mündiggewordene Welt* in which we moderns live, a world that has exchanged its minority status for responsible adulthood.[5]

Who Speaks for the Immature?

Hamann's 1784 letter to his friend Christian Jacob Kraus,[6] professor of practical philosophy and political science in Königsberg, contains an indictment of the basic Enlightenment program expressed in terms of Kant's own metaphor. Hamann finds the key to the root metaphor of immaturity and guardianship (*Unmündigkeit* and *Vormundschaft*) in a second, unacknowledged metaphor with which it is associated. Kant's essay on enlightenment identifies the

5. See, e.g., Bonhoeffer's comments in his letter to Eberhard Bethge of June 8, 1944, from Tegel prison. Dietrich Bonhoeffer, *Letters and Papers from Prison*, ed. Eberhard Bethge (New York: Macmillan, 1972), 324–29.
6. According to James C. O'Flaherty, "An especially warm friendship obtained between Hamann and Christian Jakob Kraus, who became professor of practical philosophy and of economics at the university of Königsberg, and who was, next to Kant, the most brilliant docent there. Although much younger than Hamann, Kraus was probably closer to him in his later life than anyone except Herder." *Johann Georg Hamann* (Boston: Twayne, 1979), 33.

problem as "*self-incurred* immaturity." Here, too, significant connotations of Kant's language disappear in English translation. The root of what Hamann calls "that accursed adjective *selbstverschuldet*"—*Schuld*—can mean "guilt," "debt," or "fault." Kant is saying that those in need of enlightenment are immature, deprived of the right to speak for themselves, through their own fault; and it is this claim that most arouses Hamann's ire. He returns to the issue repeatedly in the letter, and his language is peppered with allusions to *Schuld* in its various connotations. Employing one of his favorite Greek phrases, he finds the *proton pseudos*, the basic or original error of Kant's program for enlightenment, in that "accursed adjective."

Never questioning the claim that immaturity is the fundamental issue, Hamann presses the question of who is to blame for it. He uncovers a contradiction in Kant's opening words. No sooner has Kant defined *immaturity* as the *inability* to reason on one's own than he calls it *self-incurred*. But, Hamann points out, "inability is really no fault [*Schuld*]," as even Kant will acknowledge. Kant makes it into a fault, Hamann notes, by introducing categories of the *will* in his next sentence. Immaturity, Kant writes, "is *self-incurred* if its cause is not lack of understanding, but lack of resolution and courage to use it without the guidance of another. . . . Laziness and cowardice are the reasons why such a large proportion of men . . . gladly remain immature for life." Hamann seizes on the two terms of Kant's indictment of the immature— their lack of resolution (laziness) and their lack of courage (cowardice)—and turns them against the accuser.

Those whose wills in fact lack resolution and courage—the truly lazy and cowardly ones—turn out to be not the immature ones but their "enlightened" guardians, among whom is Kant himself. Hamann arrives at this conclusion by pursuing the identity of the one he calls the "indeterminate other" in Kant's essay. If, as Kant had written, "*immaturity* is the inability to use one's own understanding without the guidance of *another*," this "other" is by definition the guardian, the *Vor-mund* who speaks for the immature.[7] Hamann's suspicions are aroused by the fact that this significant figure appears *anonymously* in Kant's account, evidence for the fact that "the metaphysicians hate to call their persons by their right names." The reason for Kant's reluctance to identify the anonymous "other," Hamann surmises, is that "he reckons himself to the class of guardians," thereby exalting himself above the immature candidates for enlightenment.

Hamann now attacks the project of enlightenment head-on, calling into question the image contained in the term itself, through a series of ironic

---

7. Kant, "What Is Enlightenment?" (*AA* 8:35; Reiss 54) (emphasis original).

allusions to darkness and light, blindness and sight, night and day. He contrasts his own "pure and healthy human eyes" to the "moonlight-enlightened eyes of an *Athene glaukopis*," owl-eyed Athena who sees in the dark. The "*inability* or *fault* of the falsely accused immature one" comes not from his own laziness or cowardice but rather from the "blindness of his guardian, who purports to be able to see, and for that very reason must bear the whole responsibility for the fault." Immaturity only becomes culpable, "self-incurred," when "it surrenders to the guidance of a blind . . . guardian and leader"—in other words, to an "enlightened" guardian like Kant. Hamann closes his letter with a volley of ironic plays on "en*light*enment": he calls the Enlightenment of his century "a mere northern light," suggesting that the rationalists' program, like the aurora borealis, is both frigid and illusory—"a cold, unfruitful moonlight without enlightenment for the lazy understanding and without warmth for the cowardly will." Such nocturnal enlightenment is a "blind illumination" for the everyday citizen deprived of legal maturity, "who walks at *noon*." In closing, Hamann notes that he is writing at dusk ("*entre chien et loup*"), the liminal state between light and darkness. The French phrase was a favorite of Hamann's, for whom the "realm between day and night became a symbol of his eschatological existence between the times."[8]

The Politics of Maturity

Recovering the legal context of the metaphor of maturity and immaturity provides a clue to the important political dimensions of the controversy between Hamann and Kant. Both would agree that the enlightenment of individuals is inevitably implicated in a network of social and political forces. Kant's essay defining enlightenment puts the whole question quite explicitly in political terms, most pointedly in his announcement that "our age is the age of enlightenment, the century of *Frederick*."[9] Hamann, writing to a political scientist whom he addresses as *Domine Politice*,[10] does not overlook the implications of Kant's testimonial to their common monarch, toward whom their attitudes could hardly stand in sharper contrast. Büchsel notes that the importance of Frederick the Great as opponent in Hamann's writings has won increasing

8. Oswald Bayer, "Selbstverschuldete Vormundschaft: Hamanns Kontroverse mit Kant um *wahre* Aufklärung," in *Der Wirklichkeitsanspruch von Theologie und Religion*, ed. Dieter Henke et al. (Tübingen: Mohr Siebeck, 1976), 27–28.
9. Kant, "What Is Enlightenment?" (*AA* 8:40; Reiss 58) (emphasis original).
10. Büchsel interprets this form of address to mean that Hamann sees Kraus as one "qualified and authorized to judge political problems." "Aufklärung und christliche Freiheit," 145.

acknowledgment by scholars.[11] When Frederick assumed the throne from his father in 1740, no less an authority than Voltaire had pronounced him "Le Salomon du Nord," appointed to enlighten the eyes of the Prussian *barbares*. Voltaire's epithet, identifying the king with the Old Testament paradigm of the wise man, places Frederick in symbolic rivalry with Hamann, whom Friedrich Karl von Moser had dubbed "Magus in Norden" after those other biblical wise men, the New Testament magi.[12] Hamann, who accepted the epithet gracefully, signs the letter containing his critique of Kant with the variant *Magus in telonio*, which calls attention to his own position as Frederick's unwilling civil servant in the Königsberg customs house.

Hamann's political critique of Kantian enlightenment goes directly to the issue of power. Kant's flattering description of Frederick as "the man who first liberated mankind from immaturity"[13] betrays the *proton pseudos*, the root error of the enlighteners, and it has to do with the question of culpability introduced by Kant's "accursed adjective" *self-incurred*. The telling phrase occurs in Kant's almost incidental remark that the enlightened ruler "has at hand a well-disciplined and numerous army to guarantee public security."[14] In Hamann's sarcastic paraphrase, the purpose of the guardian's army is "to guarantee his infallibility and orthodoxy." As the "anonymous other," Hamann fingers the guardian implied by the very existence of the immature, the *Vormund* whose job it is to speak for the *Unmündige*, and singles him out for the severest censure: he twice calls him "the man of death." Without naming the king directly, Hamann lets Kraus know exactly whom he has in mind. The first clue, not decisive by itself, is the epithet "man of death," which apparently alludes to King David's encounter with the prophet Nathan in 2 Samuel 12. This supposition becomes more likely in light of Hamann's predilection for parables as the most appropriate genre for telling the truth. In the same paragraph Hamann casts Kant in the ironic role of prophet: "Who is the *other*, of whom the cosmopolitical chiliast prophesies?" But it is surely Hamann himself who intends to play Nathan to Frederick's David, prophesying in parable, allusion, and "macaronic style" in an effort to catch the conscience of the king—or, if that is expecting too much, at least to warn the consciences of his immature compatriots against the wiles of the "man of death" who has appointed himself their guardian. Such *political* pretension—backed by "a large well-disciplined army"—is the real fault: "the self-incurred guardianship and not immaturity." A more direct clue to

---

11. Büchsel, "Aufklärung und christliche Freiheit," 234n4.
12. Cited by O'Flaherty, *Johann Georg Hamann*, 25.
13. Kant, "What Is Enlightenment?" (*AA* 8:40; Reiss 58).
14. Kant, "What Is Enlightenment?" (*AA* 8:41; Reiss 59).

the identity of the "other" is Hamann's allusion to him as "this lad Absalom," another figure in the Davidic royal history, who leads an unsuccessful rebellion against his father. Hamann is surely speaking parabolically about Frederick, who as crown prince had (like Absalom) plotted against his own father, King Frederick William, and (again like Absalom) had failed. In one regard, however, Frederick fared better than his biblical prototype: although he spent some time in prison, he—unlike Absalom—survived to become king in the more conventional manner, by waiting out his father's death.

Hamann's political critique takes special aim at Kant's distinction between public and private discourse. Kant had defined their relative spheres in such a way as to virtually reverse their meaning as ordinarily understood. In Hamann's view, Kant's distinction amounts to taking away with the left hand the freedom that he has just granted with the right. "The *public* use of man's reason must always be free, and it alone can bring about enlightenment among men," Kant argues; "the *private use* of reason may quite often be very narrowly restricted, however, without undue hindrance to the progress of enlightenment."[15] Kant's odd use of these terms is governed not by the size of one's audience but rather by one's employer. Reason is used publicly, he writes, by "*a man of learning* addressing the entire *reading public*"—that is, by the self-employed intellectual. It is used privately, on the other hand, by someone performing "in a particular *civil* post or office with which he is entrusted"—that is, by an employee of the political establishment. Kant's three examples of such civil offices—the military officer, the tax collector, and the clergyman—become grist for the mill of Hamann's irony. Kant affirms the right to "argue" (*räsonniern*) to one's heart's content so long as one obeys one's political masters: "The officer says: Don't argue, get on parade! The tax-official: Don't argue, pay! The clergyman: Don't argue, believe!" The parenthetical tribute to Frederick that Kant appends is hardly calculated to reassure Hamann: "Only one ruler in the world says: *Argue* as much as you like and about whatever you like, *but obey!*"[16] Hamann's sarcastic rejoinder in the letter to Kraus goes right to the underlying political and economic relations: "So doesn't it all come to the same thing?—believe, get on parade, pay, if the d—— is not to take you. Is it not *sottise des trois parts*? And which is the greatest and most difficult? An army of priests [*Pfaffen*] or of thugs, henchmen, and purse snatchers?" For Hamann, here speaking in his proto-Marxist voice, it all comes down in the end to "the financial exploitation of immature persons" by their self-appointed political guardians. This "enlightened"

15. Kant, "What Is Enlightenment?" (*AA* 8:37; Reiss 55).
16. Kant, "What Is Enlightenment?" (*AA* 8:37; Reiss 55).

political arrangement is what Hamann, in the phrase that pithily sums up his whole critique of Kant, calls "a supremely *self-incurred guardianship.*" The guilt, in other words, has been attributed to the wrong party; Kant is blaming the victims. The onus of guilt should be removed from the oppressed and imputed to the oppressors—including their philosophical apologists.

Hamann's extended commentary on public and private comes in a postscript that is at once the most trenchant and the most difficult passage in the letter. He calls Kant's distinction "comical," but he doesn't appear to be laughing. He sees it as a distinction without a difference, but one that is nevertheless politically dangerous because it gives aid and comfort to "enlightened" tyrants. In language suggestive of the Chalcedonian definition of Christ's "two natures in one person," Hamann identifies the problem as that of "unifying the two natures of an *immature person and guardian,*" though not in the way Kant wants to do it. "Here," he says, "lies precisely the nub of the whole political problem." What follows, however, is a characteristically "macaronic" barrage of metaphor and allusion, involving a New Testament parable and passages from St. Paul, Boethius, and Kant. Apparently borrowing imagery from Jesus's parable of the king's wedding feast in Matthew 22, Hamann asks rhetorically, "What good to me is the *festive garment* of freedom when I am in a slave's smock at home?" Kantian "public" freedom is of little use to a civil servant like Hamann, who is "privately" enslaved in the king's service.

There follows the most arcane passage in the letter, in which Hamann's proto-Marxian political critique in terms of money and power appears to take on a feminist coloration as well: "Does Plato [i.e., Kant] too belong to the *fair sex*[?]—which he slanders like an old bachelor." The interpretive puzzle here is why Hamann would infer a similarity between Kant and women. Has he not already demonstrated that Kant wants to establish himself as the enlightened guardian of women and other immature persons? The key lies in Hamann's allusion to the passage in 1 Corinthians where Paul argues that "the women should keep silent in the churches" (1 Cor. 14:34). It is essential to bear in mind that Hamann, unlike many feminists today, acknowledges the authority even of scriptural passages that seem to oppose his own opinions. So the Pauline passage is presumably cited in earnest. Hamann appears, in fact, to remove any suggestion that the apostle is deprecating women by juxtaposing Boethius's association between keeping silent and being a philosopher. The implication would seem to be that women, by remaining silent in accordance with the biblical precept, behave more like philosophers than those (like Kant?) who are full of words.

Even harder to explain, however, is the apparent contradiction in the passage that immediately follows. Still speaking of women, Hamann writes, "At home (i.e., at the lectern and on the stage and in the pulpit) they may chatter to their hearts' content. There they speak as guardians and must forget everything and contradict everything as soon as, in their own self-incurred immaturity, they are to do indentured labor for the state." According to Kant's classification, the professional activities of teachers ("at the lectern"), actors ("on the stage"), and preachers ("in the pulpit") are *private*, since they involve performance "in a particular *civil* post or office" entrusted to them. But that would imply that they are *not* free to "chatter to their hearts' content" in those situations. The key to the apparent contradiction lies in the phrase "at home" (*daheim*), which Hamann has used twice already in the postscript. Kant, speaking specifically of religion, had written that the ecclesiastical teacher's use of reason is private, "since a congregation, however large it is, is never any more than a domestic [*häusliche*] gathering."[17] This identification of the congregation as domestic makes clear how Hamann could use *daheim* to refer to activities such as those "in the pulpit." Applying Kant's logic to the Pauline passage, Hamann shows the absurdity of Kant's position by drawing the conclusion that women should be able to chatter away in such "domestic" (private) places as the lectern, the stage, and the pulpit. But in those very roles, according to Kant, people speak as guardians and thus have to give up their freedom of speech as good, "private" servants of the state—thereby becoming immature through their own fault. This bizarre reversal comes about by superimposing the Pauline distinction between congregation and home on the Kantian one between public and private. Paul says that women must remain silent in the congregation but may speak at home; Kant, by making the congregation "domestic," identifies it with the realm of free speech. Here the contradiction at the heart of Kant's distinction stands exposed, for rather than allowing freedom of speech in the congregation, he subjects it to the constraints of "private" reasoning. Hamann has thus demonstrated not only the absurdity of Kant's distinction between public and private but also his violation of scriptural authority. Kantian sleight of hand has turned the "public" free use of reason into a mere "sumptuous dessert," while enslaving the "private" use, which is "the *daily bread* that we should give up for its sake." This phrase resonates with the language of the Lord's Prayer, which includes both a petition for "our daily bread" and a plea to "forgive us our debts [*Schuld*]," by which allusion Hamann returns to the underlying issue of culpability.

The feminist twist comes just at this point: "The *self-incurred immaturity is* just such a sneer as he makes at the whole fair sex, and which my three

17. Kant, "What Is Enlightenment?" (*AA* 8:38; Reiss 57).

daughters will not put up with." Hamann has shown that Kant's linkage of guilt with the social status of immaturity amounts to a slander against women, who thus come to stand for all those deprived of a political voice. By falsely blaming these victims for their *Unmündigkeit*, Kant implicitly makes himself their *Vormund*, thus acquiring the actual guilt of the "self-incurred" guardian. Hamann's transfiguration of Kant's enlightenment—his *Verklärung* of *Aufklärung*, as he puts it—leads to his radically different definition of "*true enlightenment*" as the "emergence of the immature person from a supremely *self-incurred guardianship.*" Kant is right that the problem is the liberation of the immature, but he chooses the wrong target for his critique. It is not the women and other voiceless groups who incur guilt but rather the "enlightened" monarchs and their court philosophers.

Hamann's Critique of Kantian Purism

For all its immediacy and the specificity of the issues it handles, Hamann's letter to Kraus is also a key to more general and fundamental differences between these two contemporaries. One significant clue appears near the beginning of the letter, when Hamann first speaks of Kant. In calling attention to the *Gleichnis*, the parable or metaphor at the heart of Kant's definition of enlightenment, Hamann is demonstrating his own critical method, which he calls "aesthetic,"[18] in contrast to the "dialectical" method preferred by Kant. Oswald Bayer notes the irony in this situation: "The strict 'dialectician' Kant, 'professor of logic and critic of pure reason,' employs a metaphor [*Gleichnis*] without being aware of it, thus explaining the 'Enlightenment' aesthetically."[19] No better example could be found to illustrate Hamann's relationship to Kantian philosophy, the relationship expressed technically in the title of Hamann's best-known treatment of Kant, the "Metacritique of the Purism of Reason."[20]

Hamann composed this brief but trenchant analysis of Kant's *Critique of Pure Reason* in the same year as the letter to Kraus, 1784, but did not publish

---

18. "Poetry is the mother-tongue of the human race," Hamann writes in his *Aesthetica in nuce*; and "parables [*Gleichnisse*] [are] older than reasoning." Hamann, *Sämtliche Werke*, ed. Josef Nadler (Vienna: Herder, 1949–57), 2:197; trans. in *German Aesthetic and Literary Criticism: Winckelmann, Lessing, Hamann, Herder, Schiller, Goethe*, ed. H. B. Nisbet (New York: Cambridge University Press, 1985), 141.

19. Bayer, "Selbstverschuldete Vormundschaft," 17–18.

20. Hamann, "Metakritik über den Purismum der Vernunft," in *Sämtliche Werke*, 3:281–89. A translation by Ronald Gregor Smith can be found in "Metacritique of the Purism of Reason," in *J. G. Hamann, 1730–1788: A Study in Christian Existence* (New York: Harper & Brothers, 1960).

it during his lifetime because of his friendship with Kant. Largely on the basis of Hamann's "Metacritique," Frederick Beiser calls him "the most original, powerful, and influential critic" of Kant's attempt to vindicate the "Enlightenment faith in the universality and impartiality of reason."[21] The radicalness of Hamann's critique of the Kantian critical philosophy is concentrated in the prefix "meta-," which Rudolf Unger credits him with introducing into German philosophical discussion.[22] For that tiny prefix does to Kant's project the one thing it cannot tolerate: it relativizes the critical philosophy by placing it within a more basic context of interpretation. As Beiser puts it, "The tribunal of critique spoke with such awesome authority not only because its principles were self-evident, but also because they were universal and impartial."[23] If a *meta*critique is possible, the critique loses its claim to these qualities, and thus to its foundational status.

Hamann's principal objection to Kant's philosophy, expressed in the title he chose, is its "purism"—that is, its attempt to rid knowledge of any intrinsic connection with tradition, experience, or language. Hamann foreshadows a broad range of twentieth-century thinkers who have found in language the key to philosophical conundrums. An example would be Ludwig Wittgenstein's insistence that the "meaning" of words is rooted in their actual use in ordinary language and its associated forms of life, rather than in some "essence" to be abstracted from it. Hamann's stress on tradition likewise presages the attention of later thinkers to the cultural location of ideas and systems of thought. Hamann calls language "the only, the first and the last instrument and criterion of reason" and affirms its "genealogical priority . . . over the seven holy functions of logical propositions and inferences."[24] Kant's wish to "purify" philosophy of its dependence on language rests, according to Hamann, on "nothing more than an old and cold prejudice for mathematics."[25] Hamann expresses with particular clarity the antithesis between the foundational roles of language in his own thought and reason in Kant's in a letter to Friedrich Heinrich Jacobi written in 1784, the same year as both the "Metacritique" and the letter to Kraus: "For me the question

21. Beiser, *Fate of Reason*, 8–9.
22. Rudolf Unger, *Hamann und die Aufklärung: Studien zur Vorgeschichte des romantischen Geistes im 18. Jahrhundert* (Jena: Eugen Diederichs, 1911), 1:526. However, Hamann himself is ironic in his use of "meta-," calling it "the casual synthesis of a Greek prefix." "Metacritique of the Purism of Reason" (*Sämtliche Werke*, 3:285; Smith, *J. G. Hamann*, 215).
23. Beiser, *Fate of Reason*, 8.
24. Hamann, "Metacritique of the Purism of Reason" (*Sämtliche Werke*, 3:284, 286; Smith, *J. G. Hamann*, 215, 216).
25. Hamann, "Metacritique of the Purism of Reason" (*Sämtliche Werke*, 3:285; Smith, *J. G. Hamann*, 216).

is not so much What is reason? as What is language? It is here I suspect the basis of all paralogisms and antinomies can be found which are ascribed to reason: it comes from words being held to be concepts, and concepts to be the things themselves."[26] Hamann's appeal to language and experience as the ground of reason rests on a still more basic disagreement with Kant. For if one asks why language should be the criterion of reason, Hamann appeals to the priority of the sensual over the intellectual, which amounts to an appeal to the bodily—and even sexual—basis of human language, experience, and thought. Here we encounter the most surprising of Hamann's anticipations of later thinkers. A century before Freud, the pivotal importance of sexuality was acknowledged by a thinker whose life, values, and philosophical principles are about as far from Freud's as one could possibly imagine.

Hamann's emphasis on sexuality follows from his insistence on the priority of sense over intellect.[27] Language, rather than "pure" reason, has philosophical priority because "the whole ability to think rest[s] upon language"; but language in turn depends on the body. "Sounds and letters are therefore pure forms *a priori*," he says in contrast to Kant. "Music was the oldest language, and next to the palpable rhythm of the pulse and the breath in the nostril was the original bodily image of all measurement of time and its numerical relations."[28] Hamann's point in stressing the bodily foundation of thought is not, however, to exalt sense over reason; he intends, rather, to restore the original integrity that Kant's purism threatens. Since "sensibility and understanding spring as two branches of human knowledge from one common root," he writes, Kant errs by perpetrating "an arbitrary, improper and self-willed divorce of that which nature has joined together."

Hamann's treatment of sexuality differs from other writers who use sexual imagery and analogies because, as O'Flaherty points out, "his allusions stem from an epistemological principle."[29] That principle is rooted in Hamann's holistic conception of human nature, which, W. M. Alexander argues, has been "secularized in Romanticism and distorted in Kierkegaard and existentialism."[30] Hamann's point is not to exalt will over intellect or emotions

26. Johann Georg Hamann, *Briefwechsel*, ed. Arthur Henkel (Frankfurt: Insel-Verlag, 1965), 5:264–65. I have revised the translation in Smith, *J. G. Hamann*, 249.

27. For an instructive treatment of the theme of sexuality in Hamann, see O'Flaherty, *Johann Georg Hamann*, chap. 2, esp. 38–42.

28. Hamann, "Metacritique of the Purism of Reason" (*Sämtliche Werke*, 3:286; Smith, *J. G. Hamann*, 217).

29. O'Flaherty, *Johann Georg Hamann*, 40.

30. W. M. Alexander, *Johann Georg Hamann: Philosophy and Faith* (The Hague: Martinus Nijhoff, 1966), 177.

over reason but rather to respect the integrity of what nature—and God—has joined together. The error of Kantian purism is that it violates the bodily basis of that integrity: "*Sensus* is the principle of all *intellectus*";[31] "the *heart* beats before the *head* thinks."[32] Hamann is also capable of making the point in explicitly sexual terms. "The *pudenda* of our nature," he wrote to Johann Friedrich Hartknoch (once again in 1784), "are so closely connected with the chambers of the heart and the brain that too strict an abstraction of such a natural bond is impossible."[33] Some years earlier he had confessed to Johann Gottfried Herder that "my crude imagination has never been able to picture a creative spirit without genitalia."[34] Hamann's unflinching insistence on the importance of sexuality—its *epistemological* importance, in particular—sets him apart from all the major voices of his time, whether those of Enlightenment rationalism, theological orthodoxy, or the "neologians," the theological progressives of his day.

The Theological Foundation of Hamann's Critique

Hamann's unfashionable attention to sex turns out to provide an unexpected clue to the underlying motive of his attack on Kant and the Enlightenment. At the root of his philosophical and political critique is a theological commitment to biblical revelation. The earthiness of his view of human nature and human knowledge probably owes more to his immersion in the Bible and the writings of Luther than to any contemporary influences. Hamann's break with the Enlightenment had come, after all, as a direct result of his own dramatic, if rather mysterious, conversion in London in 1758. From the day he arrived back in Königsberg to the end of his life, he demonstrated an unflagging tenacity in his adherence to a Christian sensibility that left him immune to the endeavors of his enlightened friends, including Kant, to win him back to the cause, and made him remarkably independent of the spirit of the age.

Hamann liked to describe his own vocation as "spermalogian," a term whose ambiguity links the theological and sexual themes in his thought. It is first of all a biblical term (Acts 17:18), whose literal meaning ("picking up seeds," used of birds) had come to be used metaphorically of persons to

31. Letter to Jacobi, November 14, 1784, in Hamann, *Briefwechsel*, 6:27.
32. Letter to Hans Jacob von Auerswald, July 28, 1785, in Hamann, *Briefwechsel*, 6:27; trans. from Alexander, *Johann Georg Hamann*, 177.
33. Hamann, *Briefwechsel*, 4:167; I have revised the trans. in Alexander, *Johann Georg Hamann*, 177–78.
34. Letter to Herder, May 23, 1768, in Hamann, *Briefwechsel*, 2:415.

mean "gossip," "chatterer," or "babbler."[35] Interpreters of Hamann are in general agreement, however, that he intends the sexual implications of the word as well. In his biblical commentary written shortly after his conversion in London, Hamann comments that "our reason should be impregnated by the seed of the divine word . . . and live as man and wife under one roof." The devil endeavors, he says, to disrupt this marital bliss, seeking not only "to put asunder what God has joined together" but "in our times to institute a formal divorce between them, and to titillate the reason through systems, dreams, etc."[36] The Bible should be our criterion, "our dictionary, our linguistics, on which all the concepts and speech of the Christian are founded."[37] Reason, on the other hand, plays a role for the Christian analogous to that of the law for the apostle Paul. Hamann put it this way in 1759:

> The commandment of reason is holy, just, and good. But is it given to us—to make us wise? No more than the law of the Jews was given to justify them, but rather to convince us of the opposite: how unreasonable our reason is; that our errors are to be increased by it, just as sin was increased by the law. If everywhere Paul speaks of the law one puts *reason*—the law of our century and the watchword of our wise men and scribes—then Paul will speak to our contemporaries.[38]

Twenty-four years later he used the same analogy in a letter to Jacobi: "You know that I think of reason as St. Paul does of the whole law and its righteousness—that I expect of it nothing but the recognition of error, and do not regard it as a way to truth and life."[39] Human reason, unfertilized by the Word of God, concludes the self-professed "spermalogian," is like the law without the gospel, like the letter without the life-giving spirit: while retaining its formal validity, it nevertheless kills.

Given the vast difference between Hamann's theologically grounded "linguistics" and Kant's philosophical commitment to a critical "purism," their disagreement about the Enlightenment quest for maturity was inevitable. The gulf separating Hamann from Kant and his contemporaries has not always been sufficiently taken into account by his interpreters. Even Oswald Bayer,

---

35. William F. Arndt and F. Wilbur Gingrich, *A Greek-English Lexicon of the New Testament and Other Early Christian Literature* (Chicago: University of Chicago Press, 1957), 769.
36. *Sämtliche Werke*, 1:52–53.
37. *Sämtliche Werke*, 1:243.
38. Letter to Johann Gotthelf Lindner, July 3, 1759, in Hamann, *Briefwechsel*, 1:355–56. I have revised the translation in Alexander, *Johann Georg Hamann*, 153.
39. Letter to Jacobi, November 2, 1783, in Hamann, *Briefwechsel*, 5:95, following the translation in Smith, *J. G. Hamann*, 248.

who as a theologian himself is aware of the theological basis of Hamann's critique, portrays him as a radical *Aufklärer*, one in whom "the Enlightenment is driven further, radicalized."[40] But when a position is so radicalized that its basic premise and criterion of truth is called into question, that amounts to a new position, not an extension of the old. This becomes even clearer in Hamann's attack on the ideal of "purism" so fundamental to the whole project of critical philosophy. Such a position is not just a correction of Kant but a fundamental rejection in favor of another and more adequate criterion. Hamann's method is more like Hegel's practice of showing how the dialectical tensions within a position finally cause it to collapse into its opposite. A more contemporary comparison might be deconstruction, which tries to subvert the text by turning its own unacknowledged premises against it. As Bayer himself repeatedly emphasizes, Hamann's objective is not to reform Kant but to *convert* him. It is a battle between advocates of rival absolutes, not a disagreement among fellow *Aufklärer*. Bayer is right in rejecting the interpretation of Hamann as an "irrationalist." But he apparently assumes that the only alternative to enlightenment is "irrationality." Since this term does not adequately describe Hamann's position, Bayer is forced to see him as some kind of enlightener. But Hamann speaks on behalf of a radically *different* concept of reason from that of the *Aufklärer*—one based not on human autonomy but on the "fear of the Lord."

On one point Hamann and Kant agree: the root of the issue is religious. In his essay on enlightenment, Kant explicitly identifies "*matters of religion* as the focal point of enlightenment," and argues accordingly that "religious immaturity is the most pernicious and dishonourable variety of all."[41] Their basic difference, not surprisingly, is also religious, and it is epitomized in the root metaphor of *Mündigkeit*. Just as Kant's commitment to the purism of reason led him to the metaphor of adult maturity, so Hamann's allegiance to the Bible suggested a different image: "Truly, I say to you, unless you turn and become like children, you will never enter the kingdom of heaven" (Matt. 18:3). When Hamann died in Münster in 1788, Dutch philosopher François Hemsterhuis chose as the inscription for his tombstone a passage from the apostle Paul—one that Hamann himself was fond of citing, and one that epitomizes his Christian critique of the Enlightenment:

> To the Jews an offense
> to the Greeks foolishness,

---

40. Bayer, *Zeitgenosse im Widerspruch: Johann Georg Hamann als radikaler Aufklärer* (Munich: Piper, 1988), 145.
41. Kant, "What Is Enlightenment?" (*AA* 8:41; Reiss 59).

but God elected the foolish things
of the world to confound the wise,
and God elected the weak things of
the world to confound the strong.[42]

As the Magus himself might well have added, "and God elected the immature
of the world to confound the guardians."

---

42. First Corinthians 1:23, 27, cited according to the translation in Alexander, *Johann Georg Hamann*, 13. The original Latin (from the Vulgate) can be found in Sven-Aage Jørgensen, *Johann Georg Hamann* (Stuttgart: J. B. Metzlersche Verlagsbuchhandlung, 1976), 95.

10

KANT AS CHRISTIAN APOLOGIST

The Failure of Accommodationist Theology

A strong case can be made that the dominant issues of Christian theology in the past two centuries have their roots in the remarkable half-century of German thought "from Kant to Hegel."[1] The age of German idealism in philosophy overlapped both the classical literary age of Goethe and Schiller and the rise of the Romantic movement throughout Europe. One historian of modern Christian thought, James Livingston, maintains that the "works of Kant, Schleiermacher, and Hegel alone determined the course of theology for at least the next century and a half."[2] Because these thinkers have so greatly influenced the response of Christian theology to the modern world, they remain essential reading for theologians today. Whether one expects to find paradigms useful for doing theology in our own day, or whether one seeks a therapy for the theological blunders of past generations—in either case, it would be folly to ignore these seminal modern thinkers.

Two crucial texts for understanding nineteenth- and twentieth-century Christian thought—Kant's *Religion within the Limits of Reason Alone* and

1. Richard Kroner's classic study *Von Kant bis Hegel*, 2nd ed. (Tübingen: Mohr Siebeck, 1961) is just one of the many interpretations of German idealism and related movements.
2. James C. Livingston, *Modern Christian Thought: From the Enlightenment to Vatican II* (New York: Macmillan, 1971), 143.

Schleiermacher's *Speeches on Religion*—appeared in the decade prior to 1800. These works exemplify patterns that came to typify theology in the following century. They are paradigmatic in the double sense of the term: they not only foreshadow the trends of subsequent theology but also help to bring them about; they are both the heralds of the future and its exemplary models. This paradigmatic quality lies behind such familiar epithets as Schleiermacher the "father of modern Protestant theology" and Kant the "philosopher of Protestantism." As slippery as such labels can be, they aid in the important task of recognizing the nodal points in the flow of history, of trying to see the forest as well as the individual trees. Interpretation—the name of this elusive search for illuminating patterns—is the characterizing feature of all the human sciences, including theology. In this chapter I am undertaking a project of *historical theology*, in the sense that Claude Welch differentiates it from both "theology of history" and "history of theology." That is, I approach Kant's work with explicitly theological as well as historical questions. I am concerned with the "viability of the Christian theological enterprise" and "with *how* the past illumines and contributes to the present."[3]

I will argue that Kant's *Religion within the Limits of Reason Alone* undertakes two interconnected projects not clearly distinguished by the author himself—one philosophical and descriptive, the other theological and normative. This seminal work is not simply the critical philosophy of religion that it has usually been taken to be but is also a work of theological apologetics that makes bold claims on behalf of the Christian religion. Moreover, I hope to show that Kant's reinterpretation of Christianity became the prototype for the mediating Protestant theologies of the nineteenth century and their heirs to this day, Roman Catholic as well as Protestant. The success or failure of Kant's apologetic project in *Religion within the Limits of Reason Alone* is therefore a crucial question for historical theology, with important implications for systematic and philosophical theology right up to the present. My theological thesis emerges out of these historical conclusions. Taking Nietzsche's attack on Kantian practical reason as a touchstone, I will argue that historic Christianity cannot survive Kant's attempted translation. The price of accommodating Christian doctrine and symbols in this way to the presuppositions of modernity is the sacrificing of the essential "positivity" of the gospel—a price that the church should refuse to pay.

3. Claude Welch, "The Perils of Trying to Tell the Whole Story: Current Efforts and Their Historiographical Issues," in *Papers of the Nineteenth Century Theology Working Group*, vol. 18, ed. Claude Welch and Richard Crouter (Colorado Springs: Colorado College, 1992), 64 (emphasis original).

Kant's Two Projects in the *Religion*

Gordon Michalson, in *Fallen Freedom*, his insightful study of Kant's struggle to reconcile his moral philosophy with the radical evil in human nature, offers an illuminating account of the motives underlying the whole project of Kant's philosophy of religion in the context of modern religious thought. Michalson argues that "intellectually sophisticated religious thought" of the past two centuries "has become the sustained search for a substitute for supernatural-ism in the account of faith and transcendence." In pursuit of this goal, he maintains, "this liberal tradition has been remarkably inventive in its efforts to transpose the 'real' point of the religious message out of traditional terms defined by supernatural intervention and into terms that find a secure fit in human consciousness and history." Kant plays a pivotal role in this liberal quest by setting the terms of the search and contributing key concepts. "It was Kant's genius," according to Michalson, "to show how . . . to have both science and religion without obvious intellectual sacrifice."[4]

What makes Kant's project—and Michalson's book—so interesting, how-ever, is a profound and destabilizing ambiguity at the very heart of the Kantian quest, producing in his thought what Michalson calls a "series of wobbles."[5] Michalson's account of the ambiguity in Kant's thought is illuminating and for the most part convincing, but I think he misses a key element of its mo-tivation and significance. By highlighting that element, Kant's apologetic strategy, I hope to bring into clearer focus the theological issues raised by *Religion within the Limits of Reason Alone*. Michalson believes that Kant's "wobbling" results from a retrograde element in his thought, the fact that he "has not totally thrown off the habits of mind produced by Christian culture."[6] Specifically, Kant has failed to divest himself of the "thought forms of the Reformation even as he tries to do justice to the newly emergent claims of the Enlightenment, producing a mingling of idioms that is sometimes exasperat-ing but always telling."[7] It is abundantly clear that Kant mingles the idioms of Christian orthodoxy and Enlightened modernity, and that the mixture is unstable. It is not so clear, however, either that Kant *wants* to "throw off" these Christian thought forms, or that he *ought* to do so. We might say in-stead that Kant fails to resist certain habits of mind produced by modern secular culture. Friedrich Nietzsche, a far less sympathetic interpreter than

4. Gordon E. Michalson Jr., *Fallen Freedom: Kant on Radical Evil and Moral Regeneration* (New York: Cambridge University Press, 1990), 2.

5. Michalson, *Fallen Freedom*, 28; see also 9, 89, and chap. 7.

6. Michalson, *Fallen Freedom*, 9.

7. Michalson, *Fallen Freedom*, 6–7.

Michalson of both Kant and Christianity, concludes that Kant is "in the end, an underhanded Christian."[8] The intriguing notion of Kant as *hinterlistiger Christ*, I am convinced, is borne out by a careful reading of his philosophy of religion. And Christian theologians, for reasons quite different from Nietzsche's, ought to be particularly wary of such a project.

Kant's "wobbling" in his book on religion results from his largely unacknowledged attempt to carry out two projects at once. The explicit thesis, as promised by the book's title, is the construction of what Kant calls pure rational faith. He has already argued in the *Critique of Practical Reason* that certain basic religious "postulates" are the necessary implications of reason employed practically. Or, as he puts it at the outset of *Religion within the Limits of Reason Alone*, "Morality leads unavoidably to religion."[9] He outlines the resulting natural theology in the four books of the *Religion*, which correspond generally to the traditional Christian dogmatic loci of creation and fall, justification (Christology), ecclesiology, and sanctification. The second implicit project of Kant's philosophy of religion is the identification and critique of religion "beyond the limits of reason alone." This aspect, which the Enlightenment called "positive" religion, includes all those features of traditional religion that are opaque to reason—especially teachings based on alleged historical occurrences, appeals to authority, and ritual practices not clearly based on reason or morality. The project of "depositivizing" Christian teachings runs concurrently, as a kind of subtext, to Kant's philosophy of pure rational religion.

Though the expressions *positivity* and *positive religion* seldom appear in recent writings, they have a long history in Western thought. Enlightenment thinkers before Kant were accustomed to dividing religion into *positive* and *natural* forms. This usage is dependent on two common distinctions in medieval thought. The use of *positive* and *natural* as coordinate terms rests on a long-standing distinction in the field of law. Deriving from the past participle *positus* of the Latin verb *ponere* (to put, place, lay down), *positive* laws are those laid down or "posited" by divine or human authority; they have their

8. Friedrich Nietzsche, "Die 'Vernunft' in der Philosophie" ("'Reason' in Philosophy") 6, in *Götzen-Dämmerung (Twilight of the Idols)*, in *Kritische Studienausgabe*, ed. Giorgio Colli and Mazzino Montinari (Berlin: de Gruyter, 1967–77), 6:79 (my translation).

9. Immanuel Kant, *Die Religion innerhalb der Grenzen der bloßen Vernunft*, vol. 6 of *Kant's gesammelte Schriften*, ed. Königlich Preußische Akademie der Wissenschaften (Berlin: Georg Reimer, 1914), 6. English translation available in *Religion within the Limits of Reason Alone*, trans. Theodore M. Greene and Hoyt H. Hudson (New York: Harper, 1960), 5. Subsequent references to these volumes will be made parenthetically, the page number to the German edition followed by the English edition; though the translations are my own, references to the published English translation are also provided for the convenience of the reader.

ultimate foundation in the will of the lawgiver. *Natural* laws, on the other hand, are grounded in eternal rational principles and hence are available to unaided reason. The adoption of the distinction between positive and natural into the philosophy of religion was especially convenient for Enlightenment rationalists, since their use of the term *religion* included what the Middle Ages had called *lex* or *jus*; that is, they generally assumed that religion was constituted essentially by laws or commands. Matthew Tindal, for example, argues in his *Christianity as Old as the Creation* (1730), a classic of English deism that was in Kant's library, that there is no difference between morality and religion, except that the one is "acting according to the Reason of Things consider'd in themselves; the other, acting according to the same Reason of Things consider'd as the Will of God."[10] This doctrine provides Kant with his basic definition of religion.[11]

When modern rationalists applied the old legal distinction between *positive* and *natural* to religion, they also drew on the related medieval distinction between *revealed* and *natural* theology. St. Thomas Aquinas distinguished the principles of natural reason from the principles of faith, revealed in Scripture and articulated by the fathers of the church.[12] For the rationalists of the Enlightenment, the phrase *positive religions* became a brief designation for the actual religions of the world, all of which were understood to derive their authority from some historical occurrence, usually an original teacher or founder. Since this historical origin was regularly thought to involve revelation (understood to be the supersensible receiving of propositional religious truth), *revealed* religion was usually synonymous with *positive* religion. The terminology of natural and revealed religion was the usual language of the English rationalists and the Germans before Kant.

Because the rationalists of the seventeenth and eighteenth centuries contrasted these historically revealed religions with the natural religion of reason, the term *positive* took on a pejorative connotation, which was generally maintained whenever the term was used by the German idealists and their nineteenth-century successors. With the discrediting of the Enlightenment version of natural religion, positive religion (as its counterpart) likewise ceased to be employed as a familiar category by philosophers and theologians. The first edition of *Die Religion in Geschichte und Gegenwart*, published in 1913,

---

10. Matthew Tindal, *Christianity as Old as the Creation*, ed. Günter Gawlick (1730; repr., Stuttgart–Bad Cannstatt: Friedrich Frommann Verlag [Günther Holzboog], 1967), 298.

11. "Religion is (subjectively regarded) the cognition of all our duties *as* divine commands" (*Religion within the Limits of Reason Alone*, 153/142; emphasis original, although the published English translation does not indicate it).

12. See, e.g., *Summa theologiae* 1a.1.8.

included a definition of positivity that offers a summary of its earlier usage and provides a convenient preliminary definition for its use by Kant. The element of the positive, according to this definition, refers to "what is factually given in contrast to what is derived from general concepts or principles, to what is logically constructed; thus *positive religions* are the actual, historical religions appealing to divine revelation in contrast to 'natural religion.'"[13] The omission of this entry in the third edition of this reference work (1957–65) indicates the progressive disappearance of the term in later theological discussion.[14]

Interspersed in Kant's constructive argument on behalf of his version of natural religion are polemical thrusts against positive religion. He does not treat the polemical aspect of the *Religion* with the same consistent organization that he devotes to his constructive case; but a number of factors, all of which Kant sees as threats to rational religion, reveal a generally consistent pattern. Taken together, these elements of positivity constitute a coherent structure of positive religion, a kind of antitheology with an inner logic of its own, opposed fundamentally to the Kantian theology of religion within the limits of reason alone. The difficulty of isolating Kant's own view of natural religion is due in part to the fact that it is mixed with this ongoing polemic against positive religion.

Kant's critique of positivity also serves an apologetic function in the argument of the *Religion*: he intends to reinterpret historic Christian faith by purging it of its positivity. Though Kant was exceptionally well-informed for an eighteenth-century European about other religions of the world (as is evident in a number of passages and notes in his book), it should be clear to any reader that a Christian context is assumed throughout. Kant generally avoids making explicit reference to Christian churches, creeds, theologians, and dogmas, but their presence is only thinly disguised. Since he knew that he was writing for the government censor as well as for his philosophical public, he may have had political motives for disguising the theological implications of his argument. Instead of indulging in the dubious hermeneutics of the author's mind, however, I base my conclusions on the public text of his *Religion*. What emerges is an apologetic reinterpretation of the Christian faith, whose major thesis is that essential Christianity conforms to "pure rational faith" and depends to no significant degree on "positive" doctrines or practices. He

13. "Positiv," *Die Religion in Geschichte und Gegenwart*, 1st ed., ed. Friedrich Michael Schiele and Leopold Zscharnack (1909–13), 4:1685.

14. For further discussion of the concept of positivity at the end of the eighteenth century, see Garrett Green, "Positive Religion in the Early Philosophy of the German Idealists" (PhD diss., Yale University, 1971). Chapters 1–2 analyze Kant's *Religion* at greater length than is possible here. Several passages from these two chapters appear here in slightly revised form.

can even claim that "of all the public religions which have ever existed, the Christian alone is moral" (51–52/47).

The term *positive* occurs in a few passages of the *Religion*. Kant speaks, for example, of "positive doctrines of revelation [*positiver Offenbarungslehren*]" (157/145) and of a "positive law of revelation [*positives . . . Offenbarungsgesetz*]" (187/175). Finally, he speaks very generally about believing "what is positive [*Positives*]" (188/176) in religion. More often he refers to positive religion using various terms denoting its specific aspects or manifestations: "ecclesiastical faith," "historical faith," "statutory religion," "religion of divine worship," or "revealed religion." How these terms relate to a general concept of positivity is never explicit in Kant, but it is implicit in his presentation and argument. One particularly compact sentence illustrates the close relation of these aspects of positivity: "There can be no doubt that the legislation of [God's] will ought to be solely *moral*; for statutory legislation (which presupposes a revelation) can be regarded merely as contingent and as something which never has applied or can apply to every man, hence as not binding upon all men universally" (104/95). The logic of positive religion as seen by Kant thus involves the interrelations of such elements as morality (the key term), statutory laws, revelation, contingency, and universality.

"Depositivizing" the Christian Religion

Kant's Christian apologetic is most obvious in the last book of the *Religion*, where he belatedly defines *religion* and offers a rather bewildering typology of the different varieties of religion. The project is implicit in the very definition of religion: "the cognition of all duties *as* divine commands" (153/142). The pivotal term "*as*" (whose emphasis by Kant is omitted by his English translators) stands as a kind of fulcrum between potentially equal quantities, corresponding to natural (rational or moral) religion and positive religion.[15] This definition sets up the conceptual apparatus for Kant's apologetic argument that in the case of Christianity, the two are in fact equivalent. Far from being mutually exclusive, positive and natural religion can coincide ("in this case," he writes, "the religion is *objectively* a natural one though *subjectively* a revealed one" [156/144]); and the heart of his apologetic is the claim that Christianity is the only historical example of such a happy coincidence of subject and object. Both have the same content; they differ only in form.

15. For a discussion of the important logic of the connective *as* in modern religious thought, see Garrett Green, *Imagining God: Theology and the Religious Imagination* (Grand Rapids: Eerdmans, 1998), 134–41.

The error, Kant claims, lies in trying to make what ought to be mere form—positivity—into the essential content, that is, the case of a "religion which, because of its inner constitution [*inneren Beschaffenheit*], can be regarded only as revealed" (156/144).

The more interesting and fruitful arena for observing Kant as Christian apologist, however, is not the confusing and formalistic apparatus in book four but rather the actual examples of the apologetic at work at key points throughout *Religion within the Limits of Reason Alone*. The hermeneutical key to this work is the author's constant attempt to carry out his tandem projects at once: the construction of "pure rational faith" and the argument that Christianity—stripped of its positivity—can be interpreted as such a faith. The key *theological* point at stake is the concomitant claim that the positivity of the Christian religion is merely formal and can thus be eliminated without loss to Christian truth.

The first occurrence of Kant's dual strategy is in book one, where he presents his philosophical argument that human nature is radically evil and reinterprets the Christian doctrine of original sin accordingly. No better evidence could be found against classifying Kant as a typical thinker of the Enlightenment. If naïve optimism about human nature is a characteristic feature of Enlightenment anthropology, Kant clearly violates its spirit at this point. He chooses to introduce his treatise on religion by investigating and describing the dynamics of what he calls "radical evil" in human nature. He delineates its logic with great precision, seeking on the one hand to refute the simple optimism of moralists "from *Seneca* to *Rousseau*" (20/16), but on the other hand to avoid making evil so essentially a part of human nature that the nerve of moral responsibility is severed. Concern with this delicate distinction, of course, has run throughout the history of Christian thought at least since the time of Augustine. Kant, though he struggles valiantly to reconcile moral autonomy with the idea that human beings are innately evil, emerges a Pelagian in the end.[16] Why does he arrive at a moralistic conclusion after seeing so clearly the superficiality of earlier moralists? Michalson calls radical evil "the most profound threat . . . the riderless horse in Kant's total vision" and the root of the "vicious circularity" that bedevils his entire philosophy, leading him in the end to an illegitimate appeal to divine grace.[17] While agreeing with Michalson's interpretation of Kant's argument, I would account for the

16. Space does not allow for a presentation of the evidence for this conclusion, but it has been extensively documented elsewhere. See Green, "Positive Religion," esp. 16–27. The same conclusion has been reached by Michalson (see *Fallen Freedom*, esp. 7, 102, and 132, where he comments on Kant's "basically Pelagian instincts").

17. Michalson, *Fallen Freedom*, 18, 26, 28.

Kantian religious dilemma rather differently. It is not as though he set out "to have human autonomy succeed God"[18] and then unaccountably adopted a doctrine of radical evil that could only be overcome by an illicit appeal to grace; rather, Kant is forced to confront *both* his nemeses—radical evil and divine grace—for the same reason: he does not wish to leave Christianity behind on the ash heap of history in favor of a secular ethical rationalism, but wants rather to *rescue* Christian doctrine from the paralysis of supernaturalist orthodoxy and show its compatibility, indeed virtual identity, with "pure rational faith." Radical evil and divine grace present him with such difficulties because they are the aspects of Christian teaching that stand in the greatest tension with Enlightened moral autonomy.

His dual strategy is evident in the way that Christian language and concepts—most notably original sin—emerge in the argument of book one. He does not begin, in the fashion of the theological apologist, with original sin and then seek to show its compatibility with Enlightened rationality. Rather, he begins as the critical philosopher, expounding a doctrine of radical evil "within the limits of reason alone" and then developing it in such a way that (lo and behold!) we discover that we have arrived at the very insights contained in the positive teachings of biblical faith. After constructing his philosophical account of evil, he can announce that "the foregoing agrees well with the manner of presentation [*Vorstellungsart*] that Scripture employs, whereby the origin of evil is depicted as having a *beginning* in the human race" (41/36). The distinguishing feature of the biblical treatment of evil is its presentation "in a narrative," whereby the philosophical priority of evil is translated into *temporal* categories. Once we make allowances for this formal difference, we can see that both accounts make the same point. In a highly significant footnote, Kant summarizes the key hermeneutical principle. "It is possible," he claims, "to explain how an historical account can be put to moral use without deciding whether this is the author's meaning as well or merely our own interpretation [*oder wir ihn nur hineinlegen*]" (47n/39n). He urges that historical issues be bracketed since they have "no valid relation to everyone"—that is, because they lack universality. He assigns them to "the adiaphora," the class of theologically neutral matters about which individuals may freely differ.

The dual strategy of Kant's *Religion* reappears in book two, when he turns to the solution of the problem of radical evil. Here is the culmination of his intricate attempt to preserve the moral autonomy fundamental to rational religion while showing that Christianity, rightly interpreted, contains

---

18. Michalson, *Fallen Freedom*, 140.

the same teachings. If any more evidence were needed to demonstrate Kant's apologetic interest, the presence of what amounts to a Christology in a book on the religion of reason should be the clincher. Without providing a detailed account of Kant's complete doctrine of salvation and regeneration,[19] I will focus here on a question at the very heart of the Kantian project: the issue of divine righteousness, which Kant himself calls the most difficult problem. Though he never mentions the fact explicitly, he is here dealing with the central issue of Reformation theology, as his choice of terms indicates: he refers to his own solution of the problem of divine righteousness as a "deduction of the idea of a *justification*" (76/70). His reason for *not* discussing the historical background is his desire to deal with religious problems *rationally*—"within the limits of [practical] reason alone." The entire enterprise deliberately abstracts from every particular experience and proceeds as a kind of project of thought. To put the discussion into historical perspective might compromise the universality of the project; Kant, at any rate, has little interest in the history of theology. He is, after all, trying to discover the one, true, rational meaning of religion in general.

The key problem is the following: "Whatever a man may have done in the way of adopting a good disposition, and, indeed, however steadfastly he may have persevered in conduct conformable to such a disposition, *he nevertheless started from evil*, and this debt he can by no possibility wipe out" (72/66). It is impossible, he reasons, for anyone to earn a surplus of merit after adopting a good disposition, since it is always one's duty to do every possible good; neither is there any way for one person to pay off the debt of sin accrued by another. Kant takes very seriously the state of radical evil that he described so carefully in book one. He draws the pessimistic conclusion that everyone apparently must look forward to endless punishment.

Kant's solution depends on two anthropological distinctions. First, man can be regarded both as a *physical* being ("according to his empirical character as sensible entity") and as a *moral* being ("as intelligible entity"). The other distinction is between a person before and after a "change of heart"; that is, between the "old man" in a state of radical evil (sin) and the "new man" with the perfectly good disposition. Using these two distinctions, Kant seeks to accomplish the following:

> Let us see then whether, by means of the concept of a changed moral attitude, we cannot discover in this very act of reformation such ills as the new man, whose

19. For a fuller account, see Green, "Positive Religion," chap. 1; and Michalson, *Fallen Freedom*, part 2. On most points my account and Michalson's are in close agreement. Some of the differences are addressed below.

disposition is now good, may regard as incurred by himself (in another state) and, therefore, as constituting *punishments* whereby satisfaction is rendered to divine justice. (73–74/67)

Now when a person departs from the life of the old man and enters into a state of righteousness, this amounts to a sacrifice—a sacrificial death of the old man—as well as "an entrance upon a long series of the evils of life." At this point it is important to remember that the "Son of God" in Kant's religion is merely a name for the archetype of the morally perfect disposition. Thus, the new man undertakes this sacrifice and life of trials "in the disposition of the Son of God" (74/68). Using both of the distinctions described above, Kant is able to express the matter as follows:

> Although the man . . . is *physically* the selfsame guilty person as before and must be judged as such before a moral tribunal and hence by himself; yet, because of his new disposition, he is . . . *morally* another in the eyes of a divine judge for whom this disposition takes the place of action. (74/68)

The sharp distinction between the old man and the new man allows Kant to offer real hope of salvation from radical evil without at the same time compromising his moral rigor. The distinction between physical man and moral man, on the other hand, provides a genuine continuity between the old and new man. Kant is faced with the difficult problem of trying simultaneously to affirm an absolute moral change while maintaining the personal identity of the old with the new. He is able to succeed only by relying on one of the most fundamental distinctions in his entire thought: the sensible and the intelligible. Morality (and hence religion) has to do only with the realm of the intelligible; thus, while sensibility provides the necessary substance for radical moral change, it is, strictly speaking, irrelevant to morality. This presupposition is of major importance in Kant's treatment of religious positivity.

It also has interesting immediate consequences for Kant's own theological treatment of justification. For, he says, "if we personify this idea," we can say that the Son of God himself vicariously bears the sacrifice for our sins, redeems us from the consequences of divine justice, and is the advocate for all men before the throne of divine justice. "In this mode of representation [*Vorstellungsart*]," however, "the suffering that the new man, in becoming dead to the *old*, must accept throughout life is represented [*vorgestellt*] as a death endured once for all by the representative of mankind" (74–75/69, emphasis original). Of course, if such a *Vorstellung* were to be taken literally, it would lead to morally destructive consequences as well as grave epistemo-logical problems.[20]

This deduction of justification is the key to Kant's soteriology. For he has now succeeded in solving the problem of divine righteousness by showing that a surplus of merit is after all possible.[21] The new man (alias the Son of God) sacrifices himself for the sins of the old man. Kant is able to conceive such a transaction only by once again introducing a set of dual perspectives. For "what in our earthly life . . . is ever only a *becoming*," he says in reference to the perfect moral disposition, is "credited to us exactly as if we were already in full possession of it" (75/70, emphasis original). One of the perspectives could accurately be called *sub specie Dei*, though recognition of the perspective in no way commits Kant to any assertion about God. He apparently appeals to this dual perspective when he claims that this justification of a man who has changed his moral disposition comes "from grace" but is also "fully in ac-cord with eternal righteousness" (76/70). It looks like grace from the human perspective, where only the "old man" is empirically experienced. From the supersensible vantage point, however—which reason represents as a practical idea—the justification is fully merited by the sacrifice of the "new man."

Kant no sooner completes this deduction of the idea of justification than he begins to fear its misuse. His misgivings about religious doctrines extend even to his own, and he is quick to put it into perspective. He denies that his deduction has any "*positive*" use at all (76/70).[22] It could not help one achieve a good disposition, since the premise of the deduction was that the person in question already possesses one. Likewise, it can be of no use in comforting such an individual, since the possession of a good disposition carries with it its own sense of comfort and hope. "Thus," Kant concludes, "the deduction of the idea has done no more than answer a speculative question," though it is not therefore unimportant. For if the question of a rational idea of moral justification were to be ignored, "reason could be accused of being wholly unable to reconcile with divine justice man's hope of absolution from his guilt—a reproach which might be damaging to reason in many ways, but most

20. On the importance of the concept of *Vorstellung* in Kant's theory of the imagination, see Green, *Imagining God*, 14–16.

21. Michalson puts the issue rather confusingly by speaking of a "surplus of moral debt" (*Fallen Freedom*, 107ff.). (*Any* moral debt constitutes a surplus—or rather a deficit!) As in me-dieval theology, so in Kant, the real problem is how to achieve a surplus of *merit*. The Roman Catholic claim that such a surplus accrues to the Church because of the merits of Christ and the saints became the presupposition for the doctrine of indulgences, the spark that set off Luther's Reformation.

22. Kant evidently uses the term *positive* in its more common meaning as the antithesis of *negative* rather than in the technical sense of positivity, where it is opposed to *natural*.

of all morally" (76/70). Hence negatively Kant's deduction becomes a bulwark against certain religious dangers to morality—dangers that Kant attributes to the positive elements of religion. Briefly, the lesson to be garnered is that nothing short of real moral change—no rituals, no dogmas, no worship—can bring about a person's justification.

But neither should we overlook the positive accomplishment of Kant's "deduction of the idea of a *justification*." At the very point where Christianity appears to be most definitively and hopelessly wedded to positivity—the doctrine of the satisfaction of divine justice through the sacrificial death of the Son of God—Kant has transformed the offensive teaching into the "idea" of "a" justification. In other words, even here at the heart of positive religion he has demonstrated an essential identity between Christian doctrine and "religion within the limits of reason alone." Gone are the appeals to historical particulars and empirical examples; gone, most important of all, is the apparent violation of moral autonomy. Enlightened Christians can breathe a sigh of relief: Professor Kant, the destroyer of supernaturalist orthodoxy, has revealed himself to be the apologist for a new, *true* Christianity!

Kant as "Father of Modern Theology"

By arguing that the Christian religion is the closest historical approximation we have to pure rational faith, Kant establishes himself as the progenitor of a long and distinguished tradition in modern Christian thought. Unlike Hume, whose antimetaphysical skepticism had almost wholly negative implications for traditional belief, Kant swept away the old foundations in order to establish new, more secure ones. He, of course, had announced his intention to do precisely that at the outset of the critical philosophy, in the famous dictum in the second preface to the *Critique of Pure Reason* that he had "found it necessary to deny *knowledge*, in order to make room for *faith*."[23] His interpreters have not always appreciated the extent to which it is precisely the *Christian* faith for which he thinks he has made room. *Religion within the Limits of Reason Alone*, whatever else it may be, is a sophisticated apologetic for the truth of Christianity in an age of Enlightenment.

For this reason, one could plausibly argue that Kant, rather than Schleiermacher, is the first "post-Kantian" Christian thinker, the first of many successors to try to reformulate Christian doctrine in an intellectually defensible form after the demise of metaphysical supernaturalism. "There can be no

23. Kant, *Immanuel Kant's Critique of Pure Reason*, trans. Norman Kemp Smith (New York: St. Martin's Press, 1965), 29 (Bxxx) (emphasis original).

doubt," Hans Frei has written, "that Kant's thought was the crucial dividing point for Protestant theology in the nineteenth century. His thought was like a prism, through which reflection upon all previous philosophy had to pass. All paths led to Kant."[24] The image also implies what Frei does not spell out: that all paths through the nineteenth century diverged again from their common point in Kant's thought. After gathering up the rays of precritical thought, the Kantian prism redirects them into strikingly new patterns.

The pattern to which I wish to call attention is one that shaped the methodology of theologians, especially liberal Protestants, throughout the nineteenth century and beyond. At the root of these methods is a distinction between the form and the content of Christian faith, and an accompanying conviction that for the timelessly valid *content* of Christian truth to become persuasive once again in the modern age, it must be translated out of the untenable *form* of precritical orthodoxy into a mode appropriate to critical modernity. Such theologians differ among themselves about how to correctly characterize the "bad" form of inherited Christianity, and *a fortiori* about how it ought to be trans-formed. Kant anticipates two of the most popular nineteenth-century metaphors for making the form/content distinction: the image of positivity as "only a vehicle which finally can pass over into pure religious faith" (116/107); and the metaphor of the positive "husk" that both protects and obscures the essential "kernel" of religious truth.[25] By far the commonest tendency has been to call for what amounts to a "depositivizing" of Christian teaching, even though most of these thinkers did not make explicit use of the idea of positivity.

Two of the most striking examples are exceptional in their explicit appeal to positivity, however, and both claim to do justice to the positive aspects of religion. Schleiermacher devotes the fifth of the *Speeches* to the multiplicity and particularity of "the religions." He is scathing in his indictment of the Enlightenment prejudice against positivity. "The essence of natural religion consists almost entirely in denying everything positive and characteristic in religion"; he calls natural religion "this empty formless thing."[26] The irony of Schleiermacher's apology for positivity, however, is that he defends it *in general*. "Schleiermacher," writes one commentator, "develops even the necessity

24. Hans W. Frei, "The Academic Tradition in Nineteenth-Century Protestant Theology," in *Faith and Ethics: The Theology of H. Richard Niebuhr*, ed. Paul Ramsey (New York: Harper & Row, 1965), 17.

25. See, for example, Kant's discussion of miracles in the second "General Observation." "We need not call in question any of these miracles and indeed may honor the husk [*Hülle*] which has served to bring into public current a doctrine whose authenticity rests upon a record indelibly registered in every soul and which stands in need of no miracle" (85/79–80).

26. Friedrich Schleiermacher, *On Religion: Speeches to Its Cultured Despisers*, trans. John Oman (New York: Harper, 1958), 233–34.

of the multiplicity of religions out of his concept of religion."[27] He defends the positivity not of Christianity, or of any particular religious tradition, but rather of religion itself.[28] In his own Christian systematic theology he follows a version of Kant's depositivizing methodology, first locating a religious essence in human affect or feeling and then interpreting Christian doctrines as *"accounts of the Christian religious affections set forth in speech."*[29] Without minimizing the significance of Schleiermacher's rejection of the Kantian identification of religion with morality, his program can nevertheless be seen as a methodological variation on a theme by Kant. *The* great quarrel in modern Christian thought has been about rightly distinguishing form and content. Here both Kant and Schleiermacher are on the same side of the issue: both want to interpret Scripture and doctrine as forms expressive of a prior content. That this content is rational for Kant and affective for Schleiermacher is no doubt a major difference for some purposes; but in terms of the great form/content debate they are in fundamental agreement.

The other nineteenth-century thinker who attended explicitly to the issue of positivity was Hegel. In an early fragmentary essay entitled "The Positivity of the Christian Religion," the youthful Hegel, still under the strong influence of Kant, argues for the elimination of positivity in favor of an ethical rationalism.[30] More interesting is the change in his mature viewpoint, where he argues for the necessity of religion taking on positive forms. Religion, the second form of absolute spirit, is characterized by positivity in the mode of *Vorstellung*,[31] and Hegel argues that it achieves its supreme expression in Protestant Christianity. In the end, however, he calls for the *Aufhebung* of religious positivity—even in its absolute, Christian mode—into the pure intelligibility of the concept.[32] Hegel, too, in other words, offers us another variation on a

27. Friedrich Hertel, *Das theologische Denken Schleiermachers: Untersucht an der ersten Auflage seiner Reden "Ueber die Religion"* (Zurich: Zwingli Verlag, 1965), 137 (my translation).

28. A more complete analysis of Schleiermacher on positivity can be found in Green, "Positive Religion," 264–74.

29. Schleiermacher, *The Christian Faith*, ed. and trans. H. R. Mackintosh and J. S. Stewart (New York: Harper & Row, 1963), 1:76 (§15) (emphasis original).

30. The piece was first published in Herman Nohl's edition of *Hegels theologische Jugendschriften* (1907; repr., Frankfurt: Minerva, 1966). For an English translation, see Hegel, *On Christianity: Early Theological Writings*, trans. T. M. Knox and Richard Kroner (New York: Harper & Brothers, 1961).

31. *Vorstellung*, traditionally translated as "representation," is closer to "imagination" in Kant and the German idealists. See Green, *Imagining God*, 13–18.

32. For a more extensive discussion of the young Hegel's treatment of positivity, see Green, "Positive Religion," chap. 5. For Hegel's later thought, see Stephen D. Crites, "The Problem of the 'Positivity' of the Gospel in the Hegelian Dialectic of Alienation and Reconciliation" (PhD diss., Yale University, 1961); and Crites's excellent and neglected article "The Gospel according to Hegel," *Journal of Religion* 46 (1966): 246–63.

theme by Kant, another version of the argument that the essential content of Christian truth can be translated without loss into the depositivized thought forms of modernity.

I am convinced that further variations of the theological pattern initiated by Kant and exemplified by Schleiermacher and Hegel are to be found throughout the nineteenth century and beyond, though I must leave the proof in these cases to another occasion. In every case the rejection of positivity (whether called by that name or some other) is based on a concept of religion; and religion is typically conceived to be the definitive mark of humanity. In many of the cases, this argument is coupled with an apologetic claim for the superiority of the Christian religion: Christianity, the typical argument goes, is the truest religion because it is the *most religious* religion. The liberal theology of a figure like Adolf von Harnack represents the genre in its virtually pure form. Moreover, this tradition has continued into the twentieth and twenty-first centuries as well and has come to include Roman Catholic as well as Protestant thinkers. On the Protestant side, Paul Tillich's conscious revision of Schleiermacher's program once again employs a general concept of religion (called "faith" by Tillich) to show how Christianity (especially in its Protestant manifestation) is identical with the pure form of religion itself. Catholic variations on the theme can be found, for example, in the thought of Karl Rahner and David Tracy. Each of these cases, of course, would have to be argued in detail, something I cannot do within the scope of this chapter. Instead, let me offer by way of conclusion a suggestive thesis for further exploration by others: that Kant is not only the "father" of mediating Protestant theology in the nineteenth century but also the "grandfather" of what can be termed the ecumenical liberalism of our own day.

The Failure of Accommodationist Theology

Nietzsche thought Kant to be an "underhanded Christian" because he divided reason into theoretical and practical aspects. "With his notion of 'practical reason,'" Nietzsche writes, "he invented a special kind of reason for cases in which one need not bother about reason—that is, when morality, when the sublime command 'thou shalt,' raises its voice."[33] One such case, of course, is religion—that special application of Kantian practical reason. As is so often the case, Nietzsche, approaching the matter from the side diametrically opposed to Christian orthodoxy, sees things more clearly than those

---

33. Nietzsche, *The Antichrist* §12 (KSA 6:178), cited in *The Portable Nietzsche*, trans. Walter Kaufmann (New York: Viking, 1968), 578–79.

with apologetic interests. He sees in Kant the very epitome of his contention that "the Protestant parson is the grandfather of German philosophy." Kant, exemplifying the "theologians' instinct," manages in the name of rational modernity to betray the very ideal of that modernity: "A path had been found on which one could sneak back to the old ideal."[34]

What Nietzsche describes in unflattering terms as Kant's "*Schleichweg zum alten Ideal*" is what I have been calling Kant's Christian apologetic. More generally, we can say that Kant and the tradition that follows the pattern begun by him are proposing a theological accommodationism, a method that seeks to preserve the essence of Christianity by translating it into the modern idiom. Nietzsche's discomfiture, of course, stems from his suspicion that Kant has betrayed the project of secular modernity. Christian theologians, far from finding solace in that situation, have reasons of their own for being suspicious of the Kantian program and its later imitators. For if Nietzsche suspects that Kant has sold out modern rationality, theologians may wonder whether he has not sold out Christianity. (One does not necessarily have to choose between these opposed critiques of Kant: it is possible that both are correct!)

I want to suggest by way of conclusion some reasons why theologians today ought to be suspicious of the Kantian apologetic, and by extension, of its subsequent theological variants. One of the ironies of the Kantian legacy in religious thought is that the apologetic appeal to universal reason and common human experience has led to some of the most imperialistic modern claims on behalf of Christianity. Kant speaks of "that church which contained within itself, from its first beginning, the seed and the principles of the objective unity of the true and *universal* religious faith, to which it is gradually brought nearer" (125/116, emphasis original). (Such claims, especially in the nineteenth century, were frequently linked to correlative treatments of Judaism as the archetypal "bad religion.")[35] Even in the mid-twentieth century, Tillich could argue for the superiority of specifically Protestant Christianity on the grounds that it incorporates within itself a self-critical purification of the impulse to faith.[36]

Finally, more serious than the tendency to triumphalism is the way in which theologies of accommodation so fundamentally distort the very Christian

---

34. Nietzsche, *The Antichrist* §10 (KSA 6:176), cited in Kaufmann, *Portable Nietzsche*, 576–77.

35. See, e.g., Kant's contention that "the *Jewish faith* was, in its original form, a collection of mere statutory laws upon which was established a political constitution; for whatever moral additions were then or later *appended* to it in no way whatever belong to Judaism as such." From this he concludes that "Judaism is really not a religion at all" (125/116).

36. See, e.g., Paul Tillich, *Dynamics of Faith* (New York: Harper & Brothers, 1957), 97–98.

message they seek to save. By targeting the positivity of the gospel—its concrete embodiment in historical and physical particularity—these thinkers have made a fatal misdiagnosis: intending to save the patient by excising a cancer, they set about removing the heart. The root error, I believe, lies in the false dichotomy of form and content. As theologians have increasingly come to recognize, the "essence" of Christianity—that which makes it what it is, and without which it either dies or becomes something else—lies in a particular configuration of symbolic elements, a paradigmatic structure that is unique and irreducible to other terms. The futility of projects like Kant's that seek to translate the essential content of the gospel into other terms can be compared to that of a teacher trying to teach students Chinese by offering them texts in translation. As cultural anthropologists have shown us, religions are symbolic systems that are implicated in culture in complex and unpredictable ways; they are not mere systems of thought that can be abstracted from their cultural context. Theologians like Hans Frei and George Lindbeck have tried to show how Christian theology might incorporate this view of religion. If they are right—and I am persuaded that on the key issues they are—theologians can now hope to articulate the grammar of Christian faith in ways that remain open to dialogue with modern, and even postmodern, secular thought without falling into the errors of accommodationism. As in Kant's day, the theological and secular worlds today are full of voices urging us to abandon the particularity of revelation for the sake of reason and morality ("diversity," "pluralism," and "inclusivity" are the preferred terms today). The theological task is to show the futility of such accommodation while reaffirming the integral "positivity" of Christian faith and practice.

11

MOLTMANN'S
TWO ESCHATOLOGIES

W hen theologians hear the word *hope*, they invariably think of one theologian, Jürgen Moltmann, and one book, *Theology of Hope*.[1] For the generation of theologians who came of age after the Second World War, especially those in the English-speaking world, the appearance of that volume in the 1960s represented the rebirth of the venerable theological tradition of the German universities after the traumatic hiatus of the Church Struggle, the Holocaust, and war. And even though Professor Moltmann went on to a distinguished career, in which he lectured and published on virtually the full range of theological topics, his name continues to be associated first of all with eschatology. Three decades after *Theology of Hope*, as the approaching turn of the millennium provoked a flurry of renewed attention to questions of the future and eschatology, Moltmann produced a new work of eschatology, *The Coming of God*.[2] Its appearance evoked a sense of closure to a distinguished career, of coming full circle, of returning to the beginning. Standing as bookends on a career so closely tied to the theme of

1. Jürgen Moltmann, *Theologie der Hoffnung: Untersuchungen zur Begründung und zu den Konsequenzen einer christlichen Eschatologie* (Munich: Christian Kaiser Verlag, 1964); *Theology of Hope: On the Ground and the Implications of a Christian Eschatology*, trans. James W. Leitch (New York: Harper & Row, 1967). Subsequent citations come from the English translation.

2. Moltmann, *Das Kommen Gottes: Christliche Eschatologie* (Gütersloh: Christian Kaiser Verlag, 1995); *The Coming of God: Christian Eschatology*, trans. Margaret Kohl (Minneapolis: Fortress, 1996).

hope, these two volumes of theology seemed to invite a comparison as we approached the end of a century and of a millennium, a turning point rife with eschatological associations even for those unacquainted with the Christian theological tradition.

If I were to choose an epigraph to epitomize the career of Jürgen Moltmann, I could do no better than Karl Marx's eleventh *Thesis on Feuerbach*. "The philosophers," Marx wrote in 1845, "have only *interpreted* the world, in various ways; the point, however, is to *change* it."[3] Taking Feuerbach, the philosopher who had exposed the illusory nature of religion, as his prime example, Marx accused all previous philosophy of falsifying history by trying to theorize about it in the abstract without taking into account its own entanglement in the material realities of economic and class interests. For Marx, Feuerbach (rather than some more pious philosopher, such as Kant or Hegel) was the perfect example precisely because he got things *almost* right. He supplied Marx with the basic mechanism for his own critique of religion while at the same time (so Marx believed) utterly missing its point.

Moltmann's "Early" Eschatology

Moltmann, whose theological career began as a prisoner of war in the ashes of the Third Reich, spent much of his subsequent career responding to Marx's thesis. Like many academic theologians over the past century, he was troubled by what we might call the Marxist anxiety—the worry that Marx was right about religion serving the class interests of the rich and powerful. The desire to formulate an effective theological response to the Marxist critique constitutes a persistent apologetic motive that runs like a scarlet thread through his books and articles. The first major resource that Moltmann employed in his quest was the revisionist Marxism of Ernst Bloch, who developed a philosophy of hope that opened the way to a quite different and more positive account of the role of religion in human history and society. In Bloch's concept of hope, Moltmann found the *Anknüpfungspunkt* with which to connect systematic theology to social theory.[4] So he begins *Theology of Hope* by redefining eschatology as "the doctrine of the Christian hope" and insisting that it "is not one element *of* Christianity, but it is the medium of Christian faith as such,

---

3. Karl Marx, "Theses on Feuerbach," in *Karl Marx and Friedrich Engels on Religion* (New York: Schocken Books, 1964), 72 (emphasis original).

4. *Anknüpfungspunkt*, the human point of contact for divine revelation, was the focus of a public controversy in 1934 between Karl Barth and Emil Brunner. For a fuller account, see Green, *Imagining God: Theology and the Religious Imagination* (Grand Rapids: Eerdmans, 1998), chap. 2.

the key in which everything in it is set."[5] The trouble he has with traditional eschatology is the familiar Marxist pie-in-the-sky argument: by conceiving eschatology as the "doctrine of Last Things," the church "banished from its life the future hope by which it is upheld, and relegated the future to a beyond, or to eternity," thereby severing its relationship to "all the days which are spent here, this side of the end, in history."[6] Encouraged by Bloch's thesis that hope, rather than diverting the exploited from their present suffering, can actually motivate them to resist it, Moltmann set out to show how specifically Christian hope works not to bless the status quo but to promote social change. Rather than speaking of the future abstractly, Christian hope "sets out from a definite reality in history and announces the future of that reality"—namely, the resurrected Christ. The resulting "contradiction between the resurrection and the cross" ensures the political relevance of Christian hope: "Present and future, experience and hope, stand in contradiction to each other in Christian eschatology, with the result that man is not brought into harmony and agreement with the given situation, but is drawn into the conflict between hope and experience."[7] In an unmistakable allusion to the eleventh *Thesis on Feuerbach*, Moltmann concludes that Christian theology escapes the fate of the philosophers: "The theologian is not concerned merely to supply a different *interpretation* of the world, of history and of human nature, but to *transform* them in expectation of a divine transformation."[8]

The difficulty with this attractive thesis—attractive, at least, to those whose political sympathies tilt leftward—is suggested by the redundancy in the final phrase: Why would people be motivated to transform things themselves when they are expecting a "divine transformation"? What, in other words, finally distinguishes Moltmann's expectation of future deliverance from the traditional expectation of the Last Things? Indeed, no matter how many times he asserts the politically transforming character of Christian hope, he never offers a convincing account of it, not to mention any empirical evidence that people are actually motivated in this way. More disturbing theologically is the suspicion that the thesis may arise out of a desire to quash the Marxist anxiety rather than from Scripture or Christian experience. The very aspect of Moltmann's political theology that has been most appealing to liberation theologians is thus the one about which the most serious questions must be raised. To his credit, Moltmann has not followed some of his more radical Latin American colleagues into uncritical acceptance of the "science" of

5. Moltmann, *Theology of Hope*, 16 (emphasis original).
6. Moltmann, *Theology of Hope*, 15.
7. Moltmann, *Theology of Hope*, 17, 18.
8. Moltmann, *Theology of Hope*, 84.

dialectical materialism or the ideology of class struggle. Much of the power of *Theology of Hope* comes from his careful and systematic attention both to the philosophical and theological context and to the biblical resources for his argument. His passion to vindicate the gospel in the face of Marxist critique gives that book a focus that, as we shall see, has been less evident in his later work.

Moltmann's "Later" Eschatology

The thesis of hope-inspired Christian activism persists in Moltmann's writings after *Theology of Hope*—though it undergoes some subtle changes in his second work of eschatology, written in the twilight of the twentieth century in anticipation of the coming millennial dawn. *The Coming of God* represents Moltmann's explicit return to eschatology after three decades. It would be hard to deny his claim in the preface that "this eschatology . . . is entirely in line with [the] doctrine of hope" in his first book.[9] Most of the emphases of his early eschatology are still there: the focus on hope; the emphasis on God's promises in history, along with the corresponding critiques of theologies that transpose eschatology into time or eternity; and the suspicion that eschatology all too often serves the cause of human tyranny rather than freedom. But there is nevertheless an unacknowledged shift of emphasis, particularly in the political implications of Christian eschatology.

The first change to be noted might be called the withering away of Marxism. Moltmann's "later" eschatology appeared after the demise of the Soviet empire and shows signs of the declining attachment of Western intellectuals to Marxism. An interesting symptom of this change is the treatment of Moltmann's original mentor Ernst Bloch, who appears in *The Coming of God* no longer as a Marxist but now as a Jewish thinker! Under the heading "The Rebirth of Messianic Thinking in Judaism," Moltmann uncovers a pre-Marxist Bloch, who assigned the messianic role in history not to the proletariat but to the Jews. Without ever quite saying so, Moltmann clearly thinks that the early Bloch was onto something that was unfortunately displaced in his later thinking by his allegiance to the October Revolution of 1917. He now wants to put this early Jewish Bloch into a line of development that includes Franz Rosenzweig, Gershom Scholem, and Walter Benjamin.[10] Moltmann's treatment of Marx himself also hints at a revised evaluation of his significance. In his discussion of "epochal millenarianism" in modern thought, he remarks that the views

---

9. Moltmann, *Coming of God*, xii.
10. Moltmann, *Coming of God*, 29–46.

of Feuerbach and Marx on religion and philosophy "are typically messianic and millenarian in the will towards the completion of uncompletable history. Inherent in this is the tendency towards totalitarianism."[11] In other words, Marx is significant not as the insightful critic of Christian theology but rather as a secular example of the same dangerous "messianic" thinking that has produced totalitarian political ideas in Christianity.

Related to the altered significance of Marx in Moltmann's later eschatology is the political thesis that seems to have replaced it—the very one just mentioned in connection with Marx himself. As concern with the Marxist anxiety about religion's legitimizing role in history has waned, an emphasis on the dangers of messianic political theologies has moved to the fore. No longer does Moltmann fear only the passivity of a Christianity whose hope is tied to an eschatology beyond history; in *The Coming of God* that concern has been supplemented by a fear of Christian activism in the form of what he calls presentative millenarianism or political messianism. The problem for Moltmann no longer seems to be apolitical accounts of the Christian message so much as misguided attempts to politicize the gospel in forms that tend toward totalitarianism. Albert Schweitzer got it wrong about the fate of Christian eschatology: Moltmann argues that "the eschatological history of Christianity is not a history of disappointed hope or the delay of Christ's parousia; it is a history of prematurely fulfilled hope in presentative millenarianism."[12] He develops this thesis in one of the book's most effective themes. Arguing that ancient millenarianism did not simply fade away, he shows how instead "it was transformed into a political and ecclesiastical self-confidence and sense of mission." The church of Christendom could not tolerate futurist millenarianism because it had itself become millenarian by claiming to be the earthly heir to Christ's authority. Moltmann finds the most egregious forms of this eschatological overreaching in the *totus Christus* ecclesiology of Roman Catholic and Orthodox theology, which he calls "a millenarian doctrine of the church," since the church sees itself as embodying the crucified and risen Christ, an ecclesiology that Moltmann characterizes as "an 'over-realized' eschatology . . . a triumphalist, illusory and presumptuous ecclesiology." In a trenchant summary, he identifies the error: "Before the millennium there is no rule of the saints. Only in the millennium will the martyrs rule with Christ and judge the nations."[13]

A third shift in Moltmann's eschatological thinking from the 1960s to the 1990s is more evident in its structure than its specific content. In a review of

11. Moltmann, *Coming of God*, 189.
12. Moltmann, *Coming of God*, 148.
13. Moltmann, *Coming of God*, 181, 184.

Theology of Hope at the time of its original appearance in English, Hans Frei detected a "historicism" in the book, by which he meant that for Moltmann "reality is always more historical (in some sense) than physical, and man is a historical being whose very corporeality is mediated to himself through his cultural self-transcendence."[14] While expressing admiration for the master-ful way in which Moltmann carried out his "historicist" project, Frei never-theless questioned the necessity and wisdom of tying Christian theology to the "totality claims" inherent in such a systematic project. But it is possible to see in *The Coming of God* a relativizing of the historicism of the early Moltmann, for he now organizes eschatology according to a fourfold schema in which history comprises only one movement.[15] He still defines eschatology in terms of hope, but now it unfolds in four "horizons," whose order depends on whether one is proceeding "ontically" or "noetically." The book follows the latter course, beginning with the question of the fate of the individual person, before moving on to the "history of human beings." But this second horizon in turn gives way to the cosmic question, eschatology as "hope for the new creation of the world," thus relativizing the historical by placing it between the individual and the cosmos. Thus history no longer provides the total context for eschatology, but must be coordinated with individual experience on the one hand and with the world of nature on the other. All three of these perspectives are further relativized in the final horizon of God's glory. In terms of symbolism, the later Moltmann is concerned not only with the kingdom of God (the eschatology of history) but also with the future of creation (the eschatology of nature). An apologetic context is evident here as well, for Moltmann's early concern with the Marxist anxiety has given way to a new worry about ecology—specifically the threat to creation posed by nuclear weapons and the ecological crisis.

Underlying the shift of emphasis we have noted between Moltmann's early eschatology in *Theology of Hope* and the later version in *The Coming of God* is his continuing commitment to a Christian political activism grounded in the tension between the promise embodied in the resurrection of Jesus and its eschatological fulfillment at the end of history. He is critical of traditional eschatology for encouraging Christians to wait passively for God's ultimate fulfillment of his promise in an apocalyptic future event, insisting instead on a hope that constantly motivates us to engage in political activism to transform historical reality in accordance with God's promise. As summarized by Frei in

14. Hans W. Frei, review of *Theology of Hope* by Jürgen Moltmann, in *Union Seminary Quarterly Review* 23 (1968): 269.

15. For the following, see the preface to Moltmann, *Coming of God*, esp. xiv–xvi, as well as the table of contents, where the structure is most evident.

his original review of Moltmann's theology, "Because God's promise drives history and the Church in history, the correlate of hope for the Church in the world is mission and not simply proclamation."[16] What remains unclear in both versions of his eschatology, however, is the concrete mechanism of this hope. If God has indeed promised to intervene eschatologically to triumph over sin and evil, as foreshadowed in the cross and resurrection of Jesus, whence comes the motivation that will turn hopeful waiting into political activism on behalf of God's kingdom?

The Political Captivity of Hope

At a conference on Moltmann's theology held in New York City in 1986, Hans Frei delivered a response that focused on the issue of the motivating power of Christian hope.[17] The conference included several theologians influenced by Latin American theology of liberation, who had responded positively to the political activism that is a key ingredient in Moltmann's theology of hope. Frei pressed Moltmann to explain "the character of the motion of history" and its relation to "the history of the Triune God." He formulated the question most sharply in this way: "Is the future to be created by the Spirit truly a miracle to us?" (177–78). He made clear, politely but unmistakably, that his concern was political as well as theological. He had noted at the conference "a cheerful liberationist confidence" (181) that he called into question, since it is based on "the belief that liberation is not so much a miracle but a steady motion toward [the] kingdom." Against this thesis he maintained "that the triumph of love must remain a miracle . . . in the light of the gospel" (178). Frei had made a similar criticism in his review of *Theology of Hope*, in which he linked it to "the provincialism of this outlook" because of its commitment to a dialectical view of history that has characterized "post-Kantian German theology" generally in contrast to the more empiricist outlook prevailing in Anglo-American theology. "[It] does not seem . . . divinely ordained," he wrote, "that we must swap an empiricist for an historicist, dialectical or ideological outlook before we can do theology." Here, too, the issue at stake is the miraculous character of Christian hope: "Hope, as the Christian holds it, may have to come as a genuine miracle in an empiricist context—and not as a moment in the

---

16. Frei, review of *Theology of Hope*, 267.
17. Frei, *Reading Faithfully: Writings from the Archives*, 2 vols., ed. Mike Higton and Mark Alan Bowald (Eugene, OR: Cascade Books, 2015), 1:176–82. Subsequent references to this essay will be made parenthetically.

dialectic of an all-encompassing historical process."[18] The political implications of hope are tied to this "question of the miraculousness of the promise
of love," as Frei expressed it in his 1986 response. If this promise is to be
realized, it must be truly powerful; we must "find a divine love that actually
triumphs over fate" (178–79). Conceived in this way, Christian hope implies
a different kind of political response from the revolutionary activism advocated by Moltmann and his liberationist acolytes. Appealing not to Marx
but to Abraham Lincoln ("our second greatest . . . American theologian"),[19]
Frei envisions a theology—and a politics—"that is ultimately optimistic but
insists very strongly on a tragic element in human history" (180). "There is
no such thing," he concludes, "as a Christian theology that is not a political
theology, but I think our political thinking is a divine imperative that we
have to follow in the given situation rather than programmatically across
the board, as I think liberationist theologies tend to do" (182).

Might we not carry this critique further than Frei did in 1986? Moltmann
has focused throughout his career primarily on the *political* consequences of
Christian eschatology, and his liberationist followers have made politics virtually
their only concern. Yet surely for most Christian believers over the centuries—
and for the New Testament itself—hope affects their lives at a more personal
and immediate level as well. They—we—seek relief not just from the power
and corruption of our rulers and overlords but also from the myriad assaults on
our daily lives and well-being by those around us, whether by selfish neighbors,
dishonest merchants, overbearing bosses, or unfaithful family members—in
other words, from the host of fallen humanity among whom we live. Moreover,
we face the ongoing threats of accidents, diseases, and natural disasters. And,
finally, our hope in the ultimate triumph of love is continually challenged by the
greatest threat of all—by the last enemy, death (1 Cor. 15:26). The "historicism"
that Frei detected in *Theology of Hope*, the allegiance to a sweeping dialectic of
history, has attracted many a thinker since Hegel, especially among academic
philosophers and theologians, for whom the lure of Marxism and other revolutionary political ideologies has been—and continues to be—so strong. Frei's
appeal on behalf of Anglo-American empiricism was an attempt to break the
hold of this long-standing tradition. An adequate Christian eschatology must
encompass not only our politics but the entire range of the brokenness of God's
creation, for in the midst of history, in this time between the times, we face not
only political oppression but all the evil forces of sin, death, and the devil.

18. Frei, review of *Theology of Hope*, 271.
19. Frei, "Reinhold Niebuhr, Where Are You Now That We Need You?," in *Reading Faithfully*, 1:180.

An Eschatology of Imagination?

A new and unexpected note is sounded in Moltmann's preface to *The Coming of God*, one which might have answered the question about the motivating power of Christian hope—if only he had pursued it further. For the most part, he tells us, he avoids discussions of method, not wanting to fall into the trap of "so many colleagues" who write of nothing else. Nevertheless, he says that for him "theology is not church dogmatics, and not a doctrine of faith"—so he will not be identified as the child either of Barth or of Schleiermacher. Rather, he writes, theology "is *imagination for the kingdom of God* in the world, and for the world in God's kingdom."[20] This appeal to imagination is tantalizing, but he leaves it unexplained and undeveloped. What sort of discourse is "*imagination for the kingdom of God*"? Does the theologian indulge in pious fantasy? Does he aspire to be the poet of faith rather than her philosopher? And how does imagination differ from the dogmatic discourse that Moltmann eschews? These are important questions, unavoidable ones, whose answers will determine what sort of enterprise theology takes itself to be. By skirting them, Moltmann leaves unclear how we are to take what he says when he speaks as a theologian. For example, he is critical both of theologies that dissolve eschatology into an eternity that is equally near to every moment of time, and of those that turn eschatology into time. But where does that leave his own discourse? If it describes a future that is really coming, how does he differ from those (like Schweitzer and Oscar Cullmann) who transpose eschatology into time? But if his language is not meant temporally, is he not, despite protestations to the contrary, doing what he charges Barth, Paul Althaus, and Rudolf Bultmann with doing—namely, transposing eschatology into eternity? Or is there a third option? It will only become clear when Moltmann tells us what it means to *imagine* for the kingdom of God. Until he does, he remains vulnerable to the very critique he once took so seriously, that of Karl Marx. For Marx learned from Feuerbach that imagination is the deceitful engine of religion, generating illusion and inviting bad faith. Marx therefore wanted to pluck religion, the "imaginary flowers," from the chains that bound the oppressed.[21] If Moltmann is correct—as I think he is—that theology is a discourse of imagination, then he owes us, and Marx, an explanation of how such a theology can speak the truth.[22]

20. Moltmann, *Coming of God*, xiii, xiv (emphasis original).
21. Marx, "Contribution to the Critique of Hegel's Philosophy of Right," in Karl Marx and Friedrich Engels, *On Religion* (Chico, CA: Scholars Press, 1982), 42.
22. These issues are discussed at length in chap. 3 above.

In Frei's response to Moltmann at the 1986 conference, he too invokes the role of imagination in theology. In making the point that the longed-for consummation of Christian hope must be conceived as a miracle rather than the outcome of a historical process, he cites (more than once) Paul's saying that now, in the midst of history, we "see through a glass, darkly" (1 Cor. 13:12 KJV). As Christians, he says (differentiating himself from the cheerful tone of the liberationists), we "see analogically, we see brokenly, and not schematically." Theology differs from philosophy in at least one way, since "theologians reflect conceptually not on rational constructions, . . . [but rather] on certain images." Frei particularly had in mind the powerful images of fate and chance, which "the gospel is surely in struggle against." He concludes by saying that "at the level of the Christian religious imagination, the love of the Spirit must be a love that is greater than fate . . . or chance or Manichean dualism." What we need is not a God like Hegel's, who "loves out of necessity"; we need, rather, "to find a divine love that actually triumphs over fate" (178–79).

Moltmann has given us the barest hint that theology might be conceived as imaginative discourse without offering any explanation of how this notion could be reconciled with his own account of history as "an all-encompassing historical process."[23] Frei, in response to Moltmann's schematism, points the way toward an alternative approach in his comments about the analogical nature of theology ("we see analogically, . . . brokenly, and not schematically") and his conviction that theologians reflect not on rational concepts but rather on "certain images."[24] Those insightful comments point us in the right direction, but much more needs to be done before we can do justice to the claim that theology is "imagination for the kingdom of God." The present volume is intended to be a work in progress toward that goal. Theology needs to articulate a *normative* Christian imagination rooted in the paradigmatic shape of the Scriptures of the Old and New Testaments (see chap. 1 above). In the following chapter I will show how eschatology might be reconceived as a product of the Christian theological imagination.

23. Frei, review of *Theology of Hope*, 271.
24. Frei, *Reading Faithfully*, 1:178.

12

The Eschatological Imagination

Another world to live in—whether we expect ever to pass wholly into it or no—is what we mean by having a religion.

—George Santayana, *Reason in Religion*

If in Christ we have hope in this life only, we are of all people most to be pitied.

—1 Corinthians 15:19

In the previous chapter we saw how Christian eschatology leads us to the question of theological imagination. The most prominent theological voice to address these issues since the end of World War II, that of Jürgen Moltmann, has brought us to the brink of the problem of eschatology and imagination without pursuing it or attempting to reconcile it with his own historicist theology of hope. His hints at the need to do so, like the more promising comments of Hans Frei, are an invitation to develop the eschatological implications of Christian theology conceived as an enterprise of paradigmatic imagination grounded in Scripture. The problem of imagining the future is especially intriguing and promising, for the future presents us with the purest laboratory for observing imagination in action. The reason is simple: when it comes to the future, we have few if any other resources at our disposal. How else could we have access to the future other than by imagining it? I want therefore first to reflect briefly on the formal question of imagining the future as a way of highlighting this remarkable human ability before turning to the question of content: how do Christians imagine the future concretely?

The closing years of the twentieth century saw a brief but energetic flowering of fascination with questions of the future. For Christians, especially those with a bent for theology, this premillennial fervor produced an outpouring of interest in questions of eschatology. I spent a year in the late 1990s living in the UK, where millennial fever took concrete shape as we approached the year 2000 in the proposal to build the Millennium Dome at Greenwich, where since 1851 the prime meridian has functioned as the temporal and geographical point of reference for the world. One day in 1998 I bought a newspaper to read on the train. On the front page was the latest controversy about the Millennium Dome (a recurrent topic in the British press at the time), and on that particular day the controversy involved Christians. "Church given role in Dome," announced the headline in the *Telegraph*, and the article went on to reassure readers that the archbishop of Canterbury had intervened with the planners "to ensure that Christianity is at the heart of the Millennium Dome." The dispute had to do with the design of the "Spirit Level," one of the features of the Dome's prospective interior, described by the planners as "a haven of peace and tranquillity." What seems to have disturbed the archbishop was not the projected tranquility of the government-sponsored monument to the millennium, but rather reports that "the original plans did not include the symbol of the cross." The *Telegraph* even felt called upon to comment editorially, worrying that the archbishop ("a genuinely well-meaning and gentle soul") might be "bought off" by government reassurances of a prominent Christian presence in the Dome.[1]

I continued to follow the Dome's progress after returning to the United States. (I even discovered that one could watch the Dome's construction live on the internet from anywhere in the world, thanks to a camera perched atop Canary Wharf!) My fascination with the Millennium Dome was—and still is—theologically motivated, for I sensed early on that it was an important clue to the eschatology of our late modern culture—if only I could decipher the signs. While still in the UK, I made the pilgrimage to Greenwich, where I obtained the official brochure of the Dome's sponsors—with the wonderful

---

1. *The Daily Telegraph*, April 2, 1998. It was quite an eschatological day for the *Telegraph*, which also carried a story about interior designer David Hicks, who had just died after having spent four years planning his own funeral (this one, too, prompted an editorial), as well as a small piece about the Taiwanese sect True Way, now located in Texas, whose leader had predicted that God would appear on channel 18 on local television (but didn't).

name New Millennium Experience Company—who described it as "an international icon and the largest building of its kind in the world." So what does this millennial icon tell us about its creators—which is to say, about ourselves, assuming that we live at least part of our lives as citizens of the (post)modern world?

My best guess is that the key to the Dome's meaning lies in the controversy about what to put in it, for nothing is more striking about this eschatological icon than the fact that it was conceived, designed, funded, and at least partially built before anyone had any real notion what it would contain. An American commentator called it "the world's most spectacular empty space."[2] Does this not suggest that Emptiness is precisely what the Dome expresses? Not the Buddhist kind but the modern secular sort, symbolizing the nihilism of an age that imagines itself to be the only age (that's what "secular" means, after all) and can thus imagine the future either not at all, or merely as more of the same, only bigger. The Millennium Dome thus stands as an empty symbol—rather, as a symbol of emptiness. It makes visible the impoverished imagination of late modern society in the West. As such, it is a monument to the eschatology of nihilism, an icon of the empty future. Like the numerical symbol of the year 2000 it commemorates, the Dome is a nullity, much ado about nothing (or Nothing). It is as though we still bore the imprint, deep within our common psyche, of the great time-marking and time-creating festivals of our ancestors, for clearly we felt an urge to celebrate this once-in-a-thousand-years turning of the wheel of history. But, as it turns out, we hadn't a clue about what or why we were celebrating. Instead of jockeying for exhibition space in the Spirit Level, it would have better behooved us to ask how we *as Christians* imagine the future, or whether our imaginations too have become desiccated and emptied of meaningful content.

Imagination always presupposes something not present, for its job is precisely to give us access to objects whose nonpresence would otherwise render them inaccessible. In Kant's deceptively simple definition, "*Imagination* is the faculty of representing in intuition an object that is *not itself present.*"[3] He

2. Paul Goldberger, "The Big Top," *New Yorker*, April 17 and May 4, 1998, p. 159. Goldberger, however, far from decrying the Dome's emptiness, sees it—like the Crystal Palace and the Eiffel Tower—as a virtue, but one missed by the practical politicians who control it: "monumental in the best sense of the word, yet at the same time its contents threaten to render it trite and insignificant." More intriguingly, he imagines the Dome as "the greatest revival tent in history"—without, however, telling us what it is that needs reviving or who the preacher should be.

3. Kant, *Immanuel Kant's Critique of Pure Reason*, trans. Norman Kemp Smith (New York: St. Martin's Press, 1968), B151 (emphasis original).

notes that imagination therefore belongs wholly to the realm of sensibility, since all intuition comes to us via the body's senses. In other words, we can imagine what is not present only by analogy with things that are, or have been, present to us in the world apprehended by our senses. Strictly speaking, this principle holds true even in the everyday realm of other people's sense experiences, which they can communicate to us only by appealing to our imagination—that is, by analogy to our own similar experiences. Implicit in this situation is an ambiguity that lies at the heart of imagination and makes it a two-edged sword: we necessarily imagine reality that is not present, but we may quite as easily imagine unreality (which is also "not present," though for a quite different reason). The prophet and the liar, God and the devil, both appeal to our imagination. Formally considered, imagination has the same structure in both cases. This systematic ambiguity of imagination with regard to truth is what makes the concept so useful, and at the same time so treacherous, for theology. It means that issues of trust are inextricably bound up with questions of truth: once we get over the illusion that we are in a position to test all candidates for truth by our own inner resources, we come face to face with the question, Whom shall I trust? It is also a key factor in what may be called the postmodern pathos, the cultural crisis of trust in which the hermeneutics of suspicion has become a universal contagion. When we turn to questions of eschatology and ask how Christians are to imagine the future, we feel the force of that suspicion as in no other case. The intimate relationship between truth and trust is eloquently captured by the first article of the Theological Declaration of Barmen: "Jesus Christ, as he is attested for us in Holy Scripture, is the one Word of God which we have to hear and which we have to trust and obey in life and in death."[4] The hint of eschatology in the final phrase is a reminder that the question of the future is the ultimate test of whom we will trust.

"Another World to Live In": Otherworldliness Revisited

Anthropologist Clifford Geertz begins his classic article "Religion as a Cultural System" with an epigraph from George Santayana. The power of "every living and healthy religion," the philosopher had written, "consists in its special and surprising message and in the bias which that revelation gives to life. The vistas it opens and the mysteries it propounds are another world to live in; and another world to live in—whether we expect ever to pass wholly into

4. Arthur C. Cochrane, *The Church's Confession under Hitler* (Philadelphia: Westminster, 1962), 237–42.

it or no—is what we mean by having a religion."⁵ One of the most common modern epithets for religion is "otherworldly," and it has seldom been meant as a compliment. The culture of the Enlightenment, having cast its lot with this world (which is to say, having opted for secularity), has been suspicious of religion for apparently luring people away from this world through dreams of another. Yet Santayana and Geertz are surely right that "otherworldliness" is, if not the essence, at least a prominent feature of all religion. Under the pressure of the Enlightenment critique of otherworldliness, many modern theologians, not to mention ordinary Christians in the pews, have sought to play down or even to eliminate entirely the otherworldliness of Christian faith and doctrine, which has meant the elimination or radical reinterpretation of eschatology. They have felt an apologetic pressure to declare their loyalty to *this* world while eschewing the claims that another world might make upon us, including the otherworldly aspects of Christian faith. In the previous chapter we saw how this modern tendency has shaped the theology of Jürgen Moltmann. His suspicion of the traditional attention to Last Things has led him to redirect Christian eschatology toward the political task of transforming the world here and now in the midst of history rather than waiting passively for God to intervene dramatically at the end. I believe that now is the time for Christians to reconsider the modern suspicion of otherworldliness—to ask what stake Christians have in another world, what kind of world it is, and how we apprehend it in this secular age.

Let us begin with the last question. Christians, like other religious people, apprehend another world—they call it "the world to come," "life everlasting," or "the kingdom of God"—by imagining it. They do so by employing what I call paradigmatic imagination, the human ability to grasp the constitutive pattern enabling one to apprehend something as a whole-in-parts, and to do so by analogy to something else, something immediately accessible or familiar. In formal terms, all religions are alike in this way—and not only religions, for the paradigmatic imagination functions in other areas of human life as well, including the natural sciences and the arts. In material terms, the uniquely Christian content of imagination, the normative paradigm for imagining reality, is contained in its Scriptures.⁶ (Whether other religions

---

5. Cited in Clifford Geertz, "Religion as a Cultural System," in *The Interpretation of Cultures: Selected Essays* (New York: Basic Books, 1973), 87. I have corrected a minor error in the citation; the original can be found in *The Works of George Santayana*, Triton Edition, vol. 4 (New York: Charles Scribner's Sons, 1936), 5. The context is *Reason in Religion*, in Santayana's series *The Life of Reason*; the passage cited by Geertz comes from a paragraph subtitled "All Religion Is Positive and Particular."

6. For a fuller account of how paradigmatic imagination functions in Christian life and thought, see chap. 1 above.

employ their scriptures in a similar way cannot be known a priori but is rather a matter for empirical investigation.) Lest this way of putting things sound too parochially Protestant, it should be noted that the Christian paradigm is not simply identical with the Bible; it can be found elsewhere as well, including in the doctrines, traditions, and practices of the church throughout the ages. Indeed, one could say that by definition any phenomenon—whether individual or ecclesial; textual, visual, or behavioral—is Christian insofar as it is constituted by analogy with the Christian paradigm. The most precise designation of that normative paradigm is "Jesus Christ." This name focuses the Christian imagination; it is the seed around which the myriad imagery of the Bible crystalizes into a dazzling and multifaceted whole. The authority of Scripture derives from the authority of Christ; the Bible is the rule of faith because it uniquely renders Jesus Christ to the imagination. Scripture exercises its canonical role by providing, as it were, the interactive network of images that allows us to imagine God rightly; it is the template we in the Christian community use in thinking about ourselves, the world, and the relation of both to God. That imagery has its focus and unity in Jesus Christ, whose career, narratively apprehended, is exhibited in the shape and content of the Christian Bible, starting with the complementary covenants embodied in the twofold structure of Old and New Testaments, and extending into the texture of unsubstitutable particulars that make up the individual texts.[7]

At the mention of the term "whole," someone is sure to bring up that postmodern bugaboo, "metanarratives," against whose tyranny so much ink has been spilled. Is not the Bible, that Great Story the Christian world has been telling itself for centuries, just the sort of totalizing straitjacket that Jean-François Lyotard had in mind when he defined the postmodern as "incredulity toward metanarratives"?[8] The challenge is a serious one, for it suggests that Christians might be imagining the world as a closed system that ultimately stifles freedom, spontaneity, and creativity by confining human beings to a rigid and predetermined schema. In fairness it must be admitted that some interpretations of Christianity lend credibility to this critique. An example is found in the theological interpretation of "universal history" as propounded by the young Wolfhart Pannenberg and his colleagues in the volume *Revelation as History*.[9] Claiming that "in the fate of Jesus, the end of history is experienced in advance

7. This paragraph summarizes the argument presented more fully in Green, *Imagining God: Theology and the Religious Imagination* (Grand Rapids: Eerdmans, 1998), chap. 6.

8. Lyotard, *The Postmodern Condition: A Report on Knowledge*, trans. Geoff Bennington and Brian Massumi (Minneapolis: University of Minnesota Press, 1984), xxiv.

9. Wolfhart Pannenberg, Rolf Rendtorff, Trutz Rendtorff, and Ulrich Wilkens, *Revelation as History* (New York: Macmillan, 1968). The volume was originally published in German in 1961.

as an anticipation," they reasoned that God is revealed "indirectly out of a totality of all events."[10] The evidence is available to all observers, not just Jews and Christians, because of its public nature. The resurrection of Jesus is the proleptic end of history, and thus the key that unlocks the meaning of history as a whole. As Moltmann observed in *Theology of Hope*, according to the Pannenberg thesis, "'History'. . . becomes the new summary term for 'reality in its totality.'"[11] Such a totalizing concept only works on the assumption that "universal history" describes a closed system whose pattern can be abstracted and made the object of deductive reasoning. Another case of Christianity interpreted as metanarrative—in this case, one that makes unabashed use of the term itself—is found in the work of John Milbank. Though one could hardly call his version of the Christian metanarrative a closed system (he is far too aware of postmodernism to fall into that trap), it is nevertheless totalistic in intent, aiming to replace secular social theory with Christian theology. Since modern sociology is shot through with (usually unacknowledged) "theological" assumptions, Milbank concludes that the church must reject it in favor of her own brand of Christian social theory.[12] This position "totalizes" with a vengeance, insisting that "the absolute Christian vision of ontological peace now provides the only alternative to a nihilistic outlook."[13]

The soundest theological defense against the metanarrative critique is based on the imaginative character of the Christian vision of another world. Rightly employed, the Bible offers us neither an advance report on how history will turn out, nor a "supertheory" with which to counter the theories of the secularists, but rather an alternative vision of the world in which the world is not so much completed conceptually as transformed imaginatively. To hold, in hope and expectation, to an imaginative vision of the world to come is not the same as claiming a theoretical knowledge of the totality of history. The language of the Nicene Creed is significant: "and we *look for* the resurrection of the dead; and the life of the world to come."[14] This is not

10. Pannenberg et al., *Revelation as History*, 134, 141.

11. Jürgen Moltmann, *Theology of Hope: On the Ground and Implications of a Christian Eschatology* (New York: Harper & Row, 1967), 78.

12. The debate about Milbank's theology would take us too far afield from the present task, but the question may at least be raised whether the intolerance toward other positions, Christian as well as secular, exhibited by the proponents of "radical orthodoxy" might not be a symptom of just the kind of totalizing thought toward which Lyotard and others are properly incredulous. See John Milbank, *Theology and Social Theory: Beyond Secular Reason* (Oxford: Blackwell, 1990), and the debate in *New Blackfriars*, June 1992, reprinted in part in Robin Gill, ed., *Theology and Sociology: A Reader*, new ed. (London: Cassell, 1996), 429–70.

13. Milbank, *Theology and Social Theory*, 434.

14. Philip Schaff, *The Creeds of Christendom*, 6th ed., 1877 (Grand Rapids: Baker, 1977), 1:28–29.

the language of theory but of expectation, not of prognostication but of prophecy. The point is not that as Christians we have some special source of information unavailable to people generally, on the basis of which we claim to know beforehand (pro-gnosis) what is going to happen in the future. Rather, we confess our faithfulness to that vision of the world to come contained in, and implied by, the witness of the prophets and apostles in Scripture. Our confidence is grounded, not in superior knowledge or insight, but in *trust* of those whose imaginations have illumined and captured our own. Imagining the future Christianly requires a double act of imaginative trust: we imagine the world to come by trusting the imagination of St. John of Patmos (among others), who in turn trusted that the angelic Revelation (ἀποκάλυψις) really did bear witness to Jesus Christ (Rev. 1:1). Rather than claiming theoretical foreknowledge of the future, Christians, following the model laid down by Jesus, *pray for* the coming of the kingdom.[15] Christian otherworldliness is an otherworldliness of the imagination, which necessarily remains always in tension with our immediate experience of this world. Such anticipation cannot constitute a metanarrative because *this* narrative is not yet at an end (not even "proleptically"). Strictly speaking, it is more nearly "fiction" than "fact" because it describes events that are not yet real. And that is precisely why those events can be mediated to us only by way of our imagination, and the imaginations of the biblical witnesses.

The paradigmatic imagination, by which religious people imagine another world, is *analogical*, for we are able to grasp that which is not present only by means of its *likeness* to something familiar, available, or at hand. For Christians, because their paradigm is Jesus Christ, the likenesses are necessarily historical. Christians envision the world to come by analogy with the past—a very specific past, contained in Holy Scripture. We imagine the future by imagining its likeness to this past: as new creation, heavenly Jerusalem, the return of Jesus Christ. Mircea Eliade argues that the sacred is always imagined *in illo tempore*, according to past time, the time of origin. When he applies this schema to Christianity, he gets it half right:

> The *illud tempus* evoked by the Gospels is a clearly defined historical time—the time in which Pontius Pilate was Governor of Judaea—but it was *sanctified by the presence of Christ*. When a Christian of our day participates in liturgical time, he recovers the *illud tempus* in which Christ lived, suffered,

---

15. "In the second petition, which is, 'Thy kingdom come,' we pray that Satan's kingdom may be destroyed, and that the Kingdom of grace may be advanced, ourselves and others brought into it, and kept in it, and that the Kingdom of glory may be hastened" (Westminster Shorter Catechism, q. 102).

and rose again—but it is no longer a mythical time, it is the time when Pontius Pilate governed Judaea. For the Christian, too, the sacred calendar indefinitely rehearses the same events of the existence of Christ—but these events took place in history; they are no longer facts that happened at the *origin of time*, "in the beginning." . . . This is as much as to say that history reveals itself to be a new dimension of the presence of God in the world. History becomes *sacred history* once more—as it was conceived, but in a mythical perspective, in primitive and archaic religions.[16]

Eliade rightly sees that *illud tempus* has shifted from myth to history, that Christians employ a particular historical narrative "mythically." In the Christian mythos, the "time of origins" is no longer identical with the "origin of time"—though the fact that the Fourth Gospel opens with the words "In the beginning . . ." brings the two into intimate relation with one another. The time of origin, one could say, has reappeared in the midst of time. But putting Eliade's point in this way also exposes its one-sidedness, for the Christian story goes on to say that "he will come again to judge the quick and the dead." The past becomes a paradigm of the future; in remembering the past we anticipate the future. Eliade's claim that "history reveals itself to be a new dimension of the presence of God in the world" is accurate only if we recognize that the mode of that presence is imaginative: history becomes a metaphor for God's eternal presence. It is not history generally, however, but the concrete history of Jesus Christ that is paradigmatic for the future. The relation of Christ to past and to future is figural or typological, in the sense that Hans Frei, following the lead of Erich Auerbach, showed to be the prevailing way of reading Scripture before the advent of modern critical theories.[17]

The "Delay of the Parousia"

The analogical or typological nature of the relation of past to future is also the key to the problem of the so-called delay of the parousia. Under the impact of the theory of "thoroughgoing (or consistent) eschatology" (*konsequente Eschatologie*) advanced by New Testament scholars at the end of the nineteenth century, Albert Schweitzer propounded a thesis that has haunted theologians ever since, starting with himself. "The whole history of 'Christianity' down to the present day," he wrote in 1906, "that is to say, the real inner history of

16. Mircea Eliade, *The Sacred and the Profane: The Nature of Religion*, trans. Willard R. Trask (New York: Harcourt Brace Jovanovich, 1959), 111–12 (emphasis original).

17. Hans W. Frei, *The Eclipse of Biblical Narrative: A Study in Eighteenth and Nineteenth Century Hermeneutics* (New Haven: Yale University Press, 1974), chap. 2.

it, is based on the delay of the Parousia, the non-occurrence of the Parousia, the abandonment of eschatology, the progress and completion of the 'de-eschatologising' of religion which has been connected therewith."[18] He was surely right about the effects on subsequent theology—Rudolf Bultmann's attempt to "existentialize" eschatology is a prime example—but Schweitzer's analysis misrepresents the place and role of eschatology in Christian faith and thought in both the early church and later generations. Schweitzer and the other proponents of *konsequente Eschatologie* were struck by the apparent failure of Jesus's own predictions of the end time, such as his charge to the disciples before sending them out to preach: "For truly, I say to you, you will not have gone through all the towns of Israel before the Son of Man comes" (Matt. 10:23). (Schweitzer identifies the "non-fulfilment" of this verse as "the first postponement of the Parousia.")[19] Yet one of the more remarkable phenomena of human religious behavior generally is the apparent alacrity with which religious movements shake off eschatological disappointment. Indeed some of the more vibrant religious movements—the Jehovah's Witnesses are a recent example—have their roots in millennial predictions that went unfulfilled. So too the mainstream of Christian tradition: despite Schweitzer's dire account of crisis, there is little evidence that the "delay" was in fact experienced as a crisis by Christians. Or, to the extent that there *was* a crisis, the Christian community evidently had the spiritual means to overcome it. How can that be so?

The fact that eschatological anticipation takes place in the mode of imagination has implications for the "delay of the Parousia" that have usually been overlooked by theologians. First, the analogical nature of eschatological visions means that the imagery of the temporal future functions metaphorically to represent eternity. At least since Augustine, it has generally been acknowledged by theologians that God does not create *in time* but rather *creates time* as an aspect of his creation of the world *ex nihilo*. But in that case, eschatological visions in terms of an end *time* cannot be taken literally, as though these events were scheduled to take place at some future point in time (whether or not that time can be known or predicted is irrelevant; the point is that the end, whenever it comes, is conceived in terms commensurable with past and present time). If eschatology were composed of prognostications about the future, such a compatibility of time and eternity would be appropriate.

---

18. Albert Schweitzer, *The Quest of the Historical Jesus: A Critical Study of Its Progress from Reimarus to Wrede* (New York: Macmillan, 1968), 360. Jürgen Moltmann offers a concise summary of Schweitzer's thesis and its impact on theology in *The Coming of God: Christian Eschatology*, trans. Margaret Kohl (Minneapolis: Fortress, 1996), 7–10.

19. Schweitzer, *Quest*, 360.

But since time and eternity are incommensurable, their relationship must be analogical rather than literal; in other words, temporal imagery about "future events" should be read as metaphorical language about a discontinuous and inconceivable eternity. We imagine eternity by imagining the future. The apocalyptic future is the Christian image (or one Christian image) of eternal life. Future time is a metaphor for eternity. Moltmann confuses the two by his speculations (interesting though they are) about the points of transition from eternity to time and back to eternity again.[20] Implicitly, he recognizes the imaginative character of biblical eschatology, appealing, for instance, to the indication in Revelation 5 that "the unfurled times of history will be rolled up like a scroll." But he never makes the imaginative character of eschatological vision an explicit theme, leaving the impression that Scripture's "preferred images [*Bilder*] for eternal life" are inadequate ways of describing "what is as yet hardly imaginable [*noch kaum vorstellbar*] in this impaired life."[21] In fact the language of metaphor and hyperbole, of *Bild* and *Vorstellung*, employed by the biblical witnesses is precisely the *right* way to speak about eternity, just because it is inconceivable from our temporal vantage point in history. This language is not an inadequate attempt to express what the theologian can articulate more clearly through the ordered use of conceptual discourse. Since time and eternity are incommensurable, we can pass from one to the other only by way of an imaginative gestalt switch. If we think of theology as the grammar of the Christian imagination, eschatology describes the grammar of imagining eternal life, the destiny of creation beyond time. Christians imagine eternal life *as* the future coming of God. The object of our contemplation is eternity; the medium is the eschatological vision of the world transformed in future time.

A second implication of the fact that Christians apprehend another world by imagination involves us in a different trope, *hyperbole*. Stephen Webb's proposal about the hyperbolic imagination deserves more attention from theologians than it has received. We have become accustomed to the idea that metaphor, far from being mere rhetorical ornament, enables us to say what cannot be expressed "literally"—that is, in nonmetaphoric language.[22] Webb makes the corresponding claim for hyperbole.[23] He sets out "to confront the

---

20. Moltmann, *Coming of God*, 279–95.

21. Moltmann, *Coming of God*, 294–95; cf. Moltmann, *Das Kommen Gottes: Christliche Eschatologie* (Gütersloh: Christian Kaiser / Gütersloher Verlagshaus, 1995), 324–25.

22. For a summary of the scholarly discussion of metaphor theory, see Green, *Imagining God*, 127–34.

23. Stephen H. Webb, *Blessed Excess: Religion and the Hyperbolic Imagination* (Albany: State University of New York Press, 1993). See my review in *Theology Today* 51 (April 1994): 192.

Enlightenment critique of exaggeration" by means of a "rehabilitation of hyperbole" as a way of speaking about "reality that could be expressed in no other way except through the excited and startling language of excess and extravagance."[24] Nowhere in Christian life and doctrine is the hyperbolic imagination more in evidence than in eschatology. Moltmann points out that Schweitzer "abandoned his 'historical Jesus,' the Jesus who had come to grief over his eschatological enthusiasm [*Schwärmerei*]."[25] Hyperbole, that "elegant straining of the truth," that "exaggeration on the side of truth," appears to the sober rationalist as *Schwärmerei*; but as Webb reminds us, "extravagant language does not necessarily lead to fanatical, or as the Enlightenment called it, 'enthusiastic' behavior."[26] Indeed, hyperbole finds its biblical justification, according to Webb, not in Jesus's miracles so much as his parables[27]—and we could add that many of the parables are eschatological ("The kingdom of God is like . . ."). This insight helps to explain the remarkable immunity of millenarian predictions to failure: though the prophets of "apocalypse now" have repeatedly been literally mistaken about the date of the end, might they not have been imaginatively right? Their followers believed the prophecy, though temporally inaccurate, to be hyperbolically true. Schweitzer's crisis did not derail the church's proclamation no doubt because the early Christians understood—implicitly if not explicitly—that the expectation of the Lord's imminent return was the way in which faith imagined its consummation; it was the first-century manifestation of the faithful imagination of Christians through the ages. A similar logic helps to account for the "nescience" (in Karl Rahner's term) of the man Jesus. He could predict the future no better than any other first-century Jew: "But concerning that day and hour no one knows, not even the angels of heaven, nor the Son, but the Father only" (Matt. 24:36). As Christians and theologians, we are called upon to trust, not Jesus's knowledge of the future, but his imagination, even when it assumes the hyperbolic form of those "predictions" that Schweitzer calls *Schwärmerei*. When the early church followed suit in the "faithful hyperbole" of imminent expectation and apocalyptic vision, they were imagining—and inviting us to imagine—the incommensurable and inconceivable glory of eternity opened up by Christ's death and resurrection in the most suitable language they had at their disposal, by comparing and exaggerating their sensuous and temporal experience in this world.

24. Webb, *Blessed Excess*, 22–23. "The Enlightenment," he comments, "has taught religious people to mumble, not exaggerate" (20).

25. Moltmann, *Coming of God*, 9 (I have corrected a typographical error); cf. Moltmann, *Das Kommen Gottes*, 26.

26. Webb, *Blessed Excess*, 9, 17, 18.

27. Webb, *Blessed Excess*, 23.

One further characteristic of eschatological imagination needs to be noted. In biblical accounts of the Last Things, the imagery is characteristically *visual*. Theological interpretations of imagination have sometimes gone astray by taking too literally the traditional "image of the imagination" itself and thereby assuming that all imagination is visual imagination. Virtually all of the traditional terminology—imagination, fantasy, *Einbildung*, *Vorstellung*—is based on the analogy of sight.[28] But in the case of God's future, *seeing* is in fact the appropriate mode. Just as faith is characterized by *hearing*, faith's destiny is conceived as sight (2 Cor. 5:7; cf. 1 Cor. 13:12). Thus Christian eschatology is dominated by *visions* of the future. The revelation ("apocalypse") with which the scriptural canon concludes is mainly composed of one great vision.[29] John uses aural imagery to introduce his message: "Blessed is the one who reads aloud the words of this prophecy, and blessed are those who hear" (Rev. 1:3). The content of the revelation itself, on the other hand, is visual through and through: "After this I looked, and behold . . ." (4:1); "Then I saw . . ." (5:1); "Now I watched . . ." (6:1); "After this I saw . . ." (7:1)—and so on until the great climax of chapter 21: "Then I saw a new heaven and a new earth" (21:1). The visual character of eschatological imagination makes visual art, especially painting and drawing, a favorite and especially appropriate medium for this theological locus. Expressions of the apocalyptic imagination of artists like Albrecht Dürer and Jan van Eyck rank among the most powerful commentaries on the biblical accounts of the Last Things. And the hyperbolic tone of these visions makes music and song a virtually irresistible response to them. John's apocalypse supplies the soundtrack: the four living creatures sing ceaselessly before the throne (Rev. 4:8), joined by the twenty-four elders (4:10–11) and accompanied on harps (5:8–10); the opening of each seal is heralded by an angelic trumpet fanfare (chaps. 8–9). The full chorus enters in chapter 14, when the one hundred forty-four thousand break into their "new song." Then the martyrs, also with harps, enter singing (15:2–4). (The music is also punctuated by an array of auditory special effects: e.g., "flashes of lightning, rumblings, peals of thunder, an earthquake, and heavy hail," 11:19.) Before such a vision, who can remain silent? Joseph Mangina, noting that many Christians avoid Revelation because of its "peculiar, not to say bizarre" character, points out that they have nevertheless encountered

28. See Green, *Imagining God*, 92–93.
29. Richard Bauckham notes the uniquely visual character of Revelation as compared to other apocalypses in *The Theology of the Book of Revelation* (Cambridge: Cambridge University Press, 1993), 9–10. "John's vision creates a single symbolic universe in which its readers may live for the time it takes them to read (or hear) the book." This combination of unity and visual imagery makes "Revelation distinctive among the apocalypses."

it in Christian liturgy and hymnody (e.g., Charles Wesley, Philipp Nicolai). "Christians," Mangina maintains, "are formed by the Apocalypse without realizing that it *is* the Apocalypse. The book has been among the great shapers of the Christian imagination across the centuries."[30]

Imagination and Naïveté

Because imagining the future presents us with imagination at its purest and most intensive, it offers a unique opportunity to observe the imagination in action and to reflect on its theological significance generally. One of the more attractive notions proposed for the modern interpretation of religion is captured in Paul Ricoeur's remarks about "a second naïveté."[31] The phrase has caught the attention of many a philosopher and theologian, including some who do not find Ricoeur's own attempts to reach that goal compelling. But the mere naming of the goal appeals, combining as it does a nostalgia for the lost innocence of premodern childhood with the sophisticated maturity of what Bonhoeffer called "the world come of age."[32] The qualifier "second" introduces a dialectical moment, seeming to hold out the possibility that we might recover the vitality and immediacy of the precritical "first" naïveté without abandoning our commitment to modern critical reason. Understanding imagination theologically can help us reach that goal.

Most simply put, my suggestion is that we take imagination as the mode of the second naïveté. At first glance "naïve" does not strike one as a theological attribute, but the dictionary offers some suggestive synonyms: *simple, ingenuous, unsophisticated, natural, unaffected, guileless, artless*. The list is followed by the comment that "these adjectives mean free from guile, cunning, or sham."[33] When Jesus first sets eyes on Nathaniel, he exclaims, "Behold, an Israelite indeed, in whom is no guile!" (John 1:47 RSV); and the First Letter of Peter admonishes Christians to "put away all malice and all guile" (1 Pet. 2:1 RSV). Of still greater theological interest is a passage a few verses later describing Jesus: "He committed no sin; no guile was found on his lips" (2:22 RSV)—words cited from Isaiah 53:9, one of the Servant Songs so important for the Christology of the early church. According to the apostle Paul, his opponents in Corinth made this charge: "I was crafty, you say, and got the

---

30. Joseph L. Mangina, *Revelation* (Grand Rapids: Brazos, 2010), 19–20 (emphasis original).

31. Paul Ricoeur, *The Symbolism of Evil*, trans. Emerson Buchanan (New York: Harper & Row, 1967), 351.

32. For some historical reflections on adulthood (*Mündigkeit*) as the defining metaphor of modernity, see chap. 9 above.

33. *American Heritage Dictionary of the English Language*, 3rd ed., s.v. "naïve."

better of you by guile" (2 Cor. 12:16 RSV). If naïveté means absence of guile (δόλος), it is a quality for which Christians ought to strive. One way to do so is to approach Scripture "naïvely," trusting its imagery and hyperbole to form one's own imagination. The problem with this advice is that it sounds very much like the "first" naïveté of those who eschew all use of critical reason. The duality is right there in the definition: on the one hand, "naïve" means "simple and credulous as a child; ingenuous . . . suggest[ing] the simplicity of nature"; on the other hand, "it sometimes connotes a credulity that impedes effective functioning in a practical world." The hermeneutical dilemma is brought out most clearly by the antonym *suspicious*. As Ricoeur has taught us, the modern hermeneutics of suspicion calls into question all naïve readings of Scripture and other texts. Having learned from the likes of Marx, Nietzsche, and Freud to mistrust texts, how can we ever again hear them naïvely?

The first step is to acknowledge the "otherworldly" character of faith, which means that believers will not be able to escape the tension between "this world and the next" and should beware of those who claim to avoid or to overcome it. The hermeneutical symptom of that tension is the antagonism between suspicion and naïveté, mistrust and trust. Like a wound that will not heal, it is the perennial thorn in theologians' flesh to keep them, like the apostle, "from becoming conceited." The Lord's answer to Paul is also the Lord's answer to the theologians: "My grace is sufficient for you, for my power is made perfect in weakness" (2 Cor. 12:7–9).

Liberals are right that the language we use as Christians is not "literally" true; rather, it is figurative, poetic, imaginative language. But the orthodox are right in a more important way: for the language of imagination—which is to say, biblical language—is the only language we have for thinking and speaking of God, and we receive it as the gift of the Holy Spirit. Theology deceives itself if it conceives of its task as translating the figurative language of Scripture and piety into some more nearly literal discourse about God. The theologian's job is not to tell fellow believers what they really mean; rather, it is to help the church speak more faithfully the language of the Christian imagination. The theologian is not a translator but a grammarian.

The secular world is obsessed with predictions, forecasts, and strategic plans, while the church seeks to live by faith, not knowing what the future will bring but always expecting to receive it by grace out of the hand of the God who leads us forward by his Spirit. Our very identities are part of the mystery toward which we journey, for as the apostle has said (in words they can put on my tombstone), "what we will be has not yet appeared; but we know that when he appears we shall be like him, because we shall see him as he is" (1 John 3:2).

The modern age understands itself as secular—in solidarity with this present age rather than the age to come. As a consequence, the modern imagination of the future has become desiccated, vulnerable to fads and fancies and lacking power to shape the lives and expectations of modern people. In its most extreme varieties (think of Heaven's Gate) modern imagination of the future becomes a pathetic parody of the religious imagination, a desperate expression of the gnostic hope that yet more scientific knowledge will usher in a this-worldly utopia. In its more ordinary manifestations, however, the imagination of the age is symbolized in the emptiness of the Millennium Dome. Unlike the secular future, the future imagined by Christians is not empty but is filled to overflowing with images, metaphoric and hyperbolic, of heavenly glory. Imagining the future apocalyptically is incompatible with imagining it as the indefinite extension of the present into a continuous future. The modern theological flight from otherworldliness has blinded us to the inescapable duality of the Christian life. What we as Christians have to offer the world is precisely another reality, a vision not of "one damn thing after another" but of a new heaven and a new earth. The tension, the incompatibility, between these worlds is just the point: without it, we have no gospel to preach.

PART 4

THEOLOGY OF RELIGION AND THE RELIGIONS

13

THE MYTH OF RELIGION

How to Think Christianly in a Secular World

O ne of the challenges faced by a Christian theology of paradigmatic imagination is that all of us, ordinary believers as well as theologians, already have a swarm of images in our heads and hearts besides those grounded in the Bible. In fact, an empirical study of the Christian imagination would doubtless find that many of the images that actually function as paradigms for Christians today distort or even supplant those originating in the Scriptures of the Old and New Testaments. One of the most important (I am tempted to say *the* most important) is the notion of *religion*. Just about everybody in the contemporary world, whether identifying as a Christian or not, takes for granted that Christianity is a species of religion—one religion, we say, among others. Colleges and universities study Christianity in departments of religion or religious studies, and newspapers typically have a special section devoted to religion. This way of categorizing things is so common and so familiar that most people simply take it for granted.

There are good reasons, however, for taking a closer and more critical look at this common image of religion: where it came from, why it functions culturally as it does, and whether there are grounds for calling the usual assumptions about religion into question. This task is especially important for theology, since it affects how we think about the Christian faith and how the concepts and images we employ function either to clarify or to distort our theological imagination. Some of this work has already been done, as we shall see below. The analysis needs to be historical, since the word *religion* is an ancient one that has taken on a quite different meaning since the rise of modernity.[1] The most important fact about this modern concept will come as a surprise to many: that *religion* is a *secular* term. As Western culture, beginning in the European Enlightenment, increasingly distanced itself from its Christian roots, it came to distinguish the emerging secular world from the world of religion that had for so long been culturally dominant. The concept of religion, in its modern sense, now serves as the alternative to the secular.

William Cavanaugh's *The Myth of Religious Violence* has shed a new and critical light on some of the ways in which the modern concept of religion has distorted our understanding of Christianity. The book exposes and refutes the widely held assumption that religion by its very nature tends to foster violence.[2] Some books succeed in making a convincing case for their thesis, and some fall short of the mark. But Cavanaugh's book manages to do more than the author set out to accomplish. I hope to demonstrate the implications of what might be called Cavanaugh's über-thesis. The book's stated purpose is to challenge the widespread "myth of religious violence," which he defines as "the idea that religion is a transhistorical and transcultural feature of human life, essentially distinct from 'secular' features such as politics and economics, which has a peculiarly dangerous inclination to promote violence." Cavanaugh's aim is not merely to debunk a popular misconception but also to unmask its underlying motives and unsavory political implications. "The secular nation-state," he says, "then appears as natural, corresponding to a universal and timeless truth about the inherent dangers of religion."[3] The "myth" indicated in the book's title not only misrepresents "religion" but also justifies the secular state, the major purveyor of violence in the modern age.

That's a weighty and important thesis, and *The Myth of Religious Violence* does an impressive job of demonstrating its truth. After decades of teaching modern Christian thought, I was most surprised by Cavanaugh's deconstruction of the myth of the "wars of religion" in chapter 3. (If I ever use that phrase again, it will be prefaced by a "so-called"!) He shows how the attempt to distinguish religious from political and economic factors in the European conflicts of the sixteenth and seventeenth centuries fails because its terms are anachronistic and it simply can't be squared with the historical facts. "The

1. For a fuller account of the impact of modern thought on Christian theology, see my article "Modernity," in *The Blackwell Companion to Modern Theology*, ed. Gareth Jones (Oxford: Blackwell, 2004), 162–79.

2. William T. Cavanaugh, *The Myth of Religious Violence: Secular Ideology and the Roots of Modern Conflict* (New York: Oxford University Press, 2009).

3. Cavanaugh, *Myth of Religious Violence*, 3.

story of these wars," he observes, "serves as a kind of creation myth for the modern state."[4] Not only historians should take note, for he also exposes the long tradition in American jurisprudence, including numerous Supreme Court opinions, of the self-congratulatory assumption that our constitutional "wall" separating church and state has saved us from repeating the devastating toll of religion-incited violence allegedly exacted on European society in the centuries before the founding of the American republic.

Most readers of the book will of course focus primarily on the issue of religious violence, which is, after all, the author's announced subject. Nothing I say here is meant to disparage or distract from that primary and significant concern. But Cavanaugh's unmasking of the slippery and insidious notion of "religion" assumed by purveyors of the myth of religious violence has implications that extend far beyond the specific issue of violence, and it is these implications that I wish to draw out. Cavanaugh's book, by highlighting the particular example of "religious violence," actually shows how the modern secularist notion of religion distorts and misrepresents everything it touches. The concept is not merely fuzzy and confused but pernicious, because it carries with it a hidden agenda that renders its use suspect, whether it is employed in popular, academic, or political contexts.

Critique of the concept of religion is not new. Cavanaugh draws attention to the work of Wilfred Cantwell Smith, whose 1962 book *The Meaning and End of Religion* contains an extensive history of the evolution of the concept in European thought along with a trenchant critique of its use by contemporary scholars of religion.[5] Although the word *religio* has ancient roots, it was only with the European Enlightenment of the seventeenth and eighteenth centuries that it was gradually transformed into "a new idea of religion, as a great objective something,"[6] which appears in the world in a number of specific forms called "religions." The occurrence of the plural is a linguistic marker of the new concept, along with the concomitant use of the indefinite article ("a religion"). Smith suggests that we would do better "to think of religion and the religions as adjectives rather than as nouns."[7] Most important, however, is the new generic use of the term, a development culminating at the end of the eighteenth century in Schleiermacher's *Speeches*, "the first book ever written on religion as such— . . . on religion itself as a generic something."[8]

4. Cavanaugh, *Myth of Religious Violence*, 10.
5. Wilfred Cantwell Smith, *The Meaning and End of Religion* (New York: Harper & Row, 1962).
6. Smith, *Meaning and End of Religion*, 22.
7. Smith, *Meaning and End of Religion*, 20.
8. Smith, *Meaning and End of Religion*, 45.

Smith's work as historian and critic of the term was more successful than his constructive attempts at reform, which consisted mainly of advocating use of the term *faith* instead of *religion*. This emphasis led in his subsequent writings to a doctrine of "faith" that tends to reproduce under another term the very problems raised by the generic use of "religion."

Both historians of religion and theologians have wrestled with the modern concept of religion. Karl Barth carried out a detailed historical analysis of the term, along with a spirited theological critique of the modern concept.[9] Unlike Smith, Barth does not advocate abandoning the term, even though he sees many of the same difficulties and finds even greater problems in its use by Christian theologians. Rather, he sets out to transform the concept of religion theologically by means of an original dialectical critique that first exposes the modern concept of religion as a form of *Unglaube*, faithlessness or unbelief, but then argues that God's revelation is in fact "hidden" within the phenomenon of human religion so that one can even, with appropriate qualifications, call Christianity "the true religion." Though widely misunderstood, especially by readers of the English translation, Barth's theology of religion remains the most significant treatment of the subject.[10] Even better known is Dietrich Bonhoeffer's appeal for a "nonreligious interpretation" of Christianity or even a "religionless Christianity" in his correspondence from a Berlin prison shortly before his execution in 1945. His remarks remain provocative and suggestive today, though their fragmentary and preliminary character makes it difficult to discern exactly what Bonhoeffer intended by them. His debt to Karl Barth is obvious, but they appear to differ fundamentally on the issue of whether Christianity can or should be divorced from religion.

Cavanaugh's contribution to the analysis and critique of the modern concept of religion is to show that it always functions as one pole of a duality. At issue is not only the definition of the term "religion" but also the assumption that religion, whatever it is, can and must be distinguished from secular society and culture. Cavanaugh demonstrates that the notion of the "secular," as used in contemporary discussion, always implies its correlate, "religion"—and vice versa—whether or not that connection is made explicitly. At play here is not

9. Smith cites Barth's work at one point but refers only to the negative identification of religion with *Unglaube*; he appears to be unaware of Barth's attempt to rehabilitate the term theologically.

10. Barth's most extensive and systematic theological treatment of religion is found in *Die kirchliche Dogmatik*, vol. I/2 (Zurich: Theologische Verlag Zürich, 1932–67), §17. The official English translation in *Church Dogmatics*, vol. I/2, ed. G. W. Bromiley and T. F. Torrance, trans. G. T. Thomson and Harold Knight (Edinburgh: T&T Clark, 1956), 280–361, contains serious errors and mistranslations. My new translation of §17 appears in *On Religion: The Revelation of God as the Sublimation of Religion* (New York: T&T Clark, 2006).

just the historical question of the extent to which modern society has become
more secular. Rather, the very question already assumes that our social reality
is constituted by a contrast between two realms, "religion" and the "secular."
Anyone who employs this notion of religion, Cavanaugh implies, has already
bought into the false implication that religion is something located outside of
everyday "secular" reality. Bonhoeffer saw that the theological consequence
of this move is to assume, as modern theology so often has, that God is to
be sought outside of normal life, either in a transcendent realm beyond the
secular world, or in the gaps within our secular knowledge of the world, or
deep within the interior life of the "religious" individual. He therefore urged
us to abandon the "religious interpretation" of the gospel in order to return
our attention from the periphery to the center: God, he wrote to his friend
Eberhard Bethge, "must be recognized at the centre of life, not when we are
at the end of our resources, . . . in life and not only when death comes; in
health and vigour, and not only in suffering."[11] For Christians to take seriously
Cavanaugh's deconstruction of the myth of religion (for which its alleged
tendency to violence is one index) would mean to subject that myth to a
rigorous hermeneutic of suspicion. Let me give three examples of how that
might look.

First, the enterprise now known as theology of the religions would have
to undergo a radical reappraisal. The pluralist mantra that "all religions are
different paths to the same goal" would be exposed as not just a mistaken
idea but a pernicious one that imposes on Christians and other religious
people an incoherent notion of "religion," which they are all said to share.
As Cavanaugh points out, "the category of religion does not simply describe
a new social reality but helps to bring it into being and to enforce it."[12] "Ad-
jectivally" speaking, it is obvious that people of various faith traditions do
certain things in common—for example, praying, giving alms, engaging in
corporate worship, studying holy books, thinking about ultimate questions,
and so on—which we can appropriately describe as "religious" without buying
into some essentialist concept of "religion." Scholars and religious practitioners of non-Western traditions often make the point that our conceptions of
their "religion"—"Hinduism" is a particularly apt example—are projections
of Western colonial experience and history; or, to put it bluntly, that their
religions are seen through Christian eyes. But Cavanaugh's analysis shows
that it is not only Asian and African religious cultures that are distorted by

11. Bonhoeffer, letter to Eberhard Bethge, May 29, 1944, in *Letters and Papers from Prison*
(New York: Macmillan, 1972), 312.
12. Cavanaugh, *Myth of Religious Violence*, 85.

the modern idea of religion but also the religious traditions of the West it-self. The real culprit is the modern secularist habit of trying to separate the religious from the secular.

Second, deconstructing the myth of religion would also affect its academic study, calling into question the very existence of college and university depart-ments of religion. ("Religious studies" is, ironically enough, the academy's currently preferred name for the secular study of religion, though the use of the adjective rather than the abstract noun might be viewed as a plus.) The notorious difficulty of defining religion, Cavanaugh shows, cannot be evaded as easily as religious studies scholars like to claim. He is especially effective in exposing the excuse made by many in the field: We may not be able to define it, but we know it when we see it.[13] Cavanaugh's account explains why the rise of this discipline coincides with the triumph of secularism in the university. In an earlier, more religious age, it occurred to no one to isolate "religion" in a ghetto of its own. In the light of Cavanaugh's analysis, it becomes clear that the segregation of studies deemed to be "religious" into a separate de-partment represents the academic institutionalization of the very religious/secular divide that Cavanaugh has shown to be an untenable and tendentious dogma of modern secularism.

Third, a Christian hermeneutic of suspicion toward the modern concept of religion must consider the secularization of Christian morality, the issue that is currently dividing churches with all the force of the doctrinal schisms of centuries past. I have called Cavanaugh's project a deconstruction of the modern myth of religion for good reason, for he avails himself of some of the tools and insights of postmodern critics inspired by Jacques Derrida. He shows the power of a culturally embedded dualism (secular/religious) to serve the interests of the powerful (modern secularists) against those they perceive as the others (Christians and other advocates of "religion"). Once a powerful elite succeeds in herding its opponents into a ghetto, it has not only purified itself of their influence but it also has them surrounded. Anyone who dares to advocate in the public square certain historic Christian teachings and practices now abandoned and rejected by secular society (those pertaining, say, to mar-riage or to sexual morality) knows what it feels like to live in a cultural ghetto. And as the last twentieth-century vestiges of a Christian social establishment continue to give ground to twenty-first-century secular enlightenment, the noose (to change the metaphor only slightly) continues to tighten. It is no wonder that some churches have chosen to sanctify the values of the new estab-lishment rather than risk losing their social respectability. When Cavanaugh's

---

13. Cavanaugh, *Myth of Religious Violence*, 16.

analysis is extrapolated in this way, it becomes clear that violence is not the only mythological failing attributed to the perpetrators of "religion."

One of the shrewdest distortions encouraged by the secularist attempt to separate the world into distinct secular and religious realms is that it serves to obscure what can only be called the *religious* nature of the modern secularist project itself. How else can we explain the intolerance of our secular elites who demonize as "fundamentalists" all (Christian and Muslim alike) who dare to inject their "religious" motives into our common secular culture? That they do so in the name of tolerance only makes it more obvious that their values are rooted in an absolute commitment immune to rational critique—the very attributes that Cavanaugh finds at the heart of the modern secular rejection of "religion." Maurice Cowling, in his monumental study, *Religion and Public Doctrine in Modern England*, puts it well:

> *Secularization*, so far from involving liberation from religion, has involved merely liberation from Christianity and the establishment in its place of a modern religion whose advocates so much assume its truth that they do not understand that it is a religion to which they are committed.[14]

The struggle is not between the enlightened advocates of modern secularity and the benighted followers of an absolutist and irrational religion; rather, as the letter to the Ephesians puts it, "we do not wrestle against flesh and blood, but against the rulers, against the authorities, against the cosmic powers over this present darkness" (Eph. 6:12). The modern myth of religion is a contemporary manifestation of what the New Testament calls "the world," which is governed by the principalities and powers, and about which St. Paul warned us when he wrote, "Do not be conformed to this world, but be transformed by the renewal of your mind" (Rom. 12:2). Wilfred Cantwell Smith had good instincts when he wrote, "I have come to feel that, in some ways, it is probably easier to be religious without the concept; that the notion of religion can become an enemy to piety."[15] William Cavanaugh has done us a service by showing just how cunning that enemy can be. As Christians we owe allegiance to Scripture and the Holy Spirit but not to anybody's idea of what "religion" is or ought to be.

---

14. Maurice Cowling, *Religion and Public Doctrine in Modern England* (New York: Cambridge University Press, 1980), 1:xii. I am grateful to Andrew Archie for calling my attention to this passage.

15. Smith, *Meaning and End of Religion*, 19.

14

PLURALISM AND THE RELIGIOUS IMAGINATION

Philosophical discussion about religion and the religions, as well as Christian theology of religion, has been dominated by controversy surrounding one particular approach, which generally goes under the name of pluralism. Its best known, though not its original, proponent is the late John Hick, whose 1989 book *An Interpretation of Religion* offers the fullest and most widely discussed presentation of the pluralist position. A rather lengthy literature has accumulated in which the pros and cons of the pluralist thesis are debated. I want to examine the issues raised by pluralism from a perspective that, so far as I am aware, has not previously been taken—the religious imagination. I hope to show, first, how a careful analysis of the role of imagination in religious belief and practice can clarify the situation of a religiously plural world, and second, why the pluralist theory of religion represented by Hick and his supporters is inadequate both philosophically and theologically. Finally, I will argue that the alleged moral superiority of pluralism over other positions is unfounded.

One of the chief weaknesses of religious pluralism is its thinly intellectual understanding of religion. In the opening pages of *An Interpretation of Religion*, Hick argues that religion is primarily a matter of "belief in the transcendent," or what he subsequently calls "the Real." He describes his own position as "a religious interpretation of religion," which he contrasts with "naturalistic definitions." The decisive issue between these two positions turns out to be whether or not human beings are aware of "a reality that transcends

215

ourselves and our world"; so religion is by definition intellectual affirmation of such a reality.[1] A plausible argument might conceivably be made that all (or at least most) religions involve belief in some kind of transcendent reality, but it would be much more difficult to show that such beliefs are what make them *religions* and not something else, and this thesis is rejected by most scholars of religion today. Not only is it questionable whether all religions focus centrally on such a belief, but it is not even clear that there is *any* one feature that all of them have in common, or that all are engaged in the same enterprise.

Religions as Imaginative Paradigms

As we saw in the previous chapter, the question of how to define religion has always been controversial, and discussions of it have not often proved to be illuminating; but the reductionist definition assumed by religious pluralists compels us to confront the issue if we are to offer a more adequate account of how religious traditions are related to one another. The nonfoundationalist philosophical stance generally accepted by philosophers of religion and theologians today helps to cut the Gordian knot of definitional disagreement by eliminating the need for a single definition as a necessary foundation for philosophical analysis of a phenomenon such as religion. Rather, definitions arise out of pragmatic needs and are relative to the questions being pursued at any particular time. Other ways of defining the same phenomenon will be required for the sake of answering other kinds of questions. The matter at hand is how religion is best defined relative to the question of the relationship among the world's various religious traditions. I want to propose that religion—whatever else may be said about it for other purposes—can be fruitfully defined as a particular use of imagination by human communities for purposes of orienting themselves to the whole of reality. One might well despair at this point, for I seem to be proposing to clarify one notoriously vague concept, religion, by appealing to another, imagination. And it is true, of course, that the term *imagination* has been employed in a wide variety of senses, some of which are philosophically precise but most of which are not. So I want to do briefly what I have done at greater length elsewhere[2]—to indicate in what sense religion employs imagination and what is meant by the term in this context.

---

1. John Hick, *An Interpretation of Religion: Human Responses to the Transcendent* (New Haven: Yale University Press, 1989), 1–3.
2. See chap. 1 above. For a fuller account, see Garrett Green, *Imagining God: Theology and the Religious Imagination* (Grand Rapids: Eerdmans, 1998).

The kind of imagination that plays a definitive role in religion is what I call *paradigmatic*, and I learned to think about paradigms by listening to philosophers of science. *Paradigm* comes from a Greek word meaning "pattern," and that is a good place to begin thinking about imagination. It is best conceived of as an ability (a "faculty" as the old philosophers used to say) rather than a certain part of the mind. Imagining—the verbal form puts the emphasis at the right point—is something people *do* rather than something they *have*. Imagination, at least when it is employed in its paradigmatic function, is the ability to recognize *patterns*, as the etymology of *paradigm* suggests. Sometime in the mid-twentieth century, historians and philosophers of science began to take note of the central role played by paradigms in the acquisition and transmission of knowledge in the sciences. (I have in mind especially the work of Thomas Kuhn but also of thinkers such as Norwood Russell Hanson and Paul Feyerabend.) At the heart of their insight is a logical distinction: scientists come to understand nature not piecemeal, by collecting and organizing "facts" (as the science textbooks often suggest), but rather *holistically*. This point is sometimes explained in popular fashion by invoking the motto that "the whole is greater than the sum of the parts"; but that way of putting it misses the point and may wrongly suggest that a kind of mystical insight or "sixth sense" is at work, which calls into question the rationality of science. The point about holistic logic is rather that the whole is *logically prior* to the parts. Though this claim may appear counterintuitive to common sense, which thinks of a whole as something that one constructs out of preexisting parts, holistic relationships have nevertheless been demonstrated in various ways. One of the earliest was in the field of psychology, where the Gestalt psychologists demonstrated that visual perception does not take place by associating discrete atoms of perception into composite wholes but rather by organizing perceptual input according to logically prior patterns. Kuhn cites one experiment[3] (which, he says, "provides a wonderfully simple and cogent schema for the process of scientific discovery"), in which subjects were shown a series of playing cards from an anomalous deck—containing, for example, a black three of hearts or a red ten of clubs. When the cards were shown rapidly, most subjects saw the anomalous cards in terms of their prior experience—for example, they would see the black three of hearts either as red or as a three of spades. As the exposure time increased, some of the subjects began to recognize the anomalies for what they were, often after a transitional period of confusion, but a few were never able to perceive the situation accurately.

3. Thomas S. Kuhn, *The Structure of Scientific Revolutions*, 2nd ed. (Chicago: University of Chicago Press, 1970), 62–64.

What the experiment shows is that seeing an object involves the application of patterns learned from prior experience. Since one already knows the sort of parts that make up a deck of playing cards, one tends to see the new cards according to this paradigm. Notice that paradigms are both necessary to perception and resistant to novelty; they help to explain both our perceptual successes and our failures. This feature of the experiment is just what Kuhn finds analogous to scientific discovery. He puts it this way: "novelty emerges only with difficulty."[4] But when it finally *does* emerge, it can have quite dramatic consequences, provoking one to reevaluate and reconfigure one's prior assumptions in basic ways. In the history of science, such paradigm changes produce what Kuhn calls scientific revolutions, and in the world of religion the analogy is religious conversion (for individuals) or the emergence of new religions (for whole communities).

The ability to grasp data holistically according to paradigms is what I am calling the paradigmatic imagination. It is not limited, of course, to situations of sense perception but operates at many levels of human experience, including religious belief and practice. Philosophically, examples taken from sensory experience can be employed as models for interpreting more complex varieties of paradigmatic imagination. For this reason, I propose to start with some simple examples of paradigmatic imagination operating at the level of perception in an attempt to construct a conceptual model of the religious imagination that can shed light on issues of religious pluralism.

With some trepidation I will begin with the best-known example of gestalt switches, the duck-rabbit figure (see fig. 1 in chap. 1) that was popularized by Ludwig Wittgenstein but actually originated earlier in the work of psychologist Joseph Jastrow (1863–1944). My trepidation comes from my experience that the figure so often excites interest for the wrong reasons—as an "optical illusion," for example. No one that I have read (with the possible exception of Wittgenstein himself) has done justice to the *philosophical* implications of the figure. It is useful not for its peculiarity, not as an illusion, but precisely for what it illustrates about our *ordinary* experience—namely, that we see according to implicit paradigms. What makes the figure atypical is that it carefully balances two paradigms in such a way that it is possible to see either one (though not both at the same time). We might say that it is a visual example of systematic ambiguity. The figure is instructive because in most situations what we perceive with our eyes is *not* ambiguous, which means that we are normally unaware of the "figured" nature of our perception. The duck-rabbit is thus contrived as a dramatic reminder of something that is true

4. Kuhn, *Structure of Scientific Revolutions*, 64.

of all perception; employed as a model, it shows us the constitutive role of the paradigmatic imagination.

If we were to move directly from the duck-rabbit to religious plurality—that is, take the figure as a model of religious reality—I suspect that many would see it as evidence for a pluralist philosophy of religion. After all, even though it is not possible to see both "aspects" (as Wittgenstein calls the paradigms) simultaneously, once we become aware of both, there appears to be no reason to prefer one to the other. Furthermore, both appear to be "interpretations" of the same "reality." A religious pluralist could argue that "Duckists" and "Rabbitarians" are simply employing different but equally valid images for apprehending the Real, represented in the model by the black lines on the white background. Is it not obvious that both are apprehending the same thing, however differently they may see it and speak about it? Used this way, the duck-rabbit is the equivalent of that favorite metaphor of religious plural-ists: the many paths leading to the summit of the one mountain.

But such a use of the model would be profoundly misleading. To employ the duck-rabbit in this way is to take precisely its contrived element (the per-fectly balanced ambiguity of its two aspects) as typical. The best way I know to make the point is to introduce some further examples—these taken from real life—of what we can call paradigmatic ambiguity:

(a) "In the twilight I saw the tuft of grass as a rabbit."[5]

(b) "Searching the crowd desperately, she mistook the stranger for her beloved."

(c) "Peering intently at the X-ray, the doctor pondered whether the shadow on the right lung was cancer."

(d) "Just as he released the missile, he saw to his horror that the image on the radar bore the unmistakable shape of a plane from his own air force."

(e) A box of candy arrives in the mail bearing the label "GIFT." Should you eat it? (Hint: it might be important to note whether the postmark is "London" or "Frankfurt.")

Like the duck-rabbit, each of these examples involves a situation of visual perception in which what appears before one's eyes can be seen in either of two ways. But unlike the duck-rabbit, in each of these examples the choice *matters*. It matters, first of all, because only one of the alternatives is *right*.

5. Cf. Green, *Imagining God*, 73.

Moreover, the last three cases involve real choices that may literally be matters of life and death. Abstracted from life, examples of alternative paradigms and shifting aspects appear to be "optical illusions," mere parlor games. In real-life situations, on the other hand, they may involve choices between truth and falsehood, friend and foe, life and death. I want to argue that examples such as these are better models for religious plurality than the artificially contrived and value-neutral duck-rabbit, which is excellent for demonstrating the holistic logic of paradigm shifts but tells us nothing about the actual paradigm choices we encounter in life.

Here's what our model of religion looks like so far. A religion employs paradigmatic imagination at a comprehensive level in order to tell its adherents "what the world is like" so that they might live in it rightly. Unlike other uses of imagination, in religion the imagination is pressed into service for purposes of cosmic orientation. Its concern is not to inform us about this or that particular feature of the world—its details—but rather about the world *as such*, and it performs this function by showing us the paradigm by which reality at the most comprehensive level is constituted. For one who makes that ultimate paradigm commitment, of course, quite particular consequences follow, which may affect many of life's details: for example, what to eat, whom to marry, or how to spend one's time or money. *Religious* details, however, will always turn out to be implied by the ultimate paradigm of one's faith, while other details of life in the world (we might call them *secular*) may not be. Since the potential "data" for the religious imagination include *everything*, different religions will appear to their adherents, and to outside observers, as incompatible alternatives. If a person or community sees the world Buddhistically, then for just that reason they cannot see it Christianly, since both paradigms lay claim to the same "raw materials" (just like the duck and the rabbit). This is not to deny, of course, that on many particulars the Buddhist and the Christian may agree. As these examples suggest, such cosmic paradigms may well involve beliefs in what Hick calls "transcendent reality," but such beliefs are aspects of a particular religious paradigm, not the defining characteristic of religion itself. Unlike the duck-rabbit, however, alternative religious paradigms are embedded in life, and choices among them are thus not indifferent or arbitrary—more akin to the five other examples above, yet more comprehensive in scope than any one of them.

We might pause at this point to reflect briefly on the implications of our model-under-construction for differences between the academic study of religion and the practice of religion. For the religion scholar, the various paradigms we call world religions may appear to be rather like the duck-rabbit, since they may all be entertained as theoretical possibilities and studied comparatively. From the standpoint of the religious participant, on the other hand (even if he or she should happen to be the same person as the scholar), the situation is different because one has made a concrete commitment and no longer has the luxury of detached contemplation of the alternatives. Looking at religions as cases of paradigmatic imagination thus sheds light on an important issue in the contemporary academy: how to understand the relationship of religious studies and theology. The model suggests that both perspectives are possible, but it also shows how differently they are inserted into human life, and it highlights a particular danger to which the academic study of religion is prone (we might think of it as a religious version of Heisenberg's uncertainty principle). The paradox is this: in order to compare religions formally, one must detach oneself from all of them (suspend one's imaginative commitments). But that very methodological move (phenomenologists call it *epochē*) ignores, and thus distorts, one of the defining characteristics of the very religion it is trying to explain—namely, its concrete engagement or commitment to its paradigmatic vision. If scholars of religion ignore this paradox, they may be tempted to think that the detached comparative stance is a privileged position, an Archimedean vantage point allowing the interpreter to survey dispassionately, and pass judgment on, the various religious alternatives—which in actual practice often means that the scholar may "discover" that all religions are equally valid (or invalid) and essentially interchangeable. Something like this claim is in fact made by Hick and other pluralists, who, while purporting to interpret religion "religiously," are actually ignoring one of its essential qualities.

The distortion of religion implicit in the detached perspective of religious studies shows that the model as so far developed is still incomplete, for by relying exclusively on examples of perception, it wrongly suggests that religion is mainly a matter of how one views things, as though being religious were primarily a way of observing the world rather than a way of living in it. Employing terms used by cultural anthropologist Clifford Geertz in his classic essay "Religion as a Cultural System," I would argue that the perceptual model tries to explain religion entirely in terms of its *worldview* while ignoring the complementary aspect that Geertz calls *ethos*: "the tone, character, and quality of their life, its moral and aesthetic style and mood."[6] As soon as we attend to this aspect of religion, the imaginative paradigms that constitute the various religious traditions cease to appear as arbitrary and interchangeable perspectives (like duck or rabbit) and begin to look more like real alternatives

6. Clifford Geertz, "Religion as a Cultural System," in *The Interpretation of Cultures: Selected Essays* (New York: Basic Books, 1973), 89.

among which people must choose—alternatives that are implicated in matters of right and wrong, of true and false, of salvation and damnation. And if that is the case, then it really *matters* what religious paradigm a person or community employs in order to live in the world—which brings us face to face with the issue we started with, the plurality of religions in the world today and the need to know how they are related to one another, and how one might choose among options that can differ so fundamentally on the decisive issues facing human beings.

Incommensurability in Science and Religion

In the philosophy of science from which I first learned to think about the paradigmatic imagination, one issue more than any other has been a focus of ongoing controversy. Philosophers of science like Kuhn and Feyerabend speak of the *incommensurable* nature of scientific paradigms, which has provoked their critics (especially defenders of positivist philosophy of science) to attack them for undermining the rationality of science by suggesting that proponents of different theories are unable to criticize one another's positions, or even to communicate with each other in meaningful terms. A similar debate has taken place among philosophers of religion about the alleged incommensurability of religious commitments. There is a common link between these two debates in the philosophy of Ludwig Wittgenstein, whose ideas are frequently invoked by advocates of incommensurability in both science and religion.

From the side of philosophy of religion the problem was posed by Kai Nielsen in his classic essay "Wittgensteinian Fideism." Taking aim not at Wittgenstein (about whom he remains agnostic) but at several of his disciples, Nielsen argues that these thinkers use certain ideas drawn from Wittgenstein's philosophy to effectively insulate religious belief from rational critique. Simplifying somewhat the list of eight "dark sayings" that Nielsen finds at the heart of the fideist position, one could summarize as follows.[7] Religious language, like all language games—so the argument of the "Wittgensteinian fideist" runs—cannot be detached from the forms of life in which it is embedded and which "taken as a whole are not amenable to criticism." Each form of life has its own mode of discourse, including "its own specific criteria of rationality/irrationality, intelligibility/unintelligibility, and reality/unreality." Since there is no Archimedean point from which one might evaluate a form

---

7. The following summary is based on Kai Nielsen, "Wittgensteinian Fideism," *Philosophy* 42 (1967): 192–93.

of life and its attendant language game, the job of the philosopher is not to criticize but simply to describe. Nielsen, while agreeing that one must have an insider's understanding in order to criticize religious discourse, denies that one must actually *be* a believer. He finds evidence that religious language is not "in order as it is" in the fact that "insiders can and do come to doubt the very coherence of this religious mode of life and its first-order talk."[8]

The debate among philosophers of science has proceeded along similar lines. Gerald Doppelt has attempted to describe what he calls Kuhn's epistemological relativism, which is based on the alleged *incommensurability* of differing paradigms in the history of science. He summarizes the position this way: "Kuhn's relativism hinges on his key argument that competing and historically successive scientific theories are 'incommensurable' with one another: that they are *in some sense* sufficiently different, disparate, incongruous relative to one another to block the possibility of comparative evaluation on the same scale of criteria."[9] Kuhn's positivist critics have inferred that "because rival paradigms lack any access to a common language, they cannot be meaningfully compared," which entails that a scientist can move from one paradigm to another only via "a process of 'conversion' or a 'leap of faith'—in which one is mystically converted to a new language-game." (It is worth noting that here, as so often with philosophers of science, religious metaphors appear at just this point in the argument.) The critics also "attack the holistic conception of scientific meaning . . . [as] the indispensable pillar upon which Kuhn's entire incommensurability argument rests."[10] Like the opponents of "Wittgensteinian fideism," these critics are convinced that the incommensurability thesis implies that proponents of differing paradigms are imprisoned within mutually exclusive conceptual worlds in such a way that they cannot come into meaningful conversation with one another and therefore into meaningful disagreement. Such a position, the critics charge, is unwarranted by the facts, since it does not accurately describe the real state of affairs in science (or religion, as the case may be); furthermore, it is undesirable, since it undermines the rationality of science (religion), making scientific (religious) judgments depend on a wholly arbitrary "faith" in the paradigm or form of life. As Nielsen puts it with characteristic bluntness, "To reason in such a manner is to show that one is committed to a certain metaphysical theory, come what may."[11]

8. Nielsen, "Wittgensteinian Fideism," 205.
9. Gerald Doppelt, "Kuhn's Epistemological Relativism: An Interpretation and Defense," *Inquiry* 21 (1978): 34 (emphasis original).
10. Doppelt, "Kuhn's Epistemological Relativism," 36–38.
11. Nielsen, "Wittgensteinian Fideism," 209.

A major step toward clarification of these issues has been taken by Richard Bernstein, who points out the importance of distinguishing *incommensurability* from two other terms with which it is often mistakenly assumed to be synonymous: *incomparability* and *incompatibility*.[12] He is especially effective in showing the error—frequently made by critics of Kuhn and Feyerabend, and occasionally by their supporters—of identifying incommensurability with incomparability. The point of introducing the notion of incommensurable scientific theories, Bernstein insists, was not "to call into question the possibility of *comparing* theories and rationally evaluating them, but to clarify what we are *doing* when we compare theories."[13] The point is especially clear in the case of religion, for even a proponent of the most radical difference between religions—one who believes, for example, that Islam and Christianity are utterly incommensurable and can only be understood by reference to their own paradigms—would hardly wish to deny they can be compared. For that is precisely what one is doing when asserting the radical difference between them. If we really could not compare them, how could we know that they are so different? The suspicion that some theologians harbor about the discipline of comparative religion arises not from the fact that comparativists stress the radical differences among religions but rather from their tendency to reduce them too quickly to a common set of categories (sacred and profane, sainthood, pilgrimage, myth, ritual, etc.)—that is, to treat them as commensurable. I have frequently heard the same confusion crop up when people misstate that common saying about incommensurability—"you can't add apples and oranges"—by claiming that "you can't *compare* apples and oranges," which is about as patent a falsehood as could be imagined! Arguments about reductionism, in religious studies and other disciplines, are instances of the issue of incommensurability. In the case of apples and oranges, one might plausibly treat them as commensurables by reducing them to the concept of fruit. Kuhn's point about rival scientific paradigms (and mine about differing religious paradigms) is that they assume such utterly different concepts, values, and frames of reference that they are incapable of reduction to a common set of concepts. That makes them *incommensurable* but *comparable*. (I suspect that, strictly speaking, the attribute *incomparable* can only be employed hyperbolically: "She was a woman of truly incomparable beauty!")

12. Richard J. Bernstein, *Beyond Objectivism and Relativism: Science, Hermeneutics, and Praxis* (Philadelphia: University of Pennsylvania Press, 1985), 79–108. I have previously attempted to sort out these issues in *Theology, Hermeneutics, and Imagination: The Crisis of Interpretation at the End of Modernity* (Cambridge: Cambridge University Press, 2000), 70–82; here I press further toward clarification of these matters.

13. Bernstein, *Beyond Objectivism and Relativism*, 86 (emphasis original).

The more difficult and interesting question concerns the relationship between incommensurability and incompatibility; and it is also the distinction
that gets us most directly to the issues raised by the pluralist theory of religions. Might not a pluralist grant that the various religious traditions of the
world are incommensurable, sufficiently different from one another that they
admit of no common standard of measurement, and yet compatible, on the
grounds that any one of them is capable of achieving the supreme goal of
religion? Hick, for example, argues "that each of the great traditions constitutes a context and, so far as human judgment can at present discern, a more
or less equally effective context, for the transformation of human existence
from self-centeredness to Reality-centeredness."[14] This claim, however, presupposes precisely the commensurability of the religions, for how else could Hick
or anyone else be in a position to know that they are "more or less equally
effective" in achieving their end? The concept of religion is here being used
reductively, like the concept of fruit in the case of apples and oranges (but
with less justification), subsuming the various religions under an alleged common goal of all religions, namely, "the transformation of human existence
from self-centeredness to Reality-centeredness." The problem is that if the
various religions employ incommensurable paradigms in their descriptions
of "Reality," the interpreter is unable to identify such a common goal, since
commonality implies commensurability. To deny such commonality among
the religions, however, is to offer aid and comfort to those religious "exclusivists," and their "inclusivist" fellow travelers, whom the pluralist theory of
religions sets out to discredit.

Incompatibility and Ultimacy

Let us return to the task of constructing a conceptual model of religion that
will allow us to understand the nature of the relationships among the world's
religions in an age of global pluralism. It is clear so far that each religion
is constituted essentially by its paradigmatic vision of the world; that such
paradigms are incommensurable; and that they can be meaningfully compared
with one another. What remains unclear is the issue of their mutual compatibility, the extent to which they can be understood (as religious pluralists
insist) as alternative means to the same end. The issue of compatibility or
incompatibility is so difficult to resolve because it apparently varies according to the situation. We live quite unproblematically with incommensurable

14. Hick, *Interpretation of Religion*, 369.

paradigms of various sorts in everyday life; we understand the appropriate units of measurement for all kinds of things and don't usually mix them up. For example, we might listen in a variety of ways to a speaker, suggested by such questions as these:

(a) What language is he speaking?
(b) Does he have an accent, or is it a speech impediment?
(c) What is the subject about which he is speaking?
(d) What can we learn about his feelings, character, or state of mind by listening to him?
(e) Is he an eloquent speaker?

Most of these questions are incommensurable with one another. It makes no sense, for example, to ask whether he is speaking German or about the weather, or to wonder whether he is more depressed or more eloquent. (These paradigmatic alternatives are both incommensurable and compatible.) Example (b), on the other hand, seems to pose a meaningful question about two alternatives that are commensurable but incompatible: it makes sense to argue about whether a person's speech pattern results from a regional accent or a physical handicap, and we can imagine evidence that would count toward one conclusion or the other. Example (d) might represent the mode of listening used by a therapist with a patient, and it is surely incommensurable with the other ways of listening. And some modes of hearing appear to involve special skills or personal qualities. Not everyone is equally capable of judging eloquence, or distinguishing regional French accents, or diagnosing depression. Some cases of paradigmatic perception apparently presuppose certain moral states or religious insight. When Jesus concludes a parable by saying, "He who has ears, let him hear,"[15] he is presumably making a point of this sort. Examples such as these demonstrate how mistaken those critics are who worry that people employing different paradigms are somehow isolated or imprisoned in them and unable to communicate with those who are using their imaginations differently.

Paradigmatic commitments in many areas of life, then, involve us in incommensurable ways of seeing and responding to various aspects of the world, and the successful navigation of life requires the ability to keep our paradigms straight, to use the right measuring stick for the situation at hand. But what is it about *religious* imagination in particular that makes it different from

15. E.g., Matt. 13:9, 43; Mark 4:9, 23; Luke 8:8; 14:35.

other uses of imagination? Paul Griffiths, in an essay on Christian responses to religious plurality,[16] offers a helpful analysis of what he calls the "formal and phenomenal properties" that distinguish religious construals of the world from others. His terms are *comprehensiveness, unsurpassability,* and *centrality,* and taken together, they enable us to distinguish what is uniquely religious from other aspects of culture (5). Griffiths presupposes that "a religion is . . . principally an account" (3); but for reasons that I trust are by now apparent I prefer to substitute the language of paradigmatic imagination, which encompasses the notion of giving an account but is not limited to it. The constitutive paradigm of a religion is thus comprehensive, "universal in scope" (8), encompassing all aspects of experience. Griffiths is convinced that people can "offer more than one comprehensive account at a time" (6), though the only examples he cites are "trivial" ones (those "that cannot organize a human life"). I would want to maintain that one can be committed to only one nontrivial comprehensive paradigm at once. I'm not sure whether Griffiths would agree, but the point is moot because he adds two further distinguishing marks of religious accounts to ensure that "no one can offer more than one religious account at a time" (11). To be religious, a paradigm must be not only comprehensive but also unsurpassable, so that commitment to it must be "of a non-negotiable kind" (8); and finally, it must be related to "the central questions of . . . life" (9). When these further characteristics—we could summarize by calling them ultimacy—are incorporated into our conceptual model, it becomes clear that religions are inherently "exclusivist" in the same way as the great paradigms in the history of science: it is possible to live in only one world at a time, and as Kuhn observes, "the proponents of competing paradigms practice their trade in different worlds."[17] To ask a person committed to a religious paradigm to accept the pluralist thesis would therefore amount to asking that person to ignore or discount the very quality that makes it religious in the first place.

Griffiths offers one further observation that raises a serious question about the appropriate conceptual model for religion. Having concluded that a person can commit to at most one religious account/paradigm at a time, he proposes this principle: "Bilingualism is possible, but bireligionism is not" (11). The comment is significant, since Griffiths, like many contemporary philosophers of religion and theologians, is an admirer of George Lindbeck's book *The Nature of Doctrine,* whose centerpiece is the cultural-*linguistic*

16. Paul J. Griffiths, "The Properly Christian Response to Religious Plurality," *Anglican Theological Review* 79 (1997): 3–26. Subsequent references to this article will be made parenthetically in the text.
17. Kuhn, *Structure of Scientific Revolutions,* 150.

theory of religion. At the heart of Lindbeck's influential category is a key metaphor. "A religion," he suggests, "can be viewed as a kind of cultural and/or linguistic framework or medium [paradigm] that shapes the entirety of life and thought. . . . Like a culture or language, it is a communal phenomenon that shapes the subjectivities of individuals rather than being primarily a manifestation of those subjectivities."[18] This suggestion—that religions be thought of on the model of languages—has proven exceptionally fruitful, especially by reversing the tendency of liberal theologies (Lindbeck calls them "experiential-expressivist") to view religion as the outward expression of some prior and "inward" experience. Like the anthropologists whom he credits with alerting him to this feature of religion, Lindbeck stresses the way in which religions, like languages, are external communal realities that individuals internalize so as to produce subjective experience in the first place: "A religion is above all an external word, a *verbum externum*, that molds and shapes the self and its world, rather than an expression or thematization of a preexisting self or of preconceptual experience."[19] But Griffiths's point about the ultimacy of religious paradigms shows that they lack at least one prominent feature of languages: they are not directly translatable. The linguistic model, as useful as it is in describing the grammar of religion within a community, is misleading when applied to the relations among religions. Most meanings intended by speakers of one natural language can be rendered without significant loss in another. And even where difficulties arise—for example, when a local language spoken by an agrarian people encounters the technological realities of the emerging global society—languages are surprisingly adaptive, either borrowing and naturalizing foreign words or inventing native equivalents out of indigenous linguistic resources. (To cite just one contemporary example, the word *internet* is now understood in most of the world's languages.) Religions, on the other hand, because they possess the attribute of ultimacy, are not interchangeable or substitutable like languages. Religions, in other words, are not content-neutral; they are less like ways of speaking and more like particular utterances. The differences among them are not merely formal, as the pluralist hypothesis implies.

Before leaving the issue of compatibility, we need to note one striking difference between the incompatible paradigms in the history of the sciences and those of the world's religious traditions. For all the "epistemological

18. George A. Lindbeck, *The Nature of Doctrine: Religion and Theology in a Postliberal Age* (Philadelphia: Westminster, 1984), 33.
19. Lindbeck, *Nature of Doctrine*, 34.

relativism" of Kuhn's theory of science, he never denies that science makes real progress over the course of time. Indeed, one of the strongest arguments against those critics of Kuhn who think that he imprisons scientists within self-enclosed paradigms immune to outside criticism is the undeniable fact that scientists have again and again in history abandoned older paradigms in order to adopt new ones—and have done so rationally, which is to say, on the basis of the evidence. The major religious paradigms, on the other hand, though perhaps not immortal, appear to have a better survival record. One would be hard-pressed to find a community of phlogiston chemists in the world today, since the missionary endeavors on behalf of the oxygen theory seem to have achieved a total success. Yet centuries after the Buddha transformed the religious world of India, Hindus continue to thrive alongside their Buddhist successors. And despite centuries of forced conversions, pogroms, and supersessionist theologies, Judaism survives even in the midst of Christian-dominated societies, which in their turn have not succumbed to the lure of the Islamic paradigm despite its spectacular success in some areas. Claims of progress in the history of religions, such as those of Hegel and other nineteenth-century Christian thinkers, turn out to be heavily paradigm-dependent and are consequently seldom plausible to those committed to other religious traditions. Despite the often striking similarities between scientific and religious imagination, in other words, here is at least one major point of contrast. How can we account for it? Once again, the essential quality of ultimacy that characterizes religious paradigms offers a clue. Because the objects of scientific study are natural and finite, it is possible to confirm or disconfirm scientific theories by experiment, even though what counts as a valid experiment may be in dispute between the proponents of incommensurable paradigms. Indeed, Kuhn cites the autobiographical remark by Max Planck that "a new scientific truth does not triumph by convincing its opponents and making them see the light, but rather because its opponents eventually die, and a new generation grows up that is familiar with it."[20] Yet new generations of religious believers continue to give their allegiance to ancient paradigms even in the face of successful newcomers. Religious experiments, it would appear, are more difficult to undertake and more ambiguous in their outcomes.

One way to conceive the difference between scientific and religious paradigms is suggested, surprisingly enough, by John Hick. Long before he developed his pluralist philosophy of religions, he advocated a position known as "eschatological verification," developed in response to Antony Flew's

20. Cited by Kuhn, *Structure of Scientific Revolutions*, 151.

critique of the meaningfulness of theological assertions on the grounds that they are incapable in principle of falsification. Flew had challenged theists to answer the question, "What would have to occur or to have occurred to constitute for you a disproof of the love of, or of the existence of, God?"[21] Flew, convinced that theologians had no answer to this question, argued that the thesis of God's existence is meaningless. Hick's response, building on an idea suggested by Ian Crombie, was that believers do have an answer to the question, even though by the nature of the case they cannot be in a position to know the actual outcome. In short, even though theists cannot now produce evidence of God's existence, they look forward to a state, after death, when presumably it will be clear whether they have been right in their assertion. It is not, after all, necessary to be able to actually verify or falsify an assertion in order for it to be meaningful but only to adduce conditions under which it could in principle be falsified. In the case of Christians and other theists, Hick argued, they are able to do so, even though the conditions are "eschatological." He tells a parable in which two men are traveling along a road, one of whom believes that it leads to the Celestial City while the other does not. Even though the "believer" is unable to verify his assertion along the way, it is nevertheless a meaningful assertion because the time will come when the travelers will be in a position to test it. Although our present situation is "religiously ambiguous," Hick acknowledges, we are able to conceive of "a religiously unambiguous situation"—and that is enough to establish the meaningfulness of our religious assertions.[22]

Even admitting the artificiality of "eschatological verification" as a philosophical argument, I think it can serve as a reminder of an essential quality of religions that serves to distinguish them as a category, and it is not limited to theistic believers. That quality derives from the comprehensiveness of religious paradigms, the fact that they lay claim not to this or that aspect of reality but precisely to all of it. Such a comprehensive pattern does not allow for the kind of experiment—that is, a *controlled* experiment—called for in scientific disagreements. The religious person enters into an "experiment" with all of life, meaning with his or her *own* life. As Pascal realized, religious commitment is a wager in which one quite literally bets one's life on the outcome. This quality of self-involving totality makes religion fundamentally different from the sciences, even though both depend upon the paradigmatic imagination, which accounts for their considerable similarities.

21. Antony Flew, "Theology and Falsification," in *New Essays in Philosophical Theology*, ed. Antony Flew and Alasdair MacIntyre (London: SCM, 1955), 99.

22. Hick, "Theology and Verification," in *The Existence of God*, ed. John Hick (New York: Macmillan, 1964), 260–61, 268–69.

Religion from the Inside Out: A Theological Perspective

So far our analysis has proceeded philosophically, in a manner that could be shared by members of various religious communities. (I don't mean, of course, that they would all necessarily agree with everything I've said; only that the position is not essentially shaped by a particular religious paradigm.) In conclusion I want to try out this philosophical model of how imagination functions in religion by seeing what it might look like "from the inside"— that is, from the point of view of a particular religious tradition. For this purpose I propose to look at the theology of religion of that most exclusive of exclusivist Christian theologians, Karl Barth.

Barth carried on a lifelong quarrel with "religion," but his fullest and most systematic treatment of its theological implications is found in §17 of the *Church Dogmatics*.[23] For those who come upon Barth's theology out of a background in philosophy of religion or comparative religious studies, its most surprising feature is likely to be the negativity and suspicion with which Barth treats the category of religion. One might expect a theologian, of all people, to be an apologist for religion. Yet a little historical reflection will show how groundless that expectation is, for the concept of *religion* is a modern invention, a product of the secularization of European society and the growing awareness of religious plurality since the seventeenth century.[24] Barth in fact identifies religion with faithlessness, since it represents the human attempt to establish an image of God for the purpose of justifying and sanctifying human life. Since he understands the heart of the Christian gospel to be the proclamation that God has acted on his own initiative to justify and sanctify human beings in Jesus Christ, religion competes with divine revelation rather than enabling or preparing the way for it. Nevertheless, Barth insists that revelation enters the world precisely in the form of religion, so that the two are inextricably bound up together in human life and history: "God's revelation is in fact God's presence and thus God's *hiddenness* in the world of human *religion*."[25] On the one hand, the Christian theologian must not deny that

23. For a fuller account and critical assessment of Barth's theology of religion, see Garrett Green, "Introduction: Barth as Theorist of Religion," in *On Religion: The Revelation of God as the Sublimation of Religion*, by Karl Barth, trans. Garrett Green (London: T&T Clark, 2006), 1–29.

24. See chap. 13 above. The *word* "religion" goes back to ancient times, but the concept as used today—especially in its plural form—is demonstrably modern. Cf. Wilfred Cantwell Smith, *The Meaning and End of Religion* (New York: Macmillan, 1963), chap. 1; Michel Despland, *La Religion en Occident: Evolution des idées et du vécu* (Montreal: Editions Fides, 1979).

25. Karl Barth, *Die kirchliche Dogmatik*, vol. I/2 (Zurich: Theologische Verlag Zürich, 1932–67), 307 (emphasis original); ET in Barth, *On Religion*, 35. This and subsequent citations from §17 are from my translation. The reader is warned not to trust the translation in

revelation takes the form of religion; but on the other hand, revelation rather than religion must be the guiding category in theology. Barth gives the name "religionism" to the modern theological tendency (he calls it a heresy) to reverse these priorities by treating religion as the governing theological concept. He captures the dialectical relationship that ought to obtain between them by adapting Hegel's term *Aufhebung*: revelation is the sublimation[26]—the simultaneous cancellation, overcoming, and fulfillment—of religion. Revelation, God's act of self-offering, shows religion to be human resistance to grace, idolatry that must first be removed before true knowledge and worship of God are possible. It is important to note that Barth is always careful to include *Christian* religion in this negative characterization; contrary to frequent misrepresentations of his position, he never contrasts good Christian revelation with bad non-Christian religion. The principal targets of his polemics are not proponents of the other world religions but rather Christian theologians who fall prey to the heresy of "religionism." But before we look at Barth's view of non-Christian religions, we need to understand the positive side of his theology of religion.

The key to a properly Christian understanding of religion and revelation is an analogy: "We can talk about 'true' religion," Barth writes, "only in the sense in which we talk about a 'justified sinner.'" Barth's theological roots in a rediscovery of the Protestant Reformation are evident here in his use of the doctrine of justification by faith through grace. "The true religion, like the justified man," he says, "is a creature of *grace*." As long as one holds strictly to this analogy, Barth insists that it is quite proper to state that "*the Christian religion is the true religion*." As if he could already hear the dismayed protests of the pluralists, he underscores the strictly theological nature of this assertion by stressing that it "can only be a proposition of faith," one to be uttered only while listening to God's revelation.[27]

Karl Barth's career took place in an environment marked by vigorous theological debates, first between representatives of the older theology of Protestant liberalism and the young Turks of dialectical theology, and later between Barth and his own erstwhile colleagues, especially Rudolf Bultmann and Emil Brunner. Most important of all, Barth worked out his mature theology in the shadow of National Socialism and the capitulation of the churches to

---

Church Dogmatics I/2, since it contains serious errors. For details, see my translator's preface to Barth, *On Religion*, vii–xi.

26. For a discussion of the problem of how to translate *Aufhebung*, see my introduction to Barth, *On Religion*, 5–6.

27. Barth, *Kirchliche Dogmatik*, vol. I/2, 356–57, translated in Barth, *On Religion*, 86 (emphasis original).

its influence. One must bear this context in mind in seeking to relate Barth's theology of religion to the question of Christianity's relationship to the other religions of the world. The negativity of Barth's critique of religion has more to do with "German Christians" than with Buddhists or Muslims. (The case of the Jews, of course, is a special one, which does not bear directly on our topic but serves to underscore the unique historical conditions under which Barth worked as a theologian.)

Barth nevertheless provides us with one fascinating example of the relation of Christianity to a non-Christian religion. Having established that the Christian religion is the true religion in that, and insofar as, it is the locus of the revelation of God's grace, Barth turns his attention to what he calls "the most exact, comprehensive, and plausible 'pagan' parallel to Christianity," and specifically to Reformation Christianity: the Japanese Buddhist schools known as Jōdo-shū (or Pure Land Sect) and Jōdo Shinshū (True Pure Land Sect).[28] Founded, respectively, by the monk Hōnen (1133–1212) and his disciple Shinran (1173–1263), these schools taught that one achieves the goal of rebirth in the "Pure Land," not by one's own power and striving (as earlier Buddhist schools had taught) but wholly through one's faith in the salvific power of Buddha Amida. After examining this movement (called "Japanese Protestantism" by some) in considerable detail, Barth declares it "providential" because of the lesson it teaches us: "that the Christian religion in its historical form as a mode of doctrine, life, and order *per se* can never be the thing that contains the truth—not even if the form should be that of Reformation Christianity."[29] The truth belongs to no historical form "as such," Barth insists, Christian or otherwise. The Japanese sects are "providential" not because they mirror the content of Christian teaching but because they make so crystal clear the one decisive factor in determining religious truth and error. "This one thing," Barth tells us, "is *the name Jesus Christ*." This name and nothing else gives to Christianity its truth; he calls it "the essence [*Inbegriff*] of the reality of divine revelation."[30] Having established this point, nothing remains for Barth to do but conclude his theology of religion by examining the implications of the centrality of the name Jesus Christ "from four points of view": as an act of divine creation, election, justification, and sanctification. In each case he takes pains to distinguish clearly between the divine agent and the human religious means. For example, in the case of justification he can say that "the

28. For a description of these sister schools of Japanese Buddhism, see *The Encyclopedia of Religion*, ed. Mircea Eliade (New York: Macmillan, 1987), 8:100–107.
29. Barth, *Kirchliche Dogmatik*, vol. I/2, 375, translated in Barth, *On Religion*, 104.
30. Barth, *Kirchliche Dogmatik*, vol. I/2, 376 (emphasis original), translated in Barth, *On Religion*, 105.

name Jesus Christ . . . justifies the Christian religion without its being able as a human religion to contribute even in the slightest to this reconciliation."[31] The key to getting the relationship right (as so often in Barth's theology) is his "actualism":[32] the truth of the true religion can never become a possession of its devotees and apologists because it is always and only an event, something that *happens* by the grace of God. As Barth puts it most concisely, "No religion *is* true. A religion can only *become* true."[33]

Our model of religious imagination enables us to understand Barth's "insider" argument as a Christian theologian from the "outside," as it were, with a view to the question of religious plurality. His insistence on "the name Jesus Christ" reflects the paradigmatic uniqueness of the Christian vision in contradistinction to other religious paradigms; and his refusal to identify it with another religious reality—even one so strikingly parallel as "Japanese Protestantism"—shows his awareness of the incommensurability of the two religious paradigms.[34] For "Jesus Christ" is the best shorthand account of the unique pattern according to which Christians construe the world and from which they take their bearings. This "exclusivism" (if the label even applies to such a position) is rooted not in a religious imperialism but rather in a modesty befitting the situation. One of the ironies of the debate between religious pluralists and those they call exclusivists is that each side sees in the other position an arrogance, an unjustifiable hubris, while holding its own position to be one of humility and restraint. Surely the strong appeal of pluralism to so many—including both religious believers and nonbelievers—is the widespread perception that it is the only truly tolerant position and therefore holds the moral high ground. I hope that by looking at religion through the lens of paradigmatic imagination, I have been able to show how mistaken that perception of moral superiority really is. Hick's claim to be able to judge the world's religions to be "more or less equally effective," far from being a statement of respect and toleration, could only be made by one who presumes to survey the panoply of religions from a neutral and lofty vantage point, from which their true interrelationships and their actual worth can be fairly assessed. Such a vantage point could be reached only by stepping outside all paradigms in order to see the world not in imagination but as it *really* is, or

31. Barth, *Kirchliche Dogmatik*, vol. I/2, 396, translated in Barth, *On Religion*, 124.
32. See George Hunsinger, *How to Read Karl Barth: The Shape of His Theology* (New York: Oxford University Press, 1991), 30–32.
33. Barth, *Kirchliche Dogmatik*, vol. I/2, 356 (emphasis original), translated in Barth, *On Religion*, 85.
34. Barth does not mention, and may not have known, that both Hōnen and Shinran "believed that the only means to apprehend Amida and to participate in his Original Vow was to invoke his *name*." *Encyclopedia of Religion* 8:102 (emphasis added).

else by adopting a paradigm that purports to encompass all the others. But the latter option makes of the pluralist position no more than a religion, or quasi religion, with its own paradigm-dependent account of how things are.

Where does this situation leave us in the conversation and confrontation of the religions in the world today? Since all of us necessarily see—that is, imagine—the world according to our paradigmatic commitments, we will resist the temptation to rip our eyes out of our heads in order to see more clearly while at the same time acknowledging that others view the world through quite different lenses. Insofar as we are involved in a competition (and only a Pollyanna would want to deny that we are), our aim is to "out-interpret" the opposition—to demonstrate through powerful analysis and compelling lives the beauty and truth of our vision. But because we know ourselves to be not custodians of the truth but recipients of grace, we will also acknowledge our solidarity with others on the way. All the great religious traditions of the world—and here I include the secular humanists as well—have ways of acknowledging the limitation of their vision, even as they affirm their dedication to the way they have chosen. And that means that the wisest among the faithful of all faiths can expect to learn much even from those whose ultimate commitments they cannot share. There is a place too, I think, for what I'm tempted to call an "eschatological pluralism": an earnest hope that the God we worship may see his way clear (a way that we at present cannot imagine) to bring all his human children into one kingdom at the end. But we should never confuse a hope with a theory.

15

IMAGINARY GODS
AND THE ANONYMOUS CHRIST

Having spent a significant part of my career wrestling with Karl
Barth's theology and even translating one of its most important
sections, I was both surprised and intrigued to learn that in the
archives there exist manuscripts of several sections of the dogmatics that
Barth delivered as university lectures but, for reasons unknown, never passed
on to his publisher for inclusion in *Church Dogmatics*. I first learned of their
existence in 2006 at a meeting of the Karl Barth Society of North America,
listening to a paper by Professor Wolf Krötke of the Humboldt-Universität
of Berlin.[1] He described a lengthy manuscript entitled "God and the Gods,"
which Barth had composed (but never published) to be the first section of
Church Dogmatics §42, "The Creator and His Revelation." Since this material is not widely known even among Barth scholars, I want first of all to
recapitulate Barth's treatment of this intriguing topic before considering how
this material relates to what he says about religion in his published work.
And then (since I learned from Karl Barth always to attend to *die Sache*) I
want to comment on the topic itself, asking what Barth can teach us about
the theology of religion and the religions today, when that task seems even
more pressing than it did in the previous century.

1. Wolf Krötke, "A New Impetus to the Theology of Religions from Karl Barth," paper presented to a meeting of the Karl Barth Society of North America, Washington, DC, November
2006. This paper is a translation of "Impulse für eine Theologie der Religionen im Denken Karl
Barths," later published in *Zeitschrift für Theologie und Kirche* 104 (2007): 320–35.

The topic that has long interested me most of all in Barth's writings is the theological significance of religion. I have struggled to come to terms with the way in which the modern concept of religion has affected Christian theology[2]—an influence I believe to be largely negative—and have found Barth's treatment of the issue to be especially salutary. I have also dedicated much of my theological efforts—no surprise to readers of the present volume!—to the Christian religious imagination. On this latter theme I found little of relevance in Barth's writings—that is, until I discovered what he had to say about "God and the Gods." Who knew that Barth had a sophisticated and articulate understanding of the religious imagination and its importance to Christian theology?

I first need to make a hermeneutical disclaimer. I do not intend to enter into the discussion about why Barth chose not to include this material in his *Church Dogmatics*. That question, of course, is an intriguing one, and important for certain purposes. But since my primary concern here is not biography but the subject that Barth addresses in this manuscript, I will take help wherever I can find it, especially when it comes from the pen of Karl Barth. Even if it is the case that he held this material back because he had changed his mind about the correctness of the argument (though I see no grounds for thinking so), any good student of hermeneutics knows that an author is not the final judge of his own writing. I prefer to listen to, and to take seriously, anything Barth says on this crucial topic if it can help us to think more clearly about religion and the religions, and to act more faithfully as Christians, in the twenty-first century.

Imaginary Gods

The opening sentence of Barth's section on "The Creator and His Revelation" clarifies why he must begin by talking about "the gods": "The revelation of God the Creator is the affirmation of all reality different from himself, given that it is his creature, and thereby the denial of every form of its own divinity."[3] He maintains that one feature of the doctrine of creation is a "distinguishing, delimiting, opposing, protesting function," whose job it is to distinguish "God from the gods and faith in him from the establishment and apprehension of

2. See especially chap. 13 above.
3. Karl Barth, *Unveröffentlichte Texte zur Kirchlichen Dogmatik*, ed. Hinrich Stoevesandt and Michael Trowitzsch, in *Karl Barth Gesamtausgabe*, ed. Peter Zocher, vol. 2, *Akademische Werke* (Zurich: Theologischer Verlag Zürich, 2005), 6. All quotations from this source are my translation.

any world picture, that is, from the so-called world views." The challenge is to protect the church against the modern incarnations of the two threats posed to the ancient church by Gnosticism: "the confusion of God with the gods, and faith with the world views."[4] He turns his attention to the first threat, which is our primary concern here, opening with the Wagnerian assertion that God's revelation is the *Götterdämmerung*, the twilight of the gods, in which they are divested of their authority, their claim to divinity, and their power.[5] Then he offers his first formal definition of the gods: "the exponents of the self-assertion and revelation of the Nothing."[6] They are *not* part of "the reality different from himself" that God has created. Rather, "Precisely in their divinity they are the monstrous productions and forms of the Nothing, from which the creature as such is exempted and preserved. The created world as such is not *nichtig*."[7] I have not attempted to translate Barth's term *nichtig*, which was later to be the source of major woes for Barth's translators when he published §50, "Gott und das Nichtige." I'll get to that problem shortly, but first we need to return to Barth's unpublished section to see how he structures his discussion of "God and the Gods."

The substance of Barth's argument proceeds through four topics:

1. The nature (or essence) of the gods
2. The reality of the gods
3. The possibility of the gods
4. The removal (or negation) of the gods

This arrangement reflects Barth's characteristic method of discussing the possibility of something only after first considering its reality.

The Nature of the Gods

Whatever the gods may be, Barth begins with the conviction that they are neither aspects of God himself nor parts of his creation. "In their character as gods," Barth writes, "they are not positively willed and created beings. They do not, in any case, have their divinity from him but rather without him and against him."[8] Waxing metaphorical, Barth says that they are not God's "servants and friends" but rather "intruders and enemies in his house." But

---

4. Barth, *Unveröffentlichte Texte*, 8.
5. Barth, *Unveröffentlichte Texte*, 9.
6. Barth, *Unveröffentlichte Texte*, 9.
7. Barth, *Unveröffentlichte Texte*, 13.
8. Barth, *Unveröffentlichte Texte*, 15.

the gods also have attributes that are not simply negative. Even in their "ines-sentiality," writes Barth, they nevertheless have an "essence," "a certain kind of *Dasein* and *Sosein*, a particular reality and possibility." Barth's metaphysical language here gets complicated—and interesting. While refusing to grant to the gods the true reality of either the Creator or his creatures, he nevertheless refuses simply to dismiss them as nonexistent and therefore unimportant. "We will be on our guard," he writes, "against simply saying: there are no gods."[9] This leads him to make some seemingly paradoxical—and nearly untranslatable—assertions. For example, he writes that the gods "*in ihrer ganzen Nichtigkeit nicht einfach nichts sind*"—"in their utter nullity," we might say in English, "they are not simply nothing." A bit less paradoxical, but still wholly negative: "The gods are not God and yet neither are they simply nothing." Since Barth has already called them precisely nothing, he apparently wants to distinguish between being *nothing* and being *simply nothing*. (I am tempted to say that the gods are "complexly nothing," but even theological translators have their limits!)

The paradoxical language that Barth employs here is part of the point. For in trying to characterize the nature of the gods, we are inevitably drawn into contradictions. And so Barth extends his definition of the gods: "they are creatures who, in their character as gods, are caught up in a *perversion* of their creaturehood."[10] Although their creaturely status is the *sine qua non* of their "divinity," it is not its ground or origin because it can be neither derived from, nor justified by, their creaturehood. These considerations lead to a formal definition:

> "Another god" is a creature who—either for itself alone or in combination with a group or system of its peers—is distinguished from the rest of the creaturely world and elevated above it as though it were not itself a creature, as though it had no Creator, as though it were itself the Creator and Lord of the rest of the creaturely world.[11]

This perversion of the created order unleashes powers that come neither from God nor the world of nature, constituting what Barth calls "a fatal alien middle" between the two, in which forces answerable to neither act "as if" they were God, exercising an authority that is "merely *presumed*, fictive, illusory."[12] Yet despite their illegitimacy—Barth calls them "Nothings"

9. Barth, *Unveröffentlichte Texte*, 16.
10. Barth, *Unveröffentlichte Texte*, 17 (emphasis original).
11. Barth, *Unveröffentlichte Texte*, 18.
12. Barth, *Unveröffentlichte Texte*, 19 (emphasis original).

(*Nichtse*)—they nevertheless exercise real power that can be effective and influential in the world.[13] He then describes the various forms that this unauthorized and dangerous "middle" can take. Just because we speak of "gods" in the plural does not imply that they are necessarily multiple, for they can and will congeal into a powerful mass under the direction of a single "leader"— and Barth's word *Führer* in the 1930s can hardly be coincidental!—as the gods oscillate "between multiformity and uniformity, between 'polytheism' and 'monotheism.'"[14]

The most general and fundamental way to describe the nature of the gods is this: "They are attempts, arbitrarily undertaken by the creature, to *imitate* God."[15] By attempting to elevate themselves from their proper status as creatures, raising themselves above their fellow creatures, they are trying to usurp the place of God while ironically overlooking the fact that the meaning and purpose of the creature in the first place was to be the image of God. By attempting to imitate God on their own initiative, they want to be "gracious to themselves" in defiance of God's gracious creation of the creature in his own image. In trying to do what God does, of course, they are trying to do the impossible. This ironic situation constitutes their "divinity," while at the same time ensuring that it will fail. In this way, says Barth, the gods "suffer from themselves"; they are "the inventors of all perversity." In a final rhetorical flourish Barth characterizes the nature of the gods as *"ein glänzendes Elend,"*[16] a splendid wretchedness!

The Reality of the Gods

I find the most fascinating part of this manuscript to be the section on the *reality* of the gods, for reasons that will become apparent. Putting aside for now the question of their possibility, Barth simply asks whether there *are* gods, and if so in what way. He answers with the following thesis: "All gods . . . exist only in the human imagination [*Einbildung*]."[17] And he immediately adds a crucial qualification, which deserves to be cited in full:

> The statement that something exists only in the human imagination by no means implies that it does not exist at all. Everything that exists for us, *not excluding the true and living God*, exists in any case in our imagination as well, without it therefore existing any less truly. And even what exists only in

13. Barth, *Unveröffentlichte Texte*, 19–20.
14. Barth, *Unveröffentlichte Texte*, 22.
15. Barth, *Unveröffentlichte Texte*, 22 (emphasis original).
16. Barth, *Unveröffentlichte Texte*, 27–28.
17. Barth, *Unveröffentlichte Texte*, 28.

our imagination, which is certainly to be said of the gods, exists no less truly on that account.[18]

Although I never doubted that my own work on imagination was compatible with Barth's theology, neither did I expect to find in his writings so explicit a confirmation of the main thesis of my book *Imagining God*. Barth elaborates the thesis at some length, showing how the "illumination in the encounter with the self-disclosure of God" impinges on the realm of the human imagination, which is already filled with images that exist *only* in imagination. God takes human imagination into account, showing mercy on man "and thereby also on the world of his imagination."[19] Since the reality of the gods consists only in their inclusion in human imagination, man is able to recognize them only to the extent that he "recognizes himself as *sinner* in his whole image-making activity, one who is guilty before God and stands in need of divine mercy."[20]

The precarious and paradoxical nature of the gods, who seem (Hamlet notwithstanding) both to be and not to be at the same time, makes more sense once we realize that the mode of their existence is the imagination. Barth writes that "the gods only *are* in that they *are not*; their reality is not that of God and not that of God's creatures but only that of the opposition against both."[21] That opposition exists in the human imagination, which is quite skilled at doing contradictory things. Barth goes into some detail about various forms taken by the multitude of divinities in the human imagination but stresses that there can be no end to the list. Though he doesn't cite it, one is reminded of Calvin's characterization of human nature as "a perpetual factory of idols."[22] Barth appeals at one point to Hegel to show that the gods can also behave dialectically.[23] He also shows how poets and artists, scientists and philosophers of all kinds give us glimpses of the gods and their influence on human affairs. In a rare reference to religion, he appeals to "the so-called 'primitive' religions" to make the point that "there are levels of consciousness in which the divinity of the elements and their configurations are still current to even the most modern persons, and will, moreover, always remain current. We are no doubt rather impoverished in relation to the 'primitives,' because we have forgotten—that is, repressed or artificially rationalized—so much in

18. Barth, *Unveröffentlichte Texte*, 28 (emphasis added).
19. Barth, *Unveröffentlichte Texte*, 29.
20. Barth, *Unveröffentlichte Texte*, 31 (emphasis original).
21. Barth, *Unveröffentlichte Texte*, 31 (emphasis added).
22. Calvin, *Institutes of the Christian Religion* 1.11.8.
23. Barth, *Unveröffentlichte Texte*, 35–36.

this connection that is in fact very much present."[24] It is significant that Barth puts scare quotes around "primitive," showing that he takes these religious expressions quite seriously. Psychoanalysts and poets know that Barth is on to something here, and theologians would be well-advised to take note as well.

In his final sentence on the reality of the gods, Barth anchors his argument firmly to Scripture. "The apostle did not deny but rather recognized and acknowledged" the gods, he writes, citing (in Greek) 1 Corinthians 8:5, "Indeed there are many gods and many lords." The RSV, the NIV, and the ESV all add quotation marks around "gods" and "lords"; but if Barth is right, there is no justification for doing so. Taking imagination seriously means not only the "orthodox" imagination but also the heterodox and pagan imaginations. The scare quotes are the heritage of the Enlightenment, not the Bible. Barth is warning us that not taking the reality of the gods seriously, as modern rationalism is wont to do, is to risk not taking their real power seriously.

The Possibility of the Gods

Having examined what the gods are, and in what way they are real, Barth turns to the question of how they are possible. I used to think that this jarring reversal of priorities—Barth's insistence on speaking first of the *actuality* of something before raising the apparently prior question of its *possibility*—applied only to revelation. But clearly Barth means it to apply more generally. With a fierce empiricism that would be more at home in the Anglo-Saxon world than the Continental European world, Barth refuses to speculate about the possibility of anything before he has examined its concrete actuality. And now that we have finally reached the issue of the possibility of the gods, he tells us that we are "standing before the really puzzling question of our whole context." For how do you talk about the possibility of something that is "a concrete impossibility"?[25] (An indication of just how difficult Barth found this question to be is the many passages that he wrote and crossed out in this portion of his manuscript.) Here is Barth's thesis statement: "Between Creator and creature there is something in itself impossible—taken seriously by the Creator and also not to be overlooked by the creature. The gods are a figure of this something impossible."[26]

Barth calls the possibility of the gods the *Rätselfrage*, the chief conundrum, of the whole discussion of God and the gods. The gods ought to be impossible, ought not to be at all, and yet they are. How can this be? Like many

24. Barth, *Unveröffentlichte Texte*, 38.
25. Barth, *Unveröffentlichte Texte*, 58–59.
26. Barth, *Unveröffentlichte Texte*, 59.

of the church fathers, Barth interprets sin as coming under a foreign power (*Herrschaft*: literally, "lordship"). He does not call this power Satan or the devil but rather nothingness and evil: *das Nichts, das Nichtige, Nichtigkeit, Bosheit*, and so on. In this unpublished original draft of §42, he imagines this situation as coming under the *Herrschaft* of "the gods." This habit of attributing power to nothingness is a fundamentally Augustinian way of thinking about sin and evil. Like Augustine, Barth finds that the only name he can give to this impossible possibility is *nothing*. This vocabulary of negativity may produce headaches for Barth's translators, but the point is not difficult to grasp. I have added the definite article and capitalized "the Nothing" in order to bring out the quasi-substantive (or perhaps "pseudo-substantive") quality of *das Nichts* in Barth's theology. *Das Nichtige* presents a greater problem, not because the concept is so arcane but simply because English, unlike German, lacks an adjective to accompany the noun *nothing*. (One candidate, *nihilistic*, has already been pressed into service for other purposes.) When Barth applies the qualifier *nichtig* to something, he wants to say that it partakes of the quality of the Nothing, it is "nothing-like." When he generalizes this quality as *das Nichtige*, as in the title of the published §50, he is using it to characterize the whole realm of negativity, what we might call the shadow of God's good creation.

The whole discussion of the possibility, which is to say, the impossibility, of the gods provides us with an important insight into Barth's own theological imagination—though he does not propose it merely as his own but rather as the biblical imagination that should be normative for Christian dogmatics. In Karl Barth's rendition of the scriptural imagination, God's creation is envisioned as a kind of protected space that God has opened up within the Nothing, and this means that the Nothing always threatens to overwhelm creation whenever it neglects the will of the Creator. For example, when the creature does not remain within the covenant relationship, when it tries to liberate itself from God, "then, for just this reason, the dam breaks that could have and should have protected it [the creature] from the threatening Nothing: what ought to remain excluded on the outside, on the basis of the negative decision taken in God's creating, now comes [rushing] in."[27] Another example: "It is man who has to praise the Creator, because he, in his act of creating, has snatched the creature away from nothingness and evil." A couple of sentences later, he adds this: "But it is also man who therefore has to fear the Creator, because only by his will, only by his wise and powerful election, is the creature snatched away from nothingness and evil and held over this

27. Barth, *Unveröffentlichte Texte*, 63.

abyss."[28] (This passage could have come right out of Jonathan Edwards's "Sinners in the Hands of an Angry God," one of the most frequently cited and most misunderstood sermons in the history of Christendom!)

The corresponding imagery of grace fits smoothly into this picture and completes Barth's account of the "possibility" of the gods. For the only thing that prevents man from succumbing to such powerful forces of evil is the grace of God, conceived by Barth (and Edwards) as a gracious *holding* of man, *up*holding him over the abyss of *das Nichtige*. For Barth, the human being who is upheld by God is not simply passive, since he must also actively hold on—hold on for dear life, we could say. "For everything does in fact now depend," Barth says, "on what man does"—and here we encounter another translator's dilemma: "*dass er sich also an Gott halte, von dem er gehalten ist.*"[29] Though it is difficult to reproduce in English this reciprocity of holding, we could say, "that he might hold fast to God, by whom he is upheld." When this relationship is broken—that is, when we let go—what we get is *sin*: "In letting go of God, he is already grasped and possessed by that which God has negated and rejected; he has already fallen under the domination of the nothingness and evil excluded by God."[30] Perhaps Barth's pithiest definition of sin is "*jenes Loslassen der Gnade*"—"that letting go of grace."[31] When this happens, the human creature, meant to be the guardian and keeper of creation, fails at his duty: "The watchman of this creaturely world becomes its betrayer, who opens the gate to its enemy."[32] Shifting the metaphor just a bit, "The boundary that [the creature] thereby transgresses is the boundary of the Kingdom of Nothing, of perversity, of the gods."[33]

Before we leave the question of the possibility of the gods, there is, believe it or not, something positive to be said. For in an indirect and backhanded way, even the gods give glory to God. Barth puts it this way: "Since they have their ground and possibility in the Nothing, in that creaturehood not chosen and willed but rather rejected and negated by God, they are, precisely in their negative character, the proof of the meaning and rightness of that divine choice and decision, carried out to their own detriment. In this sense they can and must also praise God." This insight carries an import greater than may at first appear. It shows that God chooses "not like a tyrant but like a skillful judge, between that which should be and remain nothing, and

28. Barth, *Unveröffentlichte Texte*, 64–65.
29. Barth, *Unveröffentlichte Texte*, 66.
30. Barth, *Unveröffentlichte Texte*, 67.
31. Barth, *Unveröffentlichte Texte*, 78.
32. Barth, *Unveröffentlichte Texte*, 68.
33. Barth, *Unveröffentlichte Texte*, 69.

that which should become something as his creature."[34] If we were unable to imagine what God might have created but chose not to create, we would be unaware of the wisdom and marvel of his actual creation. And there is more good news. Insofar as the gods have possibility, it is not God but we who give it to them. "The identity of the possibility of the gods with the possibility of human sin," Barth reasons, means that in rejecting the grace of God we are invoking the gods and thus making them a reality and a possibility in our common life.[35] But since the mercy of God confronts the fallen world in love, we can be assured that sin is overcome, and along with it the gods. Even the "terrible inconceivability" of the gods' possibility cannot separate us from the love of God. In a characteristic move, Barth's final word on the possibility of the gods is christological, reminding us that Adam the sinner is "the prophecy and archetype of Jesus Christ," in whom God himself as man replaces our perverted choice with the right one.[36]

The "Beseitigung" of the Gods

Once again I am forced initially to leave a key term untranslated because so much depends on getting it right. Krötke in his paper to the Karl Barth Society spoke of the "abolition" of the gods. I liked the sound of it because my retranslation of §17 was originally motivated by that one egregious error in the title, where the *Aufhebung* of religion was rendered as "abolition."[37] Maybe now we have found the place in Barth where something really is abolished— and who more deserving of that fate than the gods? But, alas, I've become convinced that it is not the right term here either, though for different reasons. It's important to get it right because Barth calls this fourth section "the goal of our deliberations."[38] For here we have the resolution of the problem that was developed in the first three parts. What is the solution to the problem posed by the nature, reality, and possibility of the gods?

This final section describes the negation of the gods as a fitting parallel to God's affirmation of creation. But Barth chooses an unusual term, and I believe he has selected it deliberately. Unlike religion, the gods are not *aufgehoben* but *beseitigt*. There can be no doubt that he is aware of the metaphor contained in this verb, because at one point he tells us that "the whole world

34. Barth, *Unveröffentlichte Texte*, 79–80.
35. Barth, *Unveröffentlichte Texte*, 79.
36. Barth, *Unveröffentlichte Texte*, 82.
37. My translation of §17 appears in *On Religion: The Revelation of God as the Sublimation of Religion* (New York: T&T Clark, 2006).
38. Barth, *Unveröffentlichte Texte*, 82.

of the gods" is *"beseitigt, d.h. auf die Seite gestellt."*[39] In the act of creation, the gods have simply been swept aside. (If they were abolished, after all, we would hear no more about them.) In searching for the best English equivalent, the language of sports does it best: Barth is saying that the gods have been *sidelined*—which allows us to add that they are still very much in the game! Elsewhere Barth provides us with a string of synonyms that may help to focus his meaning more sharply. God's affirmation in creation, he writes, is *"die Verneinung, die Leugnung, die Beseitigung, Überwindung und Erledigung der Götter"*—"the negation, the denial, the removal, overcoming and dispatching of the gods."[40] He intends a kind of symmetry between God's affirmation of creation and his negation of the gods, because he immediately adds that "the power of that Yes is the power of this No." For Barth, the gods represent a kind of anti-creation. In view of all the evidence, I first thought that "displacement" was the correct translation of *Beseitigung* but eventually decided it was too weak. On the one hand, Barth can say of the gods, "Whatever and however they may be elsewhere, whatever other dominion and agency they may have, here they have no place."[41] That could be taken to mean that they have been displaced: although they have no place in God's creation, they may well have a place somewhere else. On the other hand, Barth can say that God's creative activity "negates, overthrows, and destroys the gods"[42]—which comes pretty close to "abolition." In the end I settled on *removal*: God's creation of a world apart from himself, a world that he affirms and justifies, entails the *removal* of the gods. This term retains the spatial metaphor of *Beseitigung* but expresses greater finality than "displacement."

If the gods have no room in creation, from which they have been removed by the very act of creating, where *do* they have their place? Barth's answer should be evident: the gods are at home *"only* in the human imagination, in an imagination we now can and do see through as folly." Here is the *Götterdämmerung* brought about by God's revelation of the truth about himself and the world. "Here the gods are dead," Barth declares: "as dead as any Enlightenment can make them."[43] Barth does offer a few additional metaphors for the sidelining of the gods. In one rhetorical flourish he says, "Here they can only melt away like snow in the heat of the fire, they can only yield like shadows when the sun rises."[44]

39. Barth, *Unveröffentlichte Texte*, 87.
40. Barth, *Unveröffentlichte Texte*, 90.
41. Barth, *Unveröffentlichte Texte*, 105.
42. Barth, *Unveröffentlichte Texte*, 94.
43. Barth, *Unveröffentlichte Texte*, 96.
44. Barth, *Unveröffentlichte Texte*, 89.

In the final pages of this unpublished manuscript, Barth returns to Scripture, demonstrating how the theme of the removal of the gods is sounded throughout the history of Israel, from the first commandment of the Decalogue to the warnings of the prophets, culminating in the appearance of the Messiah of Israel. "The condemnation and crucifixion of Jesus," Barth writes, "was both at once: flagrant violation and powerful proclamation of the first commandment."[45] He also reiterates the link between creation and the gods: "Israel's Messiah there, the Lord of the Church here, is the mystery of the removal of the gods, because Israel's Messiah there and the Lord of the Church here is the mystery of the relationship between Creator and creature."[46] Writing at the height of National Socialism in Germany, Barth makes this bold claim: "His name, his birth, joins these two so different peoples in one people [*zu einem Volk!*] and their so different proclamation, the prophetic protest and the apostolic kerygma, in one witness."[47]

The Anonymous Christ and the Religions

Karl Barth's unpublished text on "God and the Gods" obviously deals with issues that are directly relevant to our urgent need for a theological understanding of the relationship between Christianity and the other religions of the world. It does so in terms quite different from his published theology of religion in §17 of the *Church Dogmatics* as well as his intriguing discussion in §69 of "secular parables" and "lesser lights" that we can perceive beyond the boundaries of Scripture and church. One of the more striking differences is the almost total absence of attention to *religion* in the essay on the gods. But there is also a similarity between what Barth says about religion and what he says about the gods, one that appears worrisome to some: both texts seem to make dialogue between Christians and those of other faiths more, not less, difficult. I want to address these concerns by describing what I think Karl Barth has to say to us in our twenty-first-century efforts to find an acceptable Christian theology of the religions.

Our deliberations about these matters take place today in a cultural context that I call "creeping pluralism." It has been creeping for a long time now. Dietrich Bonhoeffer thought that the process leading to *die mündiggewordene Welt*, "the world come of age," dated back at least to Hugo Grotius in the early seventeenth century, whose principle *etsi deus non daretur* serves as its

---

45. Barth, *Unveröffentlichte Texte*, 107.
46. Barth, *Unveröffentlichte Texte*, 108.
47. Barth, *Unveröffentlichte Texte*, 108.

motto.[48] I like to date its birth to 1648, when the Treaty of Westphalia ended the wars in the wake of the Reformation by establishing the principle of *cuius regio eius religio*.[49] The juxtaposed absolutes of the German principalities that resulted from the application of this principle have in our day achieved global proportions. Why should anyone credit *our* absolute, when our next-door neighbors (often quite literally today) acknowledge a rival absolute? A direct line runs from Hugo Grotius to John Hick.[50]

Even theologians sympathetic to Karl Barth do not always escape the pluralistic undertow of the age. In his paper presented to the Karl Barth Society, Krötke briefly summarizes Barth's unpublished text on "God and the Gods" and goes on to describe "the untapped potential of Karl Barth's thought for a theology of religions."[51] Krötke summarizes the pluralist option in the theology of religions, which, he points out, "seems to contribute most readily to the spirit of understanding between religions" because it "assumes that all religions are equally true in each *subjective faith perspective*."[52] But he is nevertheless quick to dismiss pluralism: "This relativistic model of the theology of religions," Krötke claims, "obviously fails to do justice to the self-understanding of any concrete religion; it is a construct of the philosophy of religion. For every religion lives from the claim that truth has disclosed itself in a particular, *concrete* way." Barth is quite right, he says, to emphasize the particularity of Christian revelation. But Krötke criticizes him for trying "to classify all religions in terms of the temptation he perceived in Christianity to put God's truth at human command through arbitrarily conceived ideas and images of God."[53] He nevertheless argues that Barth's theology contains the potential for a more open and positive approach to other religions, even though Barth did not develop it. Krötke thinks that Barth's unpublished "phenomenology of the gods" shows this untapped potential.[54]

When Krötke tries to illustrate this potential, however, he shows that he has not really left behind the spirit of pluralism after all. He speculates that Barth deleted his original §42 because he was dissatisfied with its wholly negative account of the origin of the gods, and he claims to find in Barth's text "an

---

48. Dietrich Bonhoeffer, *Letters and Papers from Prison* (New York: Macmillan, 1972), 359. The Latin phrase means "as if God did not exist."

49. The Latin phrase literally means "whose realm, his religion"—in other words, the treaty established the principle that henceforth the ruler of a region would determine its religion.

50. For a more extensive discussion of competing absolutes, see the critique of religious pluralism in chap. 14 above.

51. Krötke, "A New Impetus," 1.

52. Krötke, "A New Impetus," 3 (emphasis original).

53. Krötke, "A New Impetus," 3–4 (emphasis original).

54. Krötke, "A New Impetus," 11.

attempt to put faith in the gods . . . into a more positive relationship with the God revealed in Christ than the correlation of such faith to 'nothingness' would seem to allow."[55] The only evidence he offers for this unlikely thesis is a doctored citation from a later passage in Barth's draft. In the English version of his paper, Krötke offers the following as a translation from Barth's text:

> [The gods] are not nothing before God, neither are they condemned by him and therefore they are not reprehensible to us inasmuch as they are in their true nature genuinely creatures; to this extent they also have a share in the peace of God and his creation.[56]

In the German version of his paper Krötke cites Barth's actual words, but he also inserts an ellipsis in the middle of the sentence to indicate an omission (the English text contains no indication of the omission). Here is my translation of the passage, including the omitted portion, indicated by italics:

> [The gods] are not nothing before God and neither are they condemned by him and are therefore not condemnable for us inasmuch as they are actually and in their true nature creatures, *though ones that have been raised by the perverted imagination of man into the nature and existence of gods*; to this extent they also have a part in the peace of God and his creation.[57]

Clearly, Barth is not saying here—or anywhere else—what Krötke would like him to say. Even if we could accept the edited sentence as representative of Barth's views, it is hard to imagine that representatives of non-Christian religions would feel that the truth of their beliefs had been acknowledged or that a positive opening toward their faith had been made. If Karl Barth has anything useful to say to us today, we won't discover it by making him into a reluctant pluralist. Keith Johnson has shown how some theologians sympathetic to Barth have unwittingly provided an opening for pluralism by offering accounts of God's transcendence, which, though "consciously indebted to Karl Barth . . . implicitly open the door to Hick's line of argument" by suggesting that because we never fully comprehend God, no religion can claim superior knowledge of him.[58] Johnson argues convincingly to the contrary that the thesis of God's transcendence need not—*ought* not—lead to a pluralist account of religious truth.

55. Krötke, "A New Impetus," 12.
56. Cited in Krötke, "A New Impetus," 12.
57. Barth, *Unveröffentlichte Texte*, 276.
58. Keith E. Johnson, "Divine Transcendence, Religious Pluralism and Barth's Doctrine of God," *International Journal of Systematic Theology* 5 (2003): 200–24.

The real challenge we face is not simply how to avoid pluralism but how to provide a theologically sound alternative. To that end, I would like to look briefly at two interrelated issues: the question of God's saving activity beyond the bounds of the church, and the question of whether there are "anonymous Christians."

The best-known proposal for a theology of the religions is Karl Rahner's proposal that we can speak meaningfully of "anonymous Christians" beyond the walls of the institutional church. I won't try to summarize Rahner's well-known position, but I would like to say something about its relation to Barth's take on the same issue. In a perceptive essay comparing the views of the two theologians, Geoff Thompson argues that Barth and Rahner are really very close in their understanding of the theological issues at stake, and even in their goals, since both are convinced that the reach of God's grace is universal. "Yet," argues Thompson, "despite the common convictions and the *prima facie* close parallels . . . , the doctrinal moves by which these convictions are unfolded differ significantly, and yield two quite different positions."[59] Both are dissatisfied with the traditional doctrine, going back to the ancient church, that there is "no salvation outside the church": *extra ecclesiam nulla salus*. Rahner's solution is to affirm the doctrine while expanding the definition of *ecclesia* by positing the existence of people who, while not seeing themselves as Christians, are nevertheless on the way to salvation or may even have achieved it "anonymously"—that is, without understanding that their own way is in fact Christ's way. Barth, on the other hand, deals with the same problem by amending the formula: his principle is *extra Christum nulla salus*. Rather than attempting to expand the borders of the church, Barth directs the attention of the church to the action of Christ beyond its borders.

The contrast between Barth and Rahner brings to the fore what we might call "the case of the misplaced anonymity." Searching for "anonymous Christians" is a futile quest—and a dangerous one insofar as it tempts us to adopt a vague and abstract definition of the Christian (not to mention the presumption of baptizing by definition other human beings who have no desire, thank you very much, to be called Christians). At a crucial juncture in his critique of religion, Barth (using the example of Pure Land Buddhism) concludes that "among the religions only one thing is decisive . . . *the name Jesus Christ*."[60]

59. Geoff Thompson, "Salvation Beyond the Church's Ministry: Reflections on Barth and Rahner," in *God of Salvation: Soteriology in Theological Perspective*, ed. Ivor J. Davidson and Murray A. Rae (Burlington, VT: Ashgate, 2011), 138.

60. Barth, *On Religion: The Revelation of God as the Sublimation of Religion*, trans. Garrett Green (London: T&T Clark, 2006), 105 (cf. *KD* I/2, 376) (emphasis original). For a discussion

As Paul writes to the Romans, "if you confess with your mouth that Jesus is Lord and believe in your heart that God raised him from the dead, you will be saved. For with the heart one believes and is justified, and with the mouth one confesses and is saved" (Rom. 10:9–10). Barth's approach reorients our search by inviting us to ask not "Who are the real Christians out there?" but rather "Where is Jesus Christ out there?" If the grace of God in his self-revelation in Christ is indeed universal, then we may be sure that he is out there whether we can see him or not. The mystery is not about anonymous Christians but rather about the anonymous Christ.

This approach to the question of anonymity also has the advantage of scriptural support, for the Christ of the New Testament is given to anonymous appearances. In Jesus's parable of the last judgment in Matthew 25, it is striking that not only the goats on his left but also the sheep on his right are surprised to learn of their past encounters with the Son of Man. "Lord, when did we see you hungry and feed you, or thirsty and give you drink?" (Matt. 25:37; cf. v. 44). Those who have responded to him rightly, even though anonymously, are rewarded with eternal life. It is also worth noting that some of those whom Jesus heals do not, at least initially, know who he is. In the longest of the Gospel healing narratives, John 9, the man born blind does not even ask to be healed and has no idea who has healed him. Only after suffering interrogation and rejection by the religious establishment does he return to Jesus, who asks him, "Do you believe in the Son of Man?" He responds, "And who is he, sir, that I may believe in him?" Only after Jesus answers, "You have seen him, and it is he who is speaking to you," does he respond in faith: "He said, 'Lord, I believe,' and he worshiped him." Perhaps the most dramatic example of the anonymous Christ is in Luke 24, where on the very day of the resurrection two of Jesus's disciples fail to recognize him on the road to Emmaus. If even his own followers can encounter him anonymously, how much more likely it is that those who have never known him will fail to recognize him! Yet everything depends on our recognizing him for who he is, imagining him as the one who bears this name. "It is a matter," Barth writes, "of his existence under a quite specific *name*, which identifies him and distinguishes him from every other thing that exists, a name by which he is to be described, and by which he is to be addressed."[61] Further on, he makes this important assertion: "Really knowing him rests on the fact that

---

of Barth's comments on Pure Land Buddhism, see chap. 14 above, under "Religion from the Inside Out: A Theological Perspective."

61. Barth, *Die kirchliche Dogmatik*, vol. IV/3 (Zurich: Theologische Verlag Zürich, 1959), 49; cf. Barth, *Church Dogmatics*, vol. IV/3, trans. G. W. Bromiley (Edinburgh: T&T Clark, 1961), 46 (translation revised).

he makes himself known; adequately imagining him rests on the fact that he presents himself." This self-identification occurs in each of the biblical examples cited above.

A possible counterexample, cited by Krötke, is Paul's encounter with the Athenians in Acts 17. Krötke wants to develop a suggestion he sees in Barth that, as Krötke puts it, "the gods of the religions cannot be entirely bereft of any 'contact' or 'formal correspondence' to the true God," since they are in fact "his offspring" (Acts 17:28).[62] From this passage Krötke concludes as follows: "Even when people of other religions manage to mix the power of nothingness into their understanding of God, Christianity still has the task of *differentiating* that which is genuinely of God from that which it recognizes to be false." Krötke has managed to misrepresent both Barth and the apostle Paul at the same time. Barth follows his allusion to the gods being "his offspring" with this caveat (*not* cited by Krötke): "Yet only with the greatest irony will it be possible to say that of them." And in Paul's speech on the Areopagus, it is "we," not the gods, who are said to be "his offspring." What Paul is really doing in his speech is not reaching out in dialogue to the worshipers of pagan gods but rather attempting to introduce the Athenian adherents of the unknown god to the anonymous Christ.

Krötke and others who would like to discover a more "religion-friendly" Karl Barth are missing the utter radicality of Barth's critique of religion. It is not as though the second section of §17, "Religion as Faithlessness," were somehow replaced by the final section on "The True Religion." It has been *aufgehoben*, sublimated, according to the logic of the "negation of the negative." That sublimation, however, takes place only in Jesus Christ, and only to the extent that, by the grace of God, the church becomes "the site of the true religion to the extent that through grace it lives by grace."[63] What is missed—both by critics who accuse Barth of hostility toward other faiths and by would-be supporters of a kinder, gentler Barth—is that Barth is not an apologist for any religion, *including Christianity*. (For Barth the goal of reconciliation among the religions would be, as the saying goes, like rearranging the deck chairs on the *Titanic*.) Barth's critique is directed, not primarily against "the religions," but first and foremost against the Christian religion. He makes clear that Christianity, insofar as it is "our" religion, is *false*; only by the grace of God does it *become* true. But it becomes the truth of *Christ*, not *our* truth, not the truth of Christianity. In the opening paragraph of his section on "The True Religion" he makes this crystal clear:

62. Krötke, "A New Impetus," 13, citing Barth, *Unveröffentlichte Texte*, 23.
63. Thesis statement of §17, cited from Barth, *On Religion*, 33.

> Religion is never and nowhere true as such and in itself. On the contrary, the claim that it is true . . . is denied to every religion by God's revelation. . . . If the concept of a "true religion" is supposed to mean a truth belonging to one religion as such and in itself, it is as incapable of being realized as the concept of a "good man." . . . No religion *is* true. A religion can only *become* true.[64]

This theme is repeated throughout Barth's discussion of "The True Religion." Barth *always* includes the Christian religion in his critique of all religion. His detractors who claim that he exempts Christianity while deprecating other religions are as wrong as his would-be supporters who hope to find some positive appreciation of other religions as a basis for a more "open" dialogue. But Barth will have none of it. The job of the church is always to point away from itself and toward Jesus Christ.

Finally, I would like to address the question of where this leaves us in the global world of our own century, where people are desperate to know how the religions relate to one another, and where Christians want to know what we have to say to adherents of other religions. I have three brief comments, reminders of what we can learn from Karl Barth.

First, one of the chief worries about Barth's theology of religion is its alleged *arrogance*. But those who make this complaint are missing the point, and they have things exactly backwards. Arrogance is what we hear from religious pluralists, who tell us with utter assurance that no religion has the truth, or perhaps that all religions share in the same ultimate truth (call it "the Real"). How could one possibly be in a position to know this, even if it is true? Such a doctrine could only be proclaimed by one who occupies an exalted position beyond all mere perspectives, a vantage point from which one can survey all the religions *sub specie Dei* and report on how they are related. Karl Barth, on the other hand, can only report what he sees from his vantage point as a Christian, demonstrating the modesty of that position by refusing to pass judgment on other peoples or their faith, even suggesting that we remain alert to hear true words, echoes of the one Word of God, from any human voice. At the same time he refuses to qualify or modify the gospel that he, together with the church, hears from God's own self-disclosure in Jesus Christ. Here, I believe, he offers us a model to be emulated today.

A second, closely related, qualm is voiced by those who fear that such a forthright proclamation of Christian truth might be *offensive* to people of other faiths or of no faith. Paul writes that "we preach Christ crucified, a stumbling block to Jews and folly to Gentiles" (1 Cor. 1:23), and his word

---

64. Barth, *On Religion*, 85 (cf. *KD* I/2, 356).

for "stumbling block" is *skandalon*. Kierkegaard, who knew a thing or two about scandals, thought that there were only two possible responses to the gospel of Jesus, either faith or offense. One thing we can learn from Karl Barth (who knew his Kierkegaard) is that if we want to engage in interfaith dialogue we had better develop tough skins, because the modesty of Christian proclamation is bound to offend some listeners. If I am not mistaken, our current cultural climate ensures that Christians will increasingly find themselves giving offense. I read in the newspaper recently of a kindergartner who was forbidden by his teacher, during "show and tell," to tell the story of David and Goliath. Such incidents understandably provoke dismay and outrage among Christians. But the good news is that as the culture divests itself of its Christian roots, the words of the Bible are regaining their ability to offend.

The third truth that Karl Barth can teach us in this pluralistic age is that not only the gods but also the one God of Israel and our Lord Jesus Christ gain access to us through our imagination. At one point in his unpublished text Barth defines a god as one who "makes . . . the claim of encompassing the whole of reality."[65] The god does this by capturing our imagination, by tempting us to envision all of life according to that god's particular story or paradigm. Knowing that the battlefield is the imagination will make us better soldiers of the Lord in a secular age. As theologians, we are called to be stewards of the Christian imagination. While advertisers and politicians, talk-show hosts and how-to books, TV evangelists and college professors, are all competing to fill our minds and hearts with the images of their gods, we will go right on preaching Christ and him crucified.

Let me close with a motto from Karl Barth to keep us humble in interfaith dialogue. It caught my eye while reading his unpublished manuscript: "*Gerade auf Erwählung kann man ja nicht pochen*": "Election is one thing that nobody can brag about."[66]

---

65. Barth, *Unveröffentlichte Texte*, 53.
66. Barth, *Unveröffentlichte Texte*, 100.

PART 5

CONCLUSION

16

CHRISTIAN THEOLOGY
IN A POST-CHRISTIAN AGE

Imagination. Could there be any concept more vague, more overused, more slippery, and more subject to the whims and idiosyncrasies of its countless users? If you have any doubts, just type the word into an on-line search engine. (It took Google less than a second to come up with 543 million results.) Why would a theologian committed to doctrinal precision, theological orthodoxy, and modesty of expression want to hitch his wagon to such an out-of-control word? And then set out in search of a *normative* imagination! All I can say is that "imagination" has long seemed to me to be the *right* term, ever since I read Thomas Kuhn's book *The Structure of Scientific Revolutions* and found in it something that its author surely never intended: the key to describing for a late modern audience what it is that Christian theologians actually *do*. My only alibi—at the risk of utter circularity—is that this concept captured my imagination, and I have never ceased trying to wrestle it into theological shape. The introductory chapter to this volume is my latest attempt to summarize the results of that struggle, and the intervening chapters show how the Christian imagination works in specific situations to illumine a variety of theological issues. Thus the order of the chapters is not sequential but illustrative: not systematic steps toward a single conclusion but explorations emanating from a common center, illustrations of various ways in which Christians can employ the Bible paradigmatically to illumine the world around them in its relationship to God.

There can be little doubt that today's Christians live in an increasingly
post-Christian culture (at least those of us living in lands that were, not so
long ago, part of a culture that took its Christian foundations for granted).
Theologians have tried to adapt to this new and uncomfortable context in
various ways. When I began my theological studies half a century ago, the
rallying cry was "relevance," and the perceived need was for a theology better attuned to the emerging secular culture. Hallmarks of that era were Paul
Van Buren's book *The Secular Meaning of the Gospel* and above all Harvey
Cox's *The Secular City*, which so many of the people I knew at the end of
my first year in seminary couldn't wait to read over the summer.[1] Those
early responses to secularism reached their extreme in the so-called death-of-
God theology, championed by William Hamilton, Thomas J. J. Altizer, and
others—a movement that might better be called the death of theology.[2] In
retrospect, those days seem surprisingly cheerful, for the mood has shifted
enormously in the meantime. A pastor friend of mine now tells his congregation that "our culture is in the process of giving itself permission to persecute
Christians." Elsewhere in the world the persecution is already well underway.
Like most twentieth-century Christians, I grew up thinking of martyrdom
as Christians thrown to the lions in ancient Rome. But Christian believers
today are dying at the hands of their enemies at a far greater rate than in any
previous period in the church's history.[3]

Theologians have responded to secularization in a variety of ways, some
of them calling for politicized theologies aimed at transforming society. The
danger of this approach is that it threatens to replace the biblical theology
of redeeming grace with a this-worldly political goal (and one that inevitably
leans far to the left). In this way liberation theologies continue in more radical ways the program of theological liberalism that I call accommodationist
theology, which assumes that Christians need to find ways to reconcile their
beliefs to those of the prevailing secular culture.[4]

As our culture's departure from Christianity has continued apace, theological efforts to bridge the gap are becoming increasingly desperate, rather
like a lumberjack plummeting down a river with one foot on each of two

1. Paul M. Van Buren, *The Secular Meaning of the Gospel: Based on Analysis of Its Language*
(New York: Macmillan, 1963); Harvey Cox, *The Secular City: Secularization and Urbanization
in Theological Perspective* (New York: Macmillan, 1965).
2. Thomas J. J. Altizer and William Hamilton, *Radical Theology and the Death of God*
(Indianapolis: Bobbs-Merrill, 1966).
3. The Barnabas Fund (www.barnabasaid.org) provides detailed up-to-date information
and statistics about persecuted Christian believers around the world through its bimonthly
magazine *Barnabas Aid* and other publications.
4. See chaps. 4 and 10 above.

separating logs. On the ecclesiastical level the strain has reached the breaking point in a number of Christian denominations. No sooner had the ecumenical movement of the twentieth century achieved some remarkable reconciliations of long-standing doctrinal differences than new divisions began to open up, not in the area of doctrinal beliefs but rather in Christian moral teaching. The sexual revolution of the past century, reaching its peak in the 1960s, is now forcing Christians to decide whether the time has come to give up on accommodation to secular culture and move to a stance of moral resistance. Especially distressing are signs that many Christians today, including those holding conservative beliefs, are lending support to radical and authoritarian movements in the secular society in a desperate attempt to find allies in the struggle to survive, even when those allies reject the most basic standards of biblical Christianity. As Christians find themselves increasingly alienated from the culture around them, the temptation to hunker down in defensive hostility will continue to grow. For the sake of the gospel of Jesus Christ, this response must be vigorously resisted.

The Apologetics of Evidence

One barrier to accepting the thesis that theology fundamentally involves imagination is the continuing allegiance of so many Christians to what I call the apologetics of evidence. Whether they be theologians in the formal sense or theologically engaged laity, many Christians are convinced that the best way to advance the faith in a secular context is through apologetics, understood as advocating Christian belief on the basis of verifiable evidence. This approach is especially prevalent among those who are convinced that the crucial issues concern the relationship of science and religion.[5] Though there are many varieties of evidence-based apologetics, I want to examine the notion of "evidence" itself, a term imported from the empirical sciences. The problem with this term when put to apologetic use is that it carries with it the questionable metaphysical assumptions of the founders of modern science. The most problematic of those assumptions is the abandonment of teleology.[6] Empirical verifiability is a hallmark of modern scientific study of nature but is inapplicable to theological reasoning because it looks for evidence of God as though he were an unknown object in the world, one of his own creatures. Believers can certainly speak meaningfully about the evidence on which they base their faith, but that evidence is of another order entirely, qualitatively different from scientific

---

5. See chap. 1 above for a brief history of science and religion in the modern world.
6. See chap. 1 above, under "The Metaphysics of Modern Science."

evidence. The apologetics of evidence, by failing to make this all-important distinction, employs arguments for belief that can be laughably implausible and produce the opposite response from the one intended. One example will have to suffice. Apologists often appeal to Paul's report that the risen Jesus "appeared to more than five hundred brothers at one time" (1 Cor. 15:6) as though it constituted eyewitness evidence for the resurrection. I wonder how many of these Christians would accept similar claims made on behalf of other religions and ideologies as convincing evidence of *their* plausibility. Note also that the apostle calls these witnesses "brothers," fellow Christian believers, and is clearly not invoking them as neutral observers.

At the heart of the apologetics of evidence is the question of miracle. David Hume, writing in the midst of the European Enlightenment of the eighteenth century, offers a devastating critique of the evidence for miracles: "A miracle," he writes, "is a violation of the laws of nature; and as a firm and unalterable experience has established these laws, the proof against a miracle, from the very nature of the fact, is as entire as any argument from experience can possibly be imagined." From this statement he concludes that "no testimony is sufficient to establish a miracle unless the testimony be of such a kind that its falsehood would be more miraculous than the fact which it endeavors to establish."[7] The practitioners of the apologetics of evidence are caught in a dilemma. Wanting to propose a defense of Christian belief on rational grounds, they are unwilling to claim the resurrection of Jesus as a miracle in Hume's strong sense of the term but unable to offer a persuasive argument on any other basis. Surprisingly, Hume does not shy away from the radical implications of his argument, offering the following conclusion to his essay on miracles:

> Upon the whole, we may conclude that the Christian religion not only was at first attended with miracles, but even at this day cannot be believed by any reasonable person without one. Mere reason is insufficient to convince us of its veracity. And whoever is moved by *faith* to assent to it is conscious of a continued miracle in his own person which subverts all the principles of his understanding and gives him a determination to believe what is most contrary to custom and experience.[8]

Hume is correct in his conclusion, even given that his words drip with irony under the pressure of censorship in the Presbyterian Edinburgh of 1748. I

---

7. David Hume, "Of Miracles," in *An Inquiry concerning Human Understanding*, ed. Charles W. Hendel (Indianapolis: Bobbs-Merrill, 1955), 122–23.

8. Hume, "Of Miracles," 140–41 (emphasis original).

have never been able to decide for sure how to read his conclusion. Does he assume his words to be self-evidently absurd and therefore intend a rejection of all religion except a rationalistic deism, or is he intentionally leaving the door open for a radically faith-based religion? Either way, the important thing is that it doesn't matter! If the first interpretation is correct, he shows himself to be a dogmatic rationalist who accepts the metaphysics of modern science as the sole admissible grounds for truth. If the second interpretation is right, he sees the possibility of another option, though he clearly has no intention of adopting it for himself. His claim that faith "subverts all the principles of [our] understanding" in favor of claims that are "most contrary to custom and experience" simply shows how thoroughly his own imagination has been captured by the "scientific" rationalism of the Enlightenment.

Now picture Hume and his opponent standing before the figure of the duck-rabbit. Hume feels secure in his assertion that the object is a duck, because he can show how every detail of the figure represents a part of the duck. Nothing is omitted from his interpretation, apparently leaving no basis whatever for asserting that the figure is in fact a rabbit. Needless to say, his faith-based opponent will be able to make identical claims on behalf of the rabbit. What both sides fail to acknowledge is the necessary role of imagination: that what one sees is determined by the implicit paradigm that shapes and organizes the details into a whole. In the case of miracles in eighteenth-century rationalism, the irony is that both sides naïvely assume that they can see neutrally, from some absolute standpoint requiring no interpretation—in other words, without taking imagination into account. In the case of Hume's denial of miracles, his position is invulnerable so long as his metaphysical presuppositions are taken for granted. The bad news for his well-meaning theological opponents is that their apologetics of evidence unwittingly shackles them to the same set of presuppositions.

Imagination and Reality

The main reason that so many people today resist the thesis that theology is constituted in a basic way by imagination should be obvious. They take for granted the opposition of *imagination* and *reality*: surely what the imagination produces is *imaginary* and cannot possibly be *real*. It does not matter that this popular metaphysical dualism is demonstrably false and misleading, whether we are thinking about science or religion. The first task of Christian theology in a post-Christian age must be to take leave of the imagination-versus-reality way of thinking once and for all. The theology of paradigmatic imagination is thoroughly, aggressively *realist*. Its fundamental claim is that we cannot have reliable knowledge of the world or God without right imagination.

If the apologetics of evidence represents the Scylla in our journey toward a theology of realistic imagination, we must also steer clear of a different danger on our other flank: the rocks of Charybdis, known as *relativism*. Whereas the evidence apologists fail to acknowledge any role for imagination, the relativists are convinced that we have nothing but imagination. A famous passage from Friedrich Nietzsche sets the stage: "What, then, is truth?" he asks, and his answer sounds like an attempt to outdo Pontius Pilate:

> A mobile army of metaphors, metonyms, and anthropomorphisms—in short, a sum of human relations that have been enhanced, transposed, and embellished poetically and rhetorically, and which after long use seem firm, canonical, and obligatory to a people: truths are illusions about which one has forgotten that this is what they are.[9]

Relativism is the implicit, and sometimes explicit, epistemology of contemporary Western secularism. Since nobody can know the truth, they argue ("everything is relative" is a refrain that teachers hear ad nauseam from students), anyone claiming to know the truth must be either ignorant or bigoted. Contemporary relativism comes in two varieties, which I call soft and hard. The soft relativist is wont to say such things as "Well, that may be true for you, but it doesn't have to be true for me," a principle that removes all distinction between truth and opinion—or, expressed more bluntly, reduces truth to mere opinion.

Hard relativism adopts a more aggressive stance, taking the form of what is popularly (and confusingly) known today as "political correctness."[10] Its logic goes like this: since truth cannot be known by anyone, people who claim to speak the truth are evil and dangerous and must be silenced by any means available (including censorship, public shaming, or removal from employment). The implicit contradiction in hard relativism ought to be apparent to everyone, though plainly it is not. It goes this way: since we now *know* that all truth is relative, anyone claiming to speak the truth is in violation of, well, of the one remaining absolute—namely, that there isn't, *there can't*

---

9. Friedrich Nietzsche, "On Truth and Lie in an Extra-Moral Sense," in Walter Kaufmann, *The Portable Nietzsche* (New York: Viking, 1954), 46–47. The translation has been slightly amended.

10. Though I can't cite evidence for it, I assume that the phrase was originally meant to be ironical. If so, the irony has long since been forgotten.

be, any absolute truth. By such sleight of hand relativism becomes the new absolute.[11]

Secular relativists attempt to co-opt Wittgenstein's figure of the duck-rabbit (see fig. 1 in chap. 1) for their own purposes. More often than not, people understand this shifting-gestalt figure to be an illustration of the relativity of perception, since a viewer can learn to switch between its two "aspects" with apparent ease. But the duck-rabbit was deliberately devised by Joseph Jastrow to illustrate the basic insight of Gestalt psychology: that visual figures are not composed additively by assembling their parts into wholes but rather holistically, by grasping the pattern or paradigm that comprises the whole, allowing us to recognize its parts in the first place. The principle it illustrates might be summarized as "the priority of the whole." The figure is not meant to be a typical object of vision but quite the contrary: it is carefully contrived to balance two possible "wholes" as evenly as possible in order to demonstrate what is true but usually unobservable in all visual experience. Wittgenstein saw in this figure a way to make a philosophical point, and Thomas Kuhn applied that insight in his philosophy of science. The relativist misuses the duck-rabbit by claiming that it models reality generally. What I have tried to show, following Kuhn's lead, is just the opposite: the duck-rabbit shows us how all our experience (not just our vision) employs imagination to recognize those paradigms that enable us to see and to know what is real and not simply imaginary.[12]

Imagination and the Christian Life

Philosophy and theology are cousins, and any competent Christian theologian must be conversant with issues that philosophers have wrestled with from ancient times up to the present. Indeed, many of those philosophers have been theologians themselves, so closely are the two enterprises intertwined. In the modern age (which for good reason coincides with the beginnings of modern science), theology has been obsessed with issues of epistemology: What can we know, and how do we know that we know it, especially when the object of our knowledge is God? But there are places—very important ones—where theology must take leave of philosophy for reasons basic to the theologian's vocation.

11. The most helpful treatment of relativism and related issues that I have encountered is Richard J. Bernstein's book *Beyond Objectivism and Relativism: Science, Hermeneutics, and Praxis* (Philadelphia: University of Pennsylvania Press, 1983).

12. For a fuller discussion of the uses and abuses of the duck-rabbit figure, see chap. 14 above, under "Religions as Imaginative Paradigms."

Modern thinkers' obsession with epistemology is a good place to start. It has become customary to begin the story of modernity with René Descartes, who was both a practicing scientist and a philosopher. Descartes, as everyone who has taken Introduction to Modern Philosophy surely knows, was driven by a desire for certainty. As a scientist (a modern one, who believed that one finds the truth through observation and experiment), he wanted to secure the foundations of our knowledge. But he knew that the quest for certainty has theological consequences as well, and he took care to ensure that we first have certain knowledge of God. I am persuaded that the troubled history that goes under the label of "science and religion" has its roots here, in the desire for a certainty modeled on the kind of certainty achieved by the modern empirical sciences. In other words, the scientific quest for truth came to function as a paradigm for theology as well.

A second task for Christian theology in a post-Christian age, therefore, is to give up the quest for certainty. Perhaps it would be better to say it this way: to stop looking for certainty in the wrong places. Since God is shrouded in holy mystery, beyond our capacity for certain knowledge, any attempt to secure theological knowledge on our own is futile. Worse, the very attempt exposes our lack of faith, since God has already given us what we are seeking. Why would we continue to seek something that we have already received as a gift? Here is where the role of imagination becomes so important: by sharing his self-certainty with us, God enables us to imagine a truth beyond our own ability to know. Yes, our knowledge of God, our theology, is certain because it is grounded in God's own reality. But no, we are forever incapable of securing that knowledge, since we possess it as a gift and not as an achievement.

One of the jobs of theology is to be the guardian of the ways in which we think and speak about God. In this role theology works closely with philosophy. It is also the task of theology, however, to monitor the Christian imagination, to help the church imagine God rightly, and this enterprise is about more than just how we think. One of the chief attributes of imagination is that it governs simultaneously the ways in which we think, feel, and act; and it does so directly and concretely. The images, metaphors, and paradigms that inform our imagination do not require us first to coordinate our ideas with our emotions, and then to convert both into actions. If I imagine myself as a loser, for example, doomed to fail at everything I do, it affects how I think, determines how I feel, and governs my actions all at once. Likewise if I imagine myself as a child of God, a sinner redeemed and justified by the love of Jesus, my whole self will be conformed to that image.

Christian theology in a post-Christian age will be *hermeneutical* theology. Because of theology's paradigmatic character, its rootedness in imagination, it will devote much of its energy to interpretation. Unlike philosophy and the empirical sciences, theology is not primarily engaged in seeking theoretical knowledge or gathering empirical data. Rather, its immediate data are the images, metaphors, exemplars, and parables embedded in the biblical narratives, prophecy, and poetry; and its task is to *interpret* these imaginative elements for the church and the world. As illuminating as the duck-rabbit may be as a clue to the paradigmatic nature of our experience, it can also be misleading in its simplicity. In the sciences, after all, the paradigms are not simple visual figures but are composed of complex theories and experimental data. The guiding paradigm for Christian theology is Jesus the Messiah, but this figure must be apprehended through the complexity and apparent contradiction comprising the canon of Scripture. Jesus Christ is rendered to the imagination indirectly and cumulatively through the diversity of the biblical testimony. How can the theologian take into account everything from the ancient sagas of creation, to the violent narratives of the conquest of the land, the pessimistic ruminations of Ecclesiastes, the lyrical music of the Psalms (themselves incorporating a broad spectrum from lament to praise and thanksgiving), and culminating in the beautiful and bizarre visions of the Apocalypse? And right there in the middle are the Gospel narratives of Jesus and the apostolic preaching of the epistles. Anyone claiming that theology does not need interpretation must be a very selective reader of Scripture indeed. And lest this account seem too unrepentantly Protestant, it is important to note that theology must do its interpretive work in constant conversation with the church's two-millennium-long tradition of interpretation.

The role of Christians in a post-Christian age is to keep alive the hope that is in us, abiding in the confidence that God remains faithful to his promise. Our age is not the first time that Christian believers have needed to keep the lamp of hope burning in the midst of a seemingly hopeless situation. The church was called by Jesus to be a light to the gentiles, and that calling remains ours today. Many will be tempted to see the secular culture around us as the enemy and to adopt a defensive and embattled stance, but this temptation must be resisted at all costs. For we have a joyful message to impart, the gospel of God's love for his creation, a message that needs to be heard all the more in a faithless age. We must be prepared to continue living in faithful imagination grounded in Holy Scripture, even when the culture around us assumes that the object of our imagining is merely imaginary and that we are fools to believe it. Our response ought not follow the path of the apologetics of evidence, hoping to overcome unbelief by persuasive arguments appealing to the secular empiricism of our age. Rather, we must seek to embody the good news we are bringing through faithful thinking and faithful living, knowing that no effort of ours can compel faith in others unless their lives be transformed by God's Holy Spirit.

⊰⊱⊰⊱

I end by returning to the beginning, to this book's dedication. The last thing that needs to be said is the most important but also the most concrete and therefore the least amenable to generalization. Nothing the theologian does will have any merit unless it is instantiated in the lived experience of real people, both individuals and communities. The Christian imagination must be lived out through prayer and contemplation, corporate worship, study and private devotion, and the love of God and neighbor. It can be expressed through celebration and song, through good works and quiet reflection, and perhaps even through the writing of theological books. So varied are the possibilities that there can be no general description of the concrete forms this life may take. The Christian life is therefore best exemplified by life stories, biographies, diaries and journals, and the testimonies of individual believers. This account of theology can therefore only conclude in personal testimony, an accounting of the unique shape it has taken in one's own life. I grew up in churches that did not include personal testimonies in their worship, and I have only come to know this Christian practice late in life—especially among the prisoners with whom I now work and worship.[13] A few friends urged me not to dedicate this book to the inmates, because it was obviously not written for them, and most of them would be unable to follow its technical academic language. But I have followed my heart instead and dedicated the book to my incarcerated fellow believers. At the most obvious level, my work with them and my work as a theologian are so different from one another as to seem wholly unrelated. But I am persuaded—and my experience bears this out constantly—that the two are deeply connected. How that can be remains a mystery to me, as does every experience of grace.

---

13. For readers who may be interested, I have included a bit of my own testimony in the epilogue to chap. 5 above. A fuller account (which I have titled "How Karl Barth Sent Me to Prison") is included in Garrett Green, "Experience in Theology," in *The Routledge Companion to the Practice of Christian Theology*, ed. Mike Higton and Jim Fodor (London: Routledge, 2015), 312–32.

CREDITS

An earlier version of chapter 2 appears in Garrett Green, "Myth, History, and Imagination: The Creation Narratives in Bible and Theology," *Horizons in Biblical Theology: An International Dialogue* 12 (December 1990): 19–38, 61–63.

An earlier version of chapter 3 appears in Green, "Who's Afraid of Ludwig Feuerbach? Suspicion and the Religious Imagination," in *Christian Faith Seeking Historical Understanding: Essays in Honor of H. Jack Forstman*, ed. James O. Duke and Anthony L. Dunnavant (Macon, GA: Mercer University Press, 1997), 45–65. Reprinted by permission of Mercer University Press, 1997.

An earlier version of this chapter 4 appears in Green, "The Crisis of Mainline Christianity and the Liberal Failure of Imagination," *Reviews in Religion and Theology* (February 1996): 9–18.

An earlier version of chapter 7 appears in Green, "Barth on Beauty: The Ambivalence of Reformed Aesthetics," *Listening: Journal of Religion and Culture* 37 (Fall 2002): 147–58.

An earlier version of chapter 8 appears in Green, "The Gender of God and the Theology of Metaphor," in *Speaking the Christian God: The Holy Trinity and the Challenge of Feminism*, ed. Alvin F. Kimel Jr. (Grand Rapids: Eerdmans, 1992), 44–64. Reprinted by permission of the publisher.

An earlier version of chapter 9 appears in Green, "Modern Culture Comes of Age: Hamann versus Kant on the Root Metaphor of Enlightenment," in *What Is Enlightenment? Eighteenth-Century Answers and Twentieth-Century Questions*, ed. James Schmidt (Berkeley: University of California Press, 1996), 291–305.

An earlier version of chapter 10 appears in Green, "Kant as Christian Apologist: The Failure of Accommodationist Theology," *Pro Ecclesia* 4 (Summer 1995): 301–17.

An earlier version of chapter 12 appears in Green, "Imagining the Future," in *The Future as God's Gift: Explorations in Christian Eschatology*, ed. David Fergusson and Marcel Sarot (Edinburgh: T&T Clark, 2000), 73–87. Used by permission of Bloomsbury Publishing PLC.

An earlier version of chapter 13 appears in Green, "The Myth of Religious Violence: How to Think Christianly in a Secular World," *Pro Ecclesia* 20 (Fall 2011): 337–42.

An earlier version of chapter 14 appears in Green, "Are Religions Incommensurable? Reflections on Plurality and the Religious Imagination," *Louvain Studies* 27 (Fall 2002): 218–39.

INDEX